The Good Old Days Cookbook

beth tartan

BONANZA BOOKS
NEW YORK

This edition is published by Bonanza Books,
a division of Crown Publishers, Inc.,
by arrangement with Westover Publishing Co.
a b c d e f g h
BONANZA 1979 EDITION
Manufactured in the United States of America

Library of Congress Cataloging in Publication Data
Sparks, Elizabeth Hedgecock, 1919–
    The good old days cookbook.
    Includes index.
    1. Cookery, American.   I. Title.
TX715.S739 1979   641.5'973
ISBN 0-517-28983-0   79-13617

Book designed by Sylvan Jacobson

**To
Ruth Ellen Church**
For Many Good Days . . .

The new illustrations in this volume
were created by Don Sibley who is far too
young to have experienced the good old days
but enjoyed a brief visit to them with his pen
and ink drawings.

The art nouveau and old engravings used in
this book are there to enhance the visual
appreciation of an inordinately different
cookbook. It is hoped that the reader will
enjoy the wide range of pictorial material;
the serious; the humorous; the purely
decorative.

The marginal notes contained herein cannot
be credited to any source; they have been
said so very many times by so very many
people for so many years. They are included
with the hope that you who grew up in the
good old days will find fond memories in them
and that those of you too young to remember
will enjoy this book just a bit more.

Table of Contents

The Good Old Days Cook Book
Introduction

Man had neither clock nor calendar to mark the passage of time when times began to change. Change happened at a slow pace, creepingly slow when compared to the present pace, until the discovery of America. With that event, momentum quickened in the New World.

As it progressed—faster and faster each decade—America developed a mania for the NEW. New industries produced new products. New methods of advertising, especially electronic methods, produced demand.

The move from discomfort to comfort, from inconvenience to convenience, from labor to labor-saving devices—at the pace of a movie run at breakneck speed—seemed to offer Utopia in suburbia in the waning years of the twentieth century. Some saw America reaching a potential called The Great Society. We were the cockeyed optimists. We became fanatics of progress, a master which demands breaking with the past to seize a frenzied grasp of the future. The cost of the century's heady, exciting venture into progress brought mammoth, foreboding problems, some without apparent solutions.

In view of these overwhelming changes, Americans are pausing to ask if, in our optimism, we were not a little blinded in the race toward Utopia. A society with two cars in every garage is not coming out of the computer as America the Beautiful. The memory of America as it was in the face of the uncertainties of the future has caused a door to fling open, revealing the past, and America is caught up in a wave of nostalgia. Those who were young earlier in the century are remembering the days when movies were romantic and sentimental, when comics were innocent, when the Big Bands were the sound of the times, when families worked together to scrimp and save for the "things" they wanted. They are remembering and wondering if those were not truly The Good Old Days. Memories which have a way of acquiring a sugar coating, the way silver acquires a patina, foster a yearning for a return to days when life was simpler and tranquillity, not turbulence, was the pattern. The young, the under-30s, who tend to label anything from their parents' generation as "square" are discovering entertainment and excitement, perhaps even meaning, in old movies, phonograph records, calendars, catalogues.

In flinging open a door to the past, there is no place like the kitchen for giving birth to nostalgia, to memories. The kitchen, the heart of the home, was the place where stirring, mixing, chopping, grinding, baking, simmering, stewing, frying, and roasting produced dishes to delight the eyes, to excite the nostrils, to please the ears, and to titillate the taste. Earlier in the century fires burned brightly under pots suspended by a crane. The crane in the fireplace went the way of the churn. The wood stove went the way of the washtub and board. White ranges and refrigerators were welcomed with the same enthusiasm accorded the washing machine. The swing from the homey, fireplace kitchen to the laboratory-white kitchen with white enamel table in the center and free-standing kitchen cabinet with built-in flour sifter was rapid. Women viewed the kitchen as a special sort of emancipation from the drudgery of the dark kitchen from a dark age. And even more emancipation was to come.

Household help—the hired girl, the cook in the kitchen— almost disappeared during World War II, when many women had to cook for the first time in their lives. Often, they found the chore menial, degrading drudgery. World War II came to an end; soldiers came home, but household help did not return. The food industry, sensitive to the needs of the customer, launched a new segment of business—convenience foods, the boil-in-the-bag, the heat-and-serve, the instants. The factory took over peeling, boning, grinding, shucking, stirring, simmering—and the lady of the house could once again be the lady, and not the drudge. This was emancipation, liberation, freedom. The sign "Help Stamp Out Home Cooking" seen occasionally in a restaurant today reflects the opinion of some homemakers.

Home cooking, however, has not disappeared. Quite the contrary. O. Cedric Rowntree, president of the R. T. French Co., speaking at a luncheon for cookbook authors in New York City, put it this way: "We have taken the woman as the drudge out of the kitchen and put her back as an artist."

The story of a young woman is an example of what is happening in the kitchen. Several years ago, she was forced to stay home to care for two babies for long hours while her husband was away, with the family car. Money was scarce, and in her small world, work and boredom pushed her to the verge of "climbing the wall." Out of desperation, she stumbled into bread baking. Growing up, she had neither eaten homemade bread nor seen it made. With the help of the public library, she entered a self-prescribed course of study of breadmaking. The result is that her breadmaking skill now rivals that of a professional baker. She feeds her family breads from her oven; she dazzles guests with yeasty offerings; she teaches breadmaking courses for other young homemakers. Her breads, which rival or surpass the kind mothers used to make, have become her "thing," her status symbol. For her, breadmaking is a creative and performing art.

Her story is but one of thousands across this nation. A 1970 survey of shopping habits, as reported in the periodical *All About Food*, a *Chicago Tribune-Today* advertising publication, documents what is happening. A survey conducted in 1958 showed that only 17 per cent of the women questioned enjoyed cooking; the 1970 survey revealed that the figure rose to 49 per cent.

The reasons are of interest. First is the fact that the food industry has taken over much of the labor and a diversity of ingredients is widely available. Second is competition. Today's cooks are playing a highly competitive game—they are competing with the food industry to produce homemade dishes which taste better than the handy convenience items; they are also competing with each other. Husbands are boasting of their wives' culinary achievements with the fervor some have for the speed of a sports car. There is status in being able to say, for instance, "My wife's spun sugar holds up better than your wife's spun sugar," or, "Her beef Bourguignon is the best in the block."

Cooks also compete with food prepared in restaurants. Today's homemaker-cooks find they can produce meals from the purest, classic cuisine and serve them with appropriate wines at a lower cost, and for a more pleasurable occasion, than a meal in a restaurant—all without the hiring of a babysitter and getting through traffic.

More than anything else the new breed has discovered that food is good, and they are reveling in the discovery which is causing a renaissance in the kitchen, often the most beautiful spot in the home, and sometimes even more the center of activity than in the so-called Good Old Days.

There are other reasons for the renaissance. During World War II, soldiers learned to like the foods of the world, and when they returned home they brought back more highly developed palates which demanded new offerings. Cookbook authors responded to this interest, turning out cookbooks by the hundreds. The production, and demand, continues to satisfy a hunger which appears insatiable.

This book is for those who were young earlier in this century and who have memories of those days, and for those who are young now and in the progress of making memories.

A backward glance reveals some of the aspects of family living in earlier years.

A RECIPE WAS CALLED A RECEIPT

Earlier in this century and in the years before, cooks cooked "from scratch." That is, they cooked from basic ingredients such as flour, butter (lots of butter), and eggs. In many households, most or all of the ingredients were produced "on the place." In the "from scratch" days, a woman's place was in the home because she did not have many places to go, nor did she have many ways to travel.

Recipes were called receipts and carried mostly in the cook's head rather than in recorded form. Measures were nebulous— pinches, dashes, handfuls, glassesful, tumblersful; a cup which was any size found in the kitchen; heaping tablespoons; butter the size of a walnut; lard the size of an egg, and brine to float an egg. Pints, quarts, and pounds were more reliable measures. Printed or handwritten recipes often listed only ingredients, leaving directions for mixing and cooking to the guesswork of the cook or taking for granted the cook knew what to do with the ingredients. A recipe might suggest one cook on a quick oven or on the first fire, which meant the rolling fire built to blaze quickly in a wood range.

THEN CAME FANNIE FARMER (1857-1915)

At the age of seventeen, Fannie Farmer suffered a paralytic stroke which ended her formal education. Later she recovered enough to attend the Boston Cooking School and was graduated at the age of thirty-two. Eventually she set up her own school called Miss Farmer's School of Cookery; and soon she earned the title "the mother of level measurement," for realizing the value of standard measurements and gradually establishing them.

For ten years Fannie Farmer wrote a food column for the *Woman's Home Companion*. She also wrote the book which has been known for generations as Fannie Farmer's cookbook.

MAMA AT THE RANGE

The hearth of the big fireplace in the kitchen was the heart of the home in early America. From each side of the chimney cranes swung out for holding pots over the fire. Meat, poultry, and game were cooked on spits over the fire. Skillets on legs stood on the hearth ready to be used for frying meat or making bread. Heavy lids were used on the skillets and hot coals piled on the lids helped cook the food. Sweet potatoes, Irish potatoes, onions, and corn bread or ash cake were cooked in the ashes. Pones (cakes) of corn bread were cooked on a hoe held over the fire, thereby earning the name hoe cakes. Poundcake was baked in cast-iron poundcake bakers with heavy lids. The waffle iron for the open fire resembled a pair of scissors about a yard long with a small box on one end. Waffle batter poured into the box cooked over the fire, producing one waffle at a time.

Some kitchens had a Dutch oven built into the chimney for baking. Others had Dutch ovens built outdoors. Because of the danger of fire and to keep cooking odors out of the house, the kitchen was often a separate room apart from the big house. A screened-in outdoor "summer" kitchen was customary in some areas.

In the book *Plantation Cookery in Old Louisiana* published in 1938, Eleanore Ott wrote that her grandmother made a concession to modernity "in the shape of a monstrous stove, but she still preferred the fireplace, large enough to roast a baron of beef (about twenty pounds), and to her last day stoutly maintained that nothing was so good for baking salt-rising bread as a fireplace oven."

The Stoked Range

The green cook of 1905 was cautioned on the use of the coal range: "At all times give attention to right management of the fire; be especially careful not to have coal piled about the grate, nor to let the top of range become red-hot. Shut off drafts before the coal is burned out, and have the ovens clean and at the right temperature."

The wood-fired range was also widely used. It was black and stood on four legs. To the right was the firebox, in the center the oven and to the left the hot water box. A shelf insulated by doors and called the warming closet was at the rear above the range.

The fire was kindled in one of three ways—with paper and kindling, lightnin' (or knotty pine), or kerosene poured on stove wood. Kindling is stove wood cut into thin strips which catch fire easily. Lightnin' ignites easily because of the rosin in it. The proper management of a wood stove required skill, a bit of genius, and a touch of intuition. The amount and kind of wood used, and the opening and closing of the flue with the damper to control the blaze were important considerations.

A roaring fire was quickly built early on a cold winter morning. It was required for boiling a kettle of water, making a pot of coffee, and baking biscuits. Children who slept in cold, unheated bedrooms often dressed by its warmth.

A slow fire made with a bed of hot coals was for slow cooking on top of the range and also in the oven. The top surface of the range was sometimes used as a broiler for steaks. A layer of coarse salt formed a base for the meat.

Some of the late model wood ranges had an indicator on the front of the oven door, but the average cook tested the heat by putting her hand momentarily into the oven or by laying a piece of white paper in the oven. The degree of heat was determined by how fast the paper turned brown. Another heat indicator was a spoonful of flour placed in a shallow pie tin and set in the oven. If the flour browned in sixty seconds, the heat was right for bread. If it browned in less time, the heat had to be reduced.

Cozy in the winter, the stove was hotter than blazes in the summer when it was used for the same hot meals prepared in the winter.

DISHPAN HANDS

Dishpan hands were as much a part of the first part of the century as the Model T. Dishpan hands are rough, red, cracked hands damaged from washing dishes by hand morning, noon, and night.

Before hot and cold running water, which today gushes out at the turn of a spigot, a home had a well as a source of household water. Some wells had hand pumps; many had pulleys which drew the water up in a bucket. For dishwashing, water from the

bucket was first heated in the tea kettle and then poured into the dishpan, a big, deep pan measuring about twenty inches in diameter. Stacks of dirty dishes went into the hot water in the dishpan. With a dishcloth and a bar of soap, homemade or Octagon, each dish, one by one, was washed. Washed dishes went into a second dishpan for scalding with water from another kettle. When the chore was finished, the dishwasher, be she lady of the house or hired girl, was not only tired, she had dishpan hands.

THE APRON

The woman who did the cooking early in the century wore an apron. Often the apron covered the whole long skirt and had a bib which reached around the neck. Often, aprons had ruffles. There are women, primarily farm women, who still wear aprons as if they are uniforms. These women have used their aprons as baskets to carry "a turn" of kindling from the woodpile, to hold "a mess" of beans picked in the garden, or to carry "rosen" ears picked in the cornfield. Aprons have also been filled with hot biscuits going from range to table.

After a meal and the dishwashing were finished, the custom was to put on a clean apron before sitting down to do needlework or just to rock and talk by the fire. This was true particularly after Sunday dinner, when a woman changed to her best apron.

THE HOUSEHOLD
Before Frigidaire

When electric refrigerators first came on the market in 1916, they cost about nine hundred dollars each. By World War II the price had come down to the point that an electric refrigerator was considered indispensable to almost every household. To this day there are those who call their electric refrigerator a "Fridge," probably because Frigidaire manufactured one of the earliest models. It was a joyous day when a big, white, antiseptically clean Frigidaire was plugged into the electric outlet and the porous old wooden icebox was moved out.

The icebox had an interior that was insulated as well as possible, often with seaweed. The ice man delivered the ice which came in big chunks that weighed about 300 pounds each. Every household bought as much as the icebox held or the budget allowed. Cardboard signs indicating 25, 50, or 100 pounds were hung out to tell the iceman how much was wanted.

With his trusty pick he cut the large block into smaller blocks as the order required. Then holding the ice with ice picks or tongs he swung the block over his canvas-covered shoulder and took it inside. Once the block of ice was lowered into the icebox the ice began to melt and to drip into the drip pan on the floor. The drip pan required periodic emptying to prevent overflow.

Food was stored on shelves in the lower portion of the box. The ice chilled food sufficiently to retard spoilage and to congeal gelatin mixtures but it was never really cold. Store-bought ice cream, sold by the pint when it appeared on the market, had to be served immediately.

Commercial icehouses, nearly two thousand in number, were in operation in the early part of the century, but much ice was still cut from ponds in winter. The horse-drawn metal ice marker was pulled over a frozen pond marking the ice in neat blocks. A man with a large saw stood on the ice, cutting it into blocks the size of a small raft. He then floated the ice raft to the site of the icehouse, where it was cut into smaller chunks before storing.

By 1910, the increase in population caused polluted lakes which produced polluted ice.

The well and spring house were other ways of chilling. Butter, for instance, was placed in a well bucket and lowered into the well to chill. In a spring house, a trough was built for holding crocks of milk and butter in the cool running water.

Food was also kept cool on shelves built on the outside of the house, and in winter, there was the wonder of the cold, often very cold, back porch for storing cookie dough, the turkey, and all the special foods for holiday meals.

The Woodpile

The woodpile and woodshed were part of every farm. Their purpose was to provide a place to store wood. The woodpile was also the place for wringing chickens' necks or chopping their heads and scrubbing pots and pans. Itinerant wood sawyers traveled from farm to farm cutting logs into short lengths, ready for splitting on a chopping block into stove wood and finer pieces called kindling.

In the days of the woodpile, many a priceless antique four-poster and even canopied wooden bed went on the chopping block after the coming of the iron bedstead. The iron bedstead was a welcome object in homes plagued by bedbugs which harbored in wooden beds, as cockroaches harbored in baseboards and ants around the kitchen sink in the days before professional exterminators.

The chopping block was also a good place to crack nuts. Nuts for cracking included almonds, beechnuts, Brazil nuts, butternuts, chestnuts, chinquapins, chufas (earth almonds), filberts, ginkgo nuts, hickory nuts, pecans, and English and American walnuts. The American walnut, the wood of which is highly prized in antique furniture, is slowly disappearing in the wake of progress, but a few trees stand here and there. In autumn, the green walnuts drop to the ground and as autumn turns to winter, the green outer coating turns to brown, but few people bother anymore to gather the nuts, which just lay there wrinkling on the ground.

The Seasons

The seasons remain with us as the century moves toward the year 2000, but each merges a little deeper into the next because of controlled atmosphere, farming and shipping methods which provide produce twelve months a year, and fabrics worn in all seasons. This was not true early in the century when life was geared to the changing seasons.

The crisp golden days of autumn brought summer to an end. The harvest was in, the corn in shocks in the fields, and the pumpkins in piles. There were the joys of bobbing for apples and hayrides under the harvest moon.

The principal business of the household in winter was keeping warm. In the home with only open fireplaces, this took a bit of doing. It meant being toasted to lobster red on the front and always having a chill on the backside. It meant a pot of soup on the stove and an ever-ready pot of coffee.

Fun included popping popcorn in a wire basket over the open fire, ice skating, tobogganing, ice fishing, sledding, and snow cream.

With spring the world weary of cold and long nights came alive again. The rhubarb plants in the garden pushed tiny shoots up into the sunshine. The peony bush followed, coming up as if on cue. Irish potatoes in deep recesses in the root cellar or back under the kitchen sink sent forth green sprouts through wrinkled, lifeless skin.

A break in the weather brought a spring thaw, turning ice on lakes and ponds back into liquid to swell the streams. Farmers went again into the dormant fields. Today the tractor plows the soil, ashen and barren from the winter, turning up new soil eager to nurture tiny seeds. Before the tractor, a plow guided by strong weathered hands firmly clenched the handles which were tied behind a horse or mule did the job. Each farmer had a unique vocabulary of "Whoas" and "Giddups" to command a horse.

Anticipation was keen, after a winter devoid of fresh fruits and vegetables, for the ripening of the first bright red radish with its white bottom, the first leaves of garden lettuce to wilt with bacon drippings and vinegar, the first peas, fresh peaches, beans, berries, melons, and corn.

The rites of spring included shedding long winter underwear, called Long Johns, with the buttoned-up rumble-seat pants. Whitewashing was another rite. It was a cheap way of painting and an easy way to spruce up tree trunks, fences, and outbuildings to blend with the landscape spruced up by spring. Spring also brought the annual purge called spring cleaning. Before the vacuum cleaner came the broom. The house was swept, and scrubbed. Each windowpane and mirror shined after treatment with Bon Ami, a cleaning compound advertised with the picture of a biddy and the slogan, "It hasn't scratched yet." Can after can of Old Dutch Cleanser removed dirt. Rugs and carpets went to the clothesline for beating. Bedclothing and clothing spent days in the hot sun to rid them of cold germs and moth eggs.

In the summertime there were no tile-covered, highly chlorinated swimming pools for public use, but there were old swimming holes and the sea.

A blind man could tell the seasons, and almost the days, with his nose —in summer it was the kettle of spicy chili sauce, in fall a pot of apple butter, sage dressing at Thanksgiving, and fruit cakes at Christmas.

Summer was the time of going on picnics, making ice cream, picking blackberries, and preparing in a time of plenty for the winter ahead.

Men wore white linen suits in an effort to be cool, and ladies fanned furiously with fans to stir the air. The palm leaf fan and the folding fan were popular. Church pews held cardboard fans, most often supplied by the undertaker, who generally placed an ad on the back.

The hottest, most sultry period of the summer is Dog Days. The name comes from ancient times when the period was marked by the rising of Sirius, the Dog Star.

André Simon, founder of the International Wine and Food Society, lamented that the American diet has lost its seasonal aspects. He felt that eating strawberries, a fruit of June, in January; or endive, a winter vegetable, simultaneously with melon, a summer fruit, was not as enjoyable as foods served in their special season. In his opinion, something is lost by meals which offer the same foods month in and month out because the palate as well as the spirit anticipates the coming spring.

THE MARKETPLACE
Venders or Peddlers

At one time every kind of food was hawked by venders or peddlers. Some sold their products from horse-drawn wagons, later from trucks or the trunks of early-model cars. Many sold from pushcarts piled with everything imaginable, while others carried their wares in baskets, often several baskets or buckets hanging from a pole over the shoulders. The venders gathered in one area of the city or moved throughout the city crying and shouting their wares to would-be customers.

New York, through a third of the century, had pushcarts in numerous areas in the European tradition for a stimulating marketing experience. On Ninth Avenue were the French, the Greeks, the Irish, and the Italians. On Bleecker Street and upper First Avenue the clientele was almost exclusively Italian. Along Second Avenue were the Hungarians, the Germans, and the Czechs. On Delancey Street were the Jews and the Italians, and on Mulberry Street the Italians and the Chinese. In Times Square one found the vender of hot roast sweet potatoes and the roast chestnut vender who still exists.

Food writer Ann Batchelder recalls the hulled-corn man. (Hulled corn is similar to hominy and a favorite in New England.) The man rode in a red wagon with a box on the back pulled by an old white horse, and came once a week all through the summer. The box had a lid and a bright tin dipper, which jangled on the side, for measuring the corn. A dipperful cost three cents and filled a blue bowl used especially for the corn which, served with salt and rich creamy milk, made a suppertime dish that tasted like "ambrosia—whatever that is."

Special market days, usually Saturdays, brought farmers who

gathered in an open-air market in the European fashion with everything from masses of fresh flowers to live ducks, geese, turkeys in wooden cages, and vegetables rivaling those of the old *Les Halles* in Paris. In a Pennsylvania Dutch market, women often brought fresh *fastnachts* or doughnuts.

There were peddlers who had regular "engagements" with households. This meant the peddler called on a regular basis and brought fresh butter, eggs, and freshly killed beef, veal, and mutton, and, when available, rabbits and squirrels. The only cash some farm women had was what they called their butter-and-egg money.

THE COUNTRY STORE

The country store of yesterday is still with us today in restored villages in the country. There are also boutiques and speciality shops with decor—the potbellied stove painted a bright color, candy assortments, and bags of coffee beans ready for grinding —adapted from the old country store. The country store was usually the general store which stocked only a few groceries in the days before the wonders of modern packaging. Wrapping paper from a big roll and string hanging down from a holder were used for wrapping merchandise. There were burlap bags of coffee beans, sometimes more than one kind for hand blending, to be ground in the store or home grinder. Salt mackerel and salted spareribs came in wooden tubs. Dried beef came in great chunks to be thinly sliced at the store.

Vinegar, molasses, and kerosene came in barrels and were dispensed through spigots into jugs brought by customers. Crackers came in barrels and cheese in wheels or hoops. There were the wonders of the penny candy case. Early containers were cloth sacks for sugar and tin cans with lids for coffee. Louis Sherry's coffee, for instance, came in a square can painted gold, red, and green.

Stock might include dry goods, which meant bolts of fabrics such as calicos piled in colorful array on shelves. Other items were farm tools, buckets, nails, crocks, rope, shoes and other clothing.

The typical storekeeper wore a long apron, garters to hold up the cuffs of his shirt, and an eye shade.

The potbellied stove was the focal point of the store. Men hovered around it morning, noon, and night on chilly days and spat into the stove or on the floor under the stove. A checkers game was usually in progress inside in cold weather and outside in warm. The country store, which often included the post office, was a gathering place for the community.

THE NEIGHBORHOOD STORE

In the early part of the century, groceries came from the neighborhood grocery store, most of which, even the A & P, provided delivery service and sold on credit. Shoppers used the expression "put it on the books."

The A & P Hartfords had a vision and in 1912 opened their first and revolutionary "economy store" at 794 West Side Avenue in Jersey City, N.J. It was a cash-and-carry store without clerks to help customers fill grocery orders. And the corner was the most profitable of the A & P stores with clerks and credit. The new store put the old one out of business in six months. Within five years, more than three thousand economy stores, or almost three stores per working day, were opened. In 1925 the rate reached seven new stores a day. One of the Hartfords commented, "We went so fast that hoboes hopping off the trains got hired as managers."

In New York City, immigrants set up neighborhood shops featuring Old World specialties—Jewish dairy shops, Hungarian pork stores, Austrian pastry shops, and Italian markets with cheeses hanging from the rafters and shelves of dried fish. In San Francisco's Chinatown, the dried fish, duck, and other Chinese ingredients were displayed both indoors and out.

S. S. PIERCE OF BOSTON

In 1831, Samuel S. Pierce opened a grocery store on the corner of Court and Tremont streets in Boston. His premise was to stock his store with the finest foods he could import to the Boston harbor from anywhere in the world. Mr. Pierce did not merely place orders by letter or through agents. He personally went to Europe to seek out the best for his distinguished clientele. The windows and shelves of his store were rich with fine teas, honey, pâté from Strasbourg, biscuits from England, spices, coffee from the Far East, and wines from France. Carriages were always seen parked at the curb, while other customers arrived with market baskets on their arms.

THE SUPERMARKET

A new era in grocery merchandising came with the supermarkets of 1970 stocking six to eight thousand items, up from one thousand items in 1940. The prediction is that this figure will reach the twelve to fifteen thousand item range by the next turn of the century.

The supermarkets of 1970 have similar merchandise from coast to coast, and ordinary meals are becoming less nationalistic and regional, although the old specialties continue to appear on tables for special occasions. Each nationality has its specialties —the Russians from the Volga who became wheat farmers in Nebraska; the Basque shepherds in Nevada; the Dutch dairy farmers in Michigan; Scandinavian lumberjacks in Wisconsin and Minnesota; Mexicans in Arizona, New Mexico, and Texas; French Creoles in New Orleans; Italians; Hungarians; the Polish, Greek, and Chinese.

THE DELICATESSEN

Early in the history of our country, an Italian, Anthony Vitalli, opened the first delicatessen in Philadelphia. He sold spiced meats, imported cheeses, olives in brine, and other foreign delicacies.

In New York City the delicatessen—meaning in German "delicacies" or fine foods—was and still is common, offering sandwiches, potato salad, pickles, cheese, and cheesecake to consume on the premises or take-out. The "deli" is found in other parts of the country as well and as a department in some supermarkets.

THE TOWN DRUGSTORE

The town drugstore was a well established national institution by the turn of the century. The druggist was the first to make and use soda water, which was a vital step in the development of the ice cream soda. A man named Elias Magliore Durand, a former pharmacist in Napoleon's army, came to this country and in 1825 opened a shop near Independence Hall in Philadelphia. It is said he made the first ice cream soda. Then came the soda fountain and another national institution, the drugstore lunch.

After drugstores added fountains, round tables with curved-back chairs followed, making the drugstore the town's social center, and a whole generation grew up "sipping soda through a straw."

Coca-Cola came, adding a new dimension to sipping from soda fountain glasses—glasses which rounded at the top. In 1886, an Atlanta druggist named John S. Pemberton while trying to develop a pleasant patent medicine to sell, concocted a mixture of fruit syrup, extract of the kola nut, plain water, and extract of coca leaf. The world was not only waiting for the sunrise, as stated in a song popular earlier this century, but was also thirsty and waiting for Coca-Cola. Appearing at the right time in history started Coca-Cola on a rapid rise to success. In 1900 only the rich enjoyed themselves; everyone else was caught up in what has been called the Protestant Ethic—the idea that man's salvation came only through hard work. Soon Coca-Cola ads were telling the poor working man he deserved a few minutes to enjoy a nickel drink. The first Coke bottles were straight-sided with a paper label. By 1910 Coca-Cola was so popular that a host of imitators had appeared on the soft-drink scene. The company developed a "Mae West" bottle; a modified version is still used today.

Before the days of the electric water cooler, the drugstore was the only place ice water was readily available. This was in the period when the office water cooler was an upturned five-gallon jug or demijohn which gurgled water out into cups and men wore garters to hold up their shirt sleeves.

The story of Wall Drug in Wall, S. Dak., is an American success story. Ted Hustead was just out of the University of Nebraska School of Pharmacy. He was 28, and his wife, Dorothy, was 24. In 1931 they bought a little drugstore in Wall, population 740. The Depression came and making a living was hard, even with the family in a room in the back of the store. One hot Sunday afternoon in the summer of 1936, Dorothy Hustead thought there must be a way to stop the tourists bound for the Black Hills. She put up a sign—FREE ICE WATER.

By 1950, the Husteads were dispensing as many as five thousand glasses of ice water a day with the help of 28 employees during the tourist season. At this writing they are still dispensing.

Out of a modest beginning, the drugstore has now become a combination general store, department store and restaurant with the pharmacist hidden somewhere behind merchandise ranging from appliances to aluminum Christmas trees.

THE ICE CREAM PARLOR

The ice cream parlor with sodas, ice cream and sundaes, was a center of social life and refreshment. Blum's, the charming chain of ice cream parlors in San Francisco, resembles yesterday's parlors. Another is The Buffalo which opened in 1902 at Sedgwick and Division streets in Chicago. Since 1918 it has been at the corner of Irving Park and Pulaski roads. The Buffalo has made it with only three flavors—vanilla, chocolate, and strawberry. The decor is turn-of-the-1910s, with cherub and fan murals, leaded glass, a marble counter, and buffalo renderings.

The ice cream offered by Marshal Field & Company in Chicago is a scrumptious 22 per cent butterfat. (A butterfat content of 18 per cent is considered RICH.) Flavors are chosen from a recipe book which contains about 75 including Irish mist, whole apple pie, peanut brittle, and plum pudding.

THE BOARDING HOUSE

The boarding house reached a heyday near the end of the last century and through the first portion of this one. Taking in boarders was one of the few ways a family could supplement its income. In the case of a husband who could not or would not work it was a way for the lady of the house to earn money. This was also true of those called widow women. To ease the blow to the pride of some who had to take in boarders, the term "paying guests" was used.

Young couples frequently started married life in a boarding house where they could live more "genteelly" than they could otherwise afford. Older people retired to them and for bachelors they were permanent homes.

If there was no hotel or inn in a village, transients, such as the drummer or itinerant salesman, put up at the boarding house. The drummer of yesterday is the salesman or factory representative of today. If his visits were regular, he was taken in almost as a member of the family. Humor of the period includes jokes about the drummer and the landlord's daughter. The best boarding houses, especially where the cooking was known to be superb, had long waiting lists. The custom was to fill the table with food and everyone passed or reached for the dishes. From this practice comes the term "boarding house reach."

Fannie Farmer's claim to fame started in the boarding house her family ran. She helped with the cooking and showed such skill and interest in it that one of her younger sisters suggested she go to the Boston Cooking School and learn to teach cooking.

The most delightful boarding house of all appeared in the forties in the book, *Suds in Your Eyes*, by Mary Lasswell. The House was run by Mrs. Feeley, Miss Tinkham, and Mrs. Rasmussen with assorted boarders. The front of the house was surrounded by a fence made of beer cans. Any occasion—sad, happy, joyous, or critical was met by opening cans of beer. The good life of cold beer and good food provided by the ladies was so popular, it led to Mary Lasswell's subsequent *Mrs. Rasmussen's Book of One-Arm Cookery*.

FLOATING PALACES

The steamboats of the Mississippi and Ohio rivers were an extension of the luxurious splendor of plantation life of the last century. Patrons of the Mississippi river boats were almost exclusively from the landed aristocracy. There was also the ever-present itinerant gambler.

The architecture and appointments of the floating palaces were plush and gilt. The public rooms of the well-known steamers such as the Rob't E. Lee, the Natchez, the Frank Pargoud, the Western World, and the Grand Republic resembled grand Victorian parlors with sofas and armchairs, marble-topped tables, silver water coolers, bevel-edged mirrors, thick Turkish carpets and finely-fashioned gingerbread decorations or fretwork. Drinks were served from bars of solid mahogany with marble tops.

A voyage was of four or five days' duration. Food was served in great abundance. One ship captain instructed his dining steward that he did not want to see one inch of table cloth under the serving dishes.

The most stylish boats served dinner at six and often the entire passenger list sat down at one long table in the grand salon under ornate chandeliers burning coal oil.

On the sumptuous J. M. White as many as two hundred and fifty passengers ate at one time from Sevrès china. The napkins were of Irish linen, monogrammed J. M. W.

A veritable army of waiters brought trays of soups, entrées, fish, roasts, salads, relevés and the White was famous for its pyramids of nougat and daubes glacés. The bill for fresh fruit and nuts alone came to seven hundred dollars a week.

The menu of the M. S. Mepham, in the St. Louis-Memphis-New Orleans service, was a masterpiece of typographic and lithographic art which listed fifty meat and fish entrées and thirty cold aspics and *"pièces montées"* of elaborate and fanciful design.

Despite this bounty some super-aristocratic passengers brought aboard specialties from their own kitchen and were served aboard ship by their own servants. If another passenger reached for one of these dishes, he was politely informed it was a "private dish."

A breakfast menu lists beefsteak "plain or with onions, à la creole, Bordelaise, with mushrooms, or with tomatoes." Breakfast choices also included ham, pork chops, calves liver, mackerel, mutton chops and a dozen other meats. Twelve kinds of hot breads and cakes were listed, including waffles, muffins, flannel cakes and "dipped toast."

Before the Turn, the floating palaces enjoyed their *belle époque* and this century was to hear the sound of the steamboat whistle dwindle down to out as a faster means of travel, the train, took over transportation.

DINING CARS

The first railroad cars had neither sleeping cars nor diners. Travelers carried their own food or bought food from hawkers at train stops or the train stopped long enough for passengers to eat at a nearby boarding house or hotel, which in some cases was owned by the railroad.

In 1858, George Mortimer Pullman, a cabinetmaker from Brocton, N. Y., produced the first practical sleeping cars with a retractable upper berth which pulled up and down. The Pullman car porter brought the ladder by which a passenger climbed into the upper berth. The upper cost less than the lower berth which had the big window and more space.

A decade later, Pullman produced the first dining car which bore his name. Later a loaf of bread shaped like a car was also called Pullman.

The dining car and the sleeping cars, called hotel cars, brought the golden age of American railroad travel. Competition among carriers for passengers was fierce, and those who offered the best in dining attracted more business. Dining cars were lushly decorated with richly colored Turkish carpets, enormous French mirrors in gilded frames, fringed portieres and rare inlaid woods. Millionaires owned their own private cars, and some whole trains were decorated like fine parlors.

Early menus offered oysters on the half-shell, porterhouse steaks, quail, antelope, plover, fresh trout and terrapin with champagne available at every meal, including breakfast. The price of meals was 75 cents. Those who wanted to show off splurged on the more elaborate $1.00 dinners. That figure went up to $1.50 in 1902 when the New York Central put the Twentieth Century Limited in service. The butter served on the $1.50 dinner was produced on a model dairy farm in Vermont, owned by William Seward Webb, a Vanderbilt in-law.

All dining cars operated at loss, and many carriers urged ever-greater deficits, to provide more luxurious food. A freight solicitor named Fred Harvey, on a trip through the West, found the food in railway stations so bad he started a restaurant in the station in Topeka. He offered excellent food served on snowy-white linen by waitresses so pretty they became famous throughout the West. More than one "Harvey girl" became the wife of a lonely mining millionaire. Harvey, who also did catering for the Santa Fe Railroad, once fired a dining-car manager who had been losing only five hundred dollars a month. The manager was replaced with a man who upped the deficit to fifteen hundred so rapidly that he was made general superintendent.

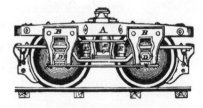

Foreigners traveling over the prairies in the West only recently won from hostile Indians were impressed with dining car menus which would have been credits to the best European hotels.

Railroads became known for their specialties. The Baltimore & Ohio was famous for terrapin stew and Chesapeake Bay seafood, which was put aboard fresh, and often live, at the beginning of each run. Fred Harvey brought culinary fame to the Santa Fe with broiled sage hen, Mexican quail, prairie chicken, and charlotte of peaches with cognac sauce. The New Haven was known for its scrod, Cotuit oysters and Maine lobsters, and for its wine and staple groceries, all purchased from the venerable S. S. Pierce Company. The Wabash was famous for a particularly succulent creamed chicken pie. The Illinois Central, the main line between the Great Lakes and New Orleans, featured Creole dishes, prepared by the secret recipes from the oldest families in the *Vieux Carré*. The Northern Pacific boasted of itself as "The Line of the Big Baked Potato." The Chicago & North Western, a Vanderbilt line for many years, offered roast Canadian goose, rabbit stew, venison steaks and mallard on its dollar dinners.

The recipes in *The Good Old Days Cookbook* have been gathered from many sources throughout the years. Most have been modernized for easy preparation by the contemporary homemaker, but some of the most quaint have been left in their original form to give an indication of the difficulties and challenges faced by home cooks in the early days of the century. That their offerings were not only good but delicious is a credit to their ingenuity and devotion.

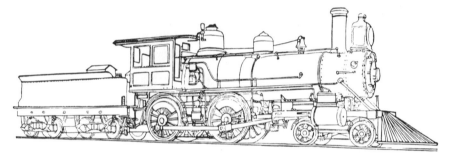

CHAPTER 1

HOME AS A FACTORY

MILK AND THE MOO COW

The family who owned a cow owned a milk factory which required little care other than milking. Milk was poured into crocks and kept as cold as possible by whatever means available. The cream rose to the top, and could be skimmed off and whipped. Milk and cream soured rather quickly in warm weather. When cream soured in the days before the electric refrigerator, it was sour cream, cream which had gone bad. By comparison, the dairy sour cream of today is sweet to the taste.

Agitating or churning cream produces butter. A churn is similar to a tall, tapered bucket with a lid. The handle of the plunger fits into a hole in the lid. Up and down, up and down the plunger is pushed by hand until small flecks of butter form. Another churn used in earlier times was a rounded bowl rocked like a cradle. The flecks of butter were gathered in a mass and pressed down into a wooden mold for shaping into a half-pound cake. The design of the mold identified the butter of a household. The liquid remaining after churning was buttermilk for drinking, for baking, or for the pigs.

Clabber—milk thickened by souring—was common, especially in warm weather. Pasteurized milk does not sour into clabber the way unpasteurized milk straight from the cow did. Clabbered milk was tangy and delicious when made into clabber cheese, a soft cheese somewhat like today's cottage cheese. Clabber was also used as a substitute for buttermilk in baking and in pancakes called clabber cakes. Firm clabber, called bonny clabber or loppered clabber, was spooned into dessert dishes and served with cream, sugar, and nutmeg or cinnamon for dessert or breakfast.

Clabber Cheese

Heat clabbered milk gently over low heat. When the clabber separates from the whey, pour in cloth; hang to drain. Whey, a watery liquid drains off, leaving the soft curds in the bag. Feed whey to pigs or discard.
For cheese, sprinkle drained curds or clabber with salt.

Cottage Cheese
1 gallon clabbered milk
1 gallon water, boiling
1 teaspoon salt
1 tablespoon heavy cream

Pour water over milk; cover, let stand for 10 minutes. Pour into cloth sack; drain. Discard whey; season curds with salt, moisten with cream. Makes about 2 cups.

Devonshire Cream

Set a pan of fresh milk, warm from the cow, in a cool place for 12 to 24 hours. Then let stand over a very slow fire and gradually bring to scalding point. Remove to a cool place, and let stand covered for 12 hours. Skim off the thick, rich cream and stir gently until smooth. Serve with honey on hot waffles.

WHEN THE FREEZER HAD A CRANK

There are two schools of thought about the proper mixture for making "cream." One is the raw egg school, which favors a mixture of beaten eggs, sugar, and pure cream flavored with vanilla. The second is the custard school, which prefers a cooked thin custard cooled before pouring into the freezing container.

The container, a metal cylinder, is filled three-fourths full with the raw egg mixture or cooked custard and fastened firmly into the center of the freezer. Alternating layers of chipped ice and ice cream salt surround the freezing container. As the crank is turned, the container revolves. A wooden spatula device, called the dasher, revolves in the opposite direction, gently agitating the cream. Easy to turn at first, once the mixture begins to freeze the turning gets harder and harder and finally so hard the crank will not move. The water is then drained from the freezer through the hole at the base. Additional ice and salt are added and packed down hard, and the freezer is covered with thick layers of a burlap bag. After the ice cream has ripened for one to two hours, comes the moment of delight when the freezer is opened and the decision is made as to who gets the supreme joy of licking the dasher.

Vanilla Ice Cream

As good as the kind made with heavy cream.
6 eggs
2 cups sugar
3 14½-ounce cans evaporated milk
¼ cup vanilla
¼ teaspoon lemon extract
¼ teaspoon salt
4 cups whole milk

Beat eggs in a 3-quart bowl with electric mixer at high speed until lemon colored. Add sugar gradually and continue to beat at medium speed until thick. Add evaporated milk, vanilla, lemon extract, salt, and milk. Stir thoroughly. Pour into a 1-gallon freezer can.

Freeze in hand-turned or motor-driven freezer, using a mixture of 8 parts crushed ice to 1 part ice cream salt. Cover with paper or heavy cloth and let stand for 1½ to 2 hours to ripen. Makes 1 gallon.

Fresh Peach Ice Cream

1 quart fresh peaches, crushed and peeled
1½ cups sugar
½ pint light cream
½ pint heavy cream
1 quart milk
1 tablespoon vanilla extract
1 teaspoon almond extract

Combine peaches and sugar, mixing well. Let stand for 10 minutes. Add light and heavy cream, milk, and extracts.

Pour into freezer can, filling ⅔ full.

Pack freezer with 1 cup ice cream salt to each 8 cups crushed ice in alternate layers. Turn until frozen. Pack down to ripen. Makes 1 gallon.

Snow Cream

1 egg
½ cup sugar
1 cup milk
1 teaspoon vanilla
1 quart fluffy snow

Beat egg until fluffy. Add sugar, milk, and vanilla. Keep the mixture cold. Run outside and get snow. Stir it gently into milk mixture. Serve at once. Makes about 2½ cups.

Freezer ice cream melted quickly once it was served in dessert dishes. The thing I remember most about it was that it was so much colder than bought ice cream.

Quick Modern Snowflake Cream

Prepare a package of instant vanilla pudding mix according to package directions, using half the amount of milk specified on the package. Stir in a quart or more of fluffy snow. Serve at once.

A HOG TO KILL

Those with the space raised little pigs into hogs as a source of meat. The pigs ate slop, served in a wooden trough, and whatever else was available. The fattened hog was killed in the cold weather of late autumn or early winter in an all-day operation with everyone helping.

Hams, shoulders, and side meat or belly were salted down as the first step in the curing process. After the hams "took" the salt, they were heavily peppered and hung in the smokehouse, an "out" building about ten feet square with a dirt floor. A fire made of logs, some still green, burned for days providing smoke for smoking the meat. After smoking, a ham required a year of hanging to cure. Lacking today's quality control in food processing, the flavor and salt content of hams varied, with some as salty as brine. Uncured or fresh hams were also called green hams. Side meat or streaked lean side meat was smoked to make bacon and also simply salted to make salt pork, fat back, or middling meat for seasoning vegetables, and occasionally, slices were fried crisply and served with cream gravy. Fresh spareribs, backbone, pork loin roast, and tenderloins were traditionally consumed first because of rapid spoilage. A sprinkling of salt helped keep the meat fresh. The liver was ground, seasoned, and made into a loaf called liver pudding, which might be called an American pâté.

Every scrap of fat was cooked in a big iron pot over an open fire. Cracklings, crisp bits of cooked fat, were pressed in the lard press to extract the last bit of lard. The remaining cracklings were added to corn bread to make crackling corn bread.

Dutch Goose

Stuffed hog's maw, which is similar to the Scotch haggis (stuffed sheep's stomach), was a prestigious dish. To prepare, clean a pig's stomach and soak in salted water. Stuff with a filling of diced potatoes, onions, and sausage. Season as desired. Sew up and boil gently in a cheesecloth for 2 hours. Leaving in the cloth, lift out and brown in the roaster, basting with butter.

Sausages

The people who came to settle America brought their sausages with them—frankfurters, bockwurst, bratwurst, thuringer, knockwurst, blood sausage, and liverwurst from Germany; bologna, salami, pepperoni, cappicola, and mortadella from Italy; Vienna sausage from Austria; Lyons sausage from France; chorizo from Spain; kielbasa from Poland. Americans also make their own sausages.

Lebanon County, Pa., is the birthplace of a fine offering, a highly seasoned beef sausage, about five inches in diameter, called Lebanon sausage. It is available at farmers' markets in the area. Sausage festivals are staged in various parts of the country. La Crosse, Wisc., has its *Oktoberfest* with bratwurst and beer. For years, Bratwurst Day, or "Brat" Day, a day when sausage was cooked over open grills in the streets, was held in Sheboygan, Wisc. The day had to be abandoned because of interference from hoodlums. New Braunfels, Tex., has a Wurstfest which lasts a week.

On the farm, scraps of meat and pods of hot red pepper were run through the sausage mill, a hand-cranked grinder mounted on a plank on four legs, all of which resembled a bench. Each sausage maker had his own blend of seasonings. A portion of the sausage was left as bulk sausage for shaping into patties for cooking; some was stuffed into casings made from a hog's carefully washed intestines.

Chitterlings, better known as "chittlins," are also made from a hog's intestines. To prepare, cut into lengths; parboil, drain, coat in flour, and fry until crisp.

Souse Meat

The head and feet of a hog make souse meat, a loaf similar to a congealed meat salad. Pork loins, in this recipe developed for today's kitchen, add more meat than the kind prepared on the farm. Souse meat is good served with crackers and beer or other beverages.

5 pigs' feet
4½ pounds pork loin roast, bone-in
1 tablespoon salt
½ teaspoon pepper
5 drops hot pepper sauce
Water
1 cup cider vinegar
3 envelopes unflavored gelatin
⅓ cup cold water
½ cup pimiento, diced and drained

Place pigs' feet and pork roast in large pot; add salt, pepper, and hot pepper sauce with water to cover. Bring water to a boil; reduce heat and simmer for 3 to 4 hours, until the meat is thoroughly cooked. Lift feet and loin from broth. Strain broth and let stand in the refrigerator overnight; the next morning remove fat from surface of broth and discard. Meanwhile, pull meat from the bones with the fingers and shred; discard bones and fat but not the skin. Bring skimmed broth to a boil; add vinegar and shredded meat and skin. Taste to determine if additional salt and pepper are needed. Simmer slowly for 30 minutes. Soften gelatin in cold water; dissolve in some of hot liquid. Add dissolved gelatin to meat mixture; stir to blend and remove from heat. Add pimiento; pour into loaf pans. Makes 5 loaves, each approximately 9 by 4½ inches.

Hog's Head Cheese

The custom in Charleston, S.C., was to make hog's head cheese, considered a must with hominy grits for breakfast at Christmas and on New Year's Day. Hog's head cheese, which is similar to souse meat, is made by boiling a hog's head with spices. The meat is minced and combined with the cooking liquid which congeals to form a loaf.

Pennsylvania Dutch Scrapple or Ponhaus

An old recipe from Lancaster County for the kind of fresh scrapple brought by farmers to the market in Philadelphia.

Make scrapple the same day the hog is butchered. Place hog's head, tongue, liver, and about ½ dozen pieces of the skin in an iron kettle. Add water to cover; cook about 2 hours or until the meat is tender and falls off the bones. The liver takes only about 30 minutes to cook; remove it when done. Lift the cooked meat out of the cooking liquid. Pull meat from bones and grind all the meat. Strain the cooking liquid and put it back in the kettle with the ground meat. Bring mixture to a boil; add seasonings. To about 3 gallons of meat and liquid, add 7 tablespoons salt and 3½ tablespoons pepper. When contents are boiling rapidly, add buckwheat flour slowly and stir very briskly until mixture thickens enough so you can make a cross in the mixture with your stirring stick. If mixture sticks too much to sides of kettle, add a small amount of lard. Pour into loaf pans and allow to become firm. To cook, cut into slices and brown on both sides in a small amount of hot lard in a heavy skillet. Serve with syrup and, if desired, scrambled eggs and fried apple slices.

Scrapple

A simple version for the modern kitchen.
½ pound bulk pork sausage
2½ cups water
¼ teaspoon salt
⅛ teaspoon pepper
⅔ cup uncooked regular Ralston cereal, or
   1 cup Instant Ralston
¼ cup flour
Shortening

In heavy skillet, cook sausage, stirring, until brown; drain off and discard fat. Add water, salt, and pepper; bring to a boil. Add cereal slowly so boiling does not stop. Boil for 5 minutes, stirring often. Rinse out a medium-size loaf pan with cold water; pour hot cereal mixture immediately into wet pan. Chill until firm. To cook, unmold, cut into ½-inch slices, and roll in flour. Cook slices in fat; brown on each side in ⅛ inch hot shortening in skillet. Serve with syrup. Makes 14 slices.

Pickled Pigs' Feet

8 pigs' feet with uppers
Water
1 quart vinegar
1 tablespoon whole cloves
4 bay leaves
1 stick cinnamon
¼ cup salt
1 teaspoon pepper
¼ cup brown sugar
1 small onion, sliced

In kettle cover pigs' feet with water; simmer for 2½ to 3 hours or until meat is tender. Lift feet out of cooking liquid, reserving 2 to 4 cups liquid; place feet in a large bowl. Combine vinegar, cloves, bay leaves, cinnamon, salt, pepper, brown sugar, and onion and simmer for 1 hour. Strain to remove spices; add 2 to 4 cups reserved cooking liquid. Pour over pigs' feet; chill for 2 days or longer.

THE MOTHER HEN

Behold the Mother Hen. She is a study in motherhood. The mother hen of yesterday had three roles: to lay eggs, to produce more chickens, and to provide food. She laid eggs, one a day when she was in the mood, some for the table and some for the market. When spring brought warmer weather, the mother hen sat on a nest of eggs until they hatched. Once her chicks, or biddies, hatched out, she cuddled them in the nest until they were sturdy enough to trail after her around the barnyard. She protected them with fierce care and would get "as mad as a settin' hen" if any were attacked. A fake egg, called the nest egg, was kept in the hen's nest as a lure to keep the hen laying in a nest familiar to the owner and to discourage her from "stealing a nest," i.e., going off under the house or barn to lay her eggs. Because hatching was a springtime happening, the young chickens were called spring chickens. In spring, people ate spring chickens; in winter they ate hens and old roosters.

The poultry industry of today has wrought wonders in the production of chickens and eggs. New breeds go through scientific cycles of egg production that are carefully charted. When the final egg on the chart is laid, a laying hen has finished her life's work and goes to the soup factory. There is no motherhood for her. She does not know what a biddy looks like. A chicken bred for food also goes through a cycle of growth. When ready for market, to market the chicken goes. No motherhood for her either. In improving chickens, new strains have replaced the familiar barnyard Dominicks, the Rhode Island Reds, and the Plymouth Rocks.

In earlier days, chickens came with feathers and most often on foot for decades before the poultry industry developed quick-growing methods which put trays of young birds, either whole or in parts, in today's refrigerator cases.

On Saturday it was the custom to go to the barnyard and catch the chicken required for Sunday dinner. It was then killed by wringing its neck or chopping it off with an ax. A skilled neck wringer held the chicken firmly by the head, gave a quick flip over the wrist, and the headless chicken went flopping around in the woodpile.

Next there were the feathers to reckon with. Some picked chicken dry; others scalded it first. Scalding meant pouring boiling water over the bird and letting it stand briefly. Off came the feathers, leaving the tiny pin feathers which had to be removed one by one, usually with the help of a knife. Once those were reckoned with, the downy hairs remained on the naked chicken. The hairs required singeing, accomplished by holding the chicken over two or three tablespoonfuls of burning wood alcohol in a plate or saucer. It was also done with lighted paper, such as tightly rolled newspaper. Care was taken to avoid smoking the bird.

Once the exterior was cleaned there were the entrails and the windpipe to contend with. To remove these, openings were cut in the rump and the neck. The skilled chicken cleaner reached in and pulled out all the entrails

On Saturday I watched our cook wring a chicken's neck. She did it with a magician's sleight of hand. One minute the chicken was alive and the next minute, ready for scalding with a kettle of hot water.

Inside a hen there were often as many as seven or eight unlaid eggs—we called them unborn eggs —in varying sizes. The unborn eggs went into the chicken gravy. It was fun to fish them out of the gravy boat.

in one solid mass. Care was required not to break the gall, which contains a green substance that, if allowed to touch the chicken, makes it "as bitter as gall."

The gizzard is a dandy little package built by nature to resemble a winter coat with a zip-out lining. In cleaning, the gizzard was cut open revealing a collection of sandy particles. The edge of the inner lining was easily removed, taking with it the sandy particles and leaving a nice clean gizzard.

The whole chicken or cut-up pieces, carefully salted for preservation, was then ready for the icebox. It is easy to see that one chicken, and often many more were required, took a good bit of time on Saturday. Instructions for the "green cook" in 1905 included how to draw and truss a chicken. Trussing, getting it in shape for baking, meant sewing up the cavities with a trussing needle and a double thickness of white twine. Wings were placed in the position of the arms under the heads of today's sunbather.

Chicken every sunday was routine in many homes. The usual dish was roast chicken, also called baked hen, and most often it was stuffed. Stuffing preferences included a forcemeat of another fowl, veal, or pork, or a mixture of any of these, and all the bread and potato stuffings. Sage was the favored seasoning for stuffing. The sage came from a shrub which grew in the garden. The plant with wrinkled whitish-green leaves was cut back in late summer and the cuttings were dried. Before they were used, the cuttings were pulverized by rubbing them between the hands.

Baked Hen

This is a modern workable recipe for the Sunday favorite.

    1 3½- to 5-pound roasting chicken
    Water
    2 bay leaves
    A few celery tops
    5 or 6 whole peppercorns
    ½ cup onion, diced
    2 to 3 cups celery, diced
    ¼ cup chicken fat or margarine
    ½ pound white bread, crumbled
    ½ 8-ounce package corn bread dressing mix
    1¼ teaspoons salt or to taste
    ¼ teaspoon black pepper
    1 tablespoon fresh sage, finely pulverized, or
        1 teaspoon poultry seasoning

Place chicken in a pot with water to cover. Add bay leaves, celery tops, and peppercorns. Bring water to a boil. Reduce heat to simmer and cover pot. Continue to cook for 1 to 1½ hours or until the chicken is tender but not overcooked. Remove from broth.

For dressing, cook diced onion and celery in chicken fat or margarine in skillet until golden. Add to crumbled bread, dressing mix, salt, pepper, and sage or poultry seasoning. Add broth to moisten bread mixture.

It should be fairly moist (the testing of the recipe took almost 6 cups of broth). Mix and spread into greased shallow baking pan about 10 to 15 inches. Bake dressing in a 325-degree oven for about 45 minutes. Rub the drained chicken with a stick of butter or margarine to hasten browning, and place on top of the dressing. Raise oven temperature to 375 degrees and bake until chicken is hot and brown. Meanwhile, allow broth to boil, uncovered, to reduce in volume. Use broth to make gravy, following the proportion of 2 tablespoons each of fat and flour to each cup of liquid. The fat can be chicken fat. Season with salt and pepper, using a heavy hand with the pepper. Add diced giblets and 3 diced hard-cooked eggs. Serve from the gravy boat.

Chicken Pie

Chicken pie is also an old favorite, perhaps more favored for church suppers than for Sunday dinners. Chicken pie can be made in a variety of ways. Pennsylvania Dutch chicken pot pie is sometimes boiled and sometimes baked. It may consist of stewed chicken with dumplings or noodles. It is also sometimes baked in a pastry crust. Another version common to several other parts of the country has a base and topping of pastry dough with a third layer of pastry in the center. When cooked, it resembles a dumpling or a noodle.

The secret of chicken pie, according to an old cook, is the rich flavor of a large stewing chicken made richer with the addition of butter.

> 1 2½- to 3-pound chicken
> Water
> ¼ cup celery tops, chopped
> 3 or 4 whole peppercorns
> 1½ teaspoons salt
> 2 chicken bouillon cubes
> ½ cup (1 stick) butter or margarine, melted
> ½ teaspoon black pepper
> 1 cup flour
> 3 teaspoons baking powder
> 1 cup milk
> 1 10-ounce can cream of chicken soup

Place chicken in a pot with water to cover. Add celery tops, peppercorns, 1 teaspoon salt, and bouillon cubes. Bring to a boil. Reduce heat to simmer and cover pot. Cook chicken until done, about 45 minutes. Remove from broth. Separate meat and shred with fingers; discard bones. Twirl skin in electric blender and add to shredded chicken. Place chicken in a 13- by 7-inch baking dish that is 2 inches deep. Pour melted butter or margarine over chicken. Meanwhile, allow broth to boil vigorously to reduce in volume. Sift flour with baking powder and remaining ½ teaspoon salt. Add milk and blend until smooth. Spread flour mixture evenly over chicken. This forms a crust-like topping.

In a saucepan, blend chicken soup with 1¾ cups chicken broth. Heat to boiling and pour over flour mixture. Bake in a 425-degree oven for about 1 hour or until lightly browned.

Grandmother made chicken pie in what she called a dirt dish. It was a deep earthenware dish. She stuck little rolls of pastry into the chicken filling and added dots of butter with a heavy hand.

Fried Chicken

Great platters of fried chicken appear on American tables and find their way to suppers and picnics. Although fried chicken goes under many names— Southern fried, Maryland fried, and Kentucky fried— the truth is that most fried chicken is prepared in virtually the same way. A young chicken is cut into pieces and coated in seasoned flour. It is then either deep fried or browned in shallow fat with butter added to aid browning. Steaming chicken that has been browned in shallow fat makes it softer, more moist, and tender. To steam, add a small amount of water to the browned pieces in a skillet. Cover and allow to steam for about 15 minutes. Remove cover to allow water to evaporate and pieces to re-crisp.

Fried chicken without cream gravy is not fried chicken for many tastes. In lean times, when there was a limited quantity of chicken and meat, a lot of gravy and mashed potatoes accompanied the meat so no one went hungry. But, cream gravy is going the way of other rich offerings in an age plagued by calories and cholesterol.

Cream Gravy

Cream gravy is simply medium-thick white sauce flavored with chicken drippings. Use 2 tablespoons fat (drippings) and 2 tablespoons flour to each cup milk. Blend flour into drippings in a skillet removed from the burner. Flour blends into fat or drippings more smoothly if fat is cold or warm rather than hot. Add milk. Blend and place skillet over medium heat. Cook, stirring, until smooth and thick. Use a wire whisk to banish lumps. Season to taste with salt and pepper.

In the Ozarks the custom is to blend a tablespoon or more of native pecans rubbed to a powder into chicken gravy.

Another old favorite is chicken fried bread, also called chicken biscuits, which consists of squares or rounds of baking powder biscuit dough fried until brown and crisp in the same fat used for frying the chicken.

Maryland cooks turn out fine chicken fricassees, both white and brown, and fricassee is the star of countless New England Sunday dinners. White chicken fricassee is stewed chicken with cream and butter, often seasoned with blades of mace. For brown fricassee, pieces of chicken are first coated in flour and browned before the sauce is added.

Country Captain

President Franklin D. Roosevelt liked a chicken dish called Country Captain which was part of the fare served when he was in residence at Warm Springs, Ga. Of East Indian origin, it is thought the dish found its way into this country along with spice shipments to Savannah.

> 1 2½- to 3-pound young chicken
> ¼ cup flour
> 1 teaspoon salt
> ¼ teaspoon pepper
> ⅓ cup butter
> 1 small onion, finely chopped
> ⅓ cup green pepper, slivered
> 1 clove garlic, crushed
> 1½ teaspoons curry powder
> ½ teaspoon thyme
> 1 teaspoon lemon rind, grated
> 1 1-pound can tomatoes
> 2 tablespoons currants
> ¼ cup cashew nuts
> ¼ cup chutney

Cut chicken into pieces and coat in mixture of flour, salt, and pepper. Brown in butter in large, heavy skillet. Remove chicken from skillet. To skillet, add onion, green pepper, garlic, curry powder, thyme, and lemon rind; cook, stirring, for a few minutes. Add tomatoes and chicken and cook slowly for 25 minutes or until chicken is tender. If mixture becomes dry, add small quantities of water. Add currants; heat and serve with cashew nuts and chutney. Serves 4.

TURTLES AND TERRAPINS

There are fewer turtles now than earlier in the century because of pollution and other products of progress. The fortunate, however, may still find turtles in various parts of the country—particularly in sprawling rural areas close to water. To catch a turtle in a lake, drive sturdy wooden stakes around the edge of the lake. For a turtle hook, use a large fishhook tied to the wooden stakes with a strong cord, and for bait, use tough meat, like neck meat from beef or a fish head. Set the hooks preferably at twilight. The next morning check on the turtle catch. Turtles are also caught by graveling—feeling with the hands under water along a creek bank.

Turtle meat is fried like chicken, cooked like country style steak, and made into soups and stews, but the taste differs from that of either beef, veal, pork, or chicken.

Turtle, particularly green turtle, is considered a fine delicacy. The "cow" turtle is preferred to the "bull" turtle, which is generally coarse in texture.

During the last half of the nineteenth century, the terrapin developed from food for slaves and apprentices into one of the highest priced delicacies. In 1910 the average wholesale prices for marketable specimens were from $2.50 to $8.00, the figures steadily rising with the diminishing supply. Terrapins from the mouth of the Chesapeake River were choice. The most prized terrapins are those called "full cows," or females full of eggs.

A popular way of cooking terrapin is over hot coals. The meat is done when the under shell comes off. To eat, remove only the gall and eat the whole contents from the inverted upper shell. Season the meat with butter, salt, and pepper. Before hibernation, the terrapin empties the stomach and is consequently clean, although a fastidious taste prefers to have the terrapin thoroughly washed, and the entrails and lights as well as the gall sack removed.

FROGS

The custom was to go gigging for frogs at night. The frogs were speared with a sharp spear, such as a pitchfork. The legs were then cut off and cooked like fried chicken.

OPOSSUM

The ideal time to hunt opossum, usually shortened to 'possum, is on a nippy autumn night. After dark, opossums come out of hollow trees or other hiding places to search for food. The success of the hunt depends on dogs trained to follow the opossums and to "tree" them. Once the opossum is in a tree, a light flashed in his eyes immobilizes him. Someone climbs the tree, grabs the opossum, and puts it in a burlap sack. Sometimes the opossum, seized by a nerve spasm, falls out of the tree and appears to be dead. He is actually "playing 'possum," and as soon as the spasm ends, he scurries away toward freedom.

Early in the century, the opossum was a "new" dish among whites in the North. Tasting somewhat like young pig, it was generally roasted or baked and served with sweet potatoes.

SORGHUM

Sorghum, a syrup similar to molasses, is made from the juice squeezed from sugar cane. On the farm the juice is extracted by feeding the stalks between two rollers similar to the rollers on an old washing machine. Power to make the rollers rotate comes from a pole fastened on one end to the rollers and on the other to a mule. The mule walks in a circle and causes the rollers to turn. The extracted juice is turned into open tin trays over a wood fire. About one and one-half hours of simmering and skimming off the scum is required for the syrup to become sorghum.

A cruet of sorghum was a common table fixture and sopping was a common practice. To sop, place a big hunk of soft butter on a plate. Pour sorghum into the butter and blend. Sop up with a biscuit. The Delta Queen, at this writing, still stops at Hawesville, Ky., the sorghum capital of the U.S.A., to let passengers off to buy jars of sorghum.

PICKING BLACKBERRIES

Blackberries grow wild on tall, thin bushes full of sharp briars that rip the skin when touched. The briar patch was immortalized in Joel Chandler Harris's Uncle Remus stories. Blackberry bushes grow in thickets, which in some areas are fairly abundant. In Oregon and Washington the bushes are found growing on logged-over or burned-over land in the mountains.

Blackberries are ripe in the hottest days of summer. Searching for berries is a sweaty, sweltering job plagued by the ubiquitous chiggers and snakes.

Chiggers are minute critters which dig into the skin and itch like the dickens. A coating of lard over the skin is said to discourage them. A straw hat protects against sunstroke and old cotton stockings over the arms ward off the briars.

Among joys of picking blackberries are seeing the bucket fill, berry by berry; the songs of the birds; the midday chant of the cicada; the chirp of crickets; the soft whistle of Mother Rabbit to her young; and the trickle of a brook. A bucket of blackberries brings the final joys—pies, cobblers, wines, cordial, jam, and jelly.

The wild dewberry, similar in shape to the blackberry, is more red in color and has a larger portion of fruit to seed than the blackberry. The wild dewberry is now scarce to nonexistent.

Blackberry Roll

> 2 cups flour, sifted
> 2 teaspoons baking powder
> 1 teaspoon salt
> 2 tablespoons sugar
> ⅓ cup plus 4 tablespoons butter
> 1 egg
> ⅓ cup milk, approximate
> 1 pint of blackberries, sweetened with ⅔ to
> ¾ cup sugar

Sift together flour, baking powder, salt, and sugar. Cut in ⅓ cup butter with pastry blender or two knives until mixture resembles crumbs. Beat egg; add with sufficient milk to make soft dough; mix lightly. Turn out on lightly floured board and knead just enough to make the dough cling together. Roll out to a thickness of about ¼ inch. Spread with remaining soft butter. Cover with sweetened blackberries. Roll up like a jelly roll. It is a good idea to roll the dough on wax paper, as the dough is tender and rich and difficult to lift into the baking pan. Lifting wax paper, turn roll over into baking pan. Bake in a 400-degree oven for 25 minutes or until golden brown. Cut into slices and serve warm with berry sauce or thick cream.

Armed with buckets—some lard buckets and some water buckets— the children went forth like an army to fight chiggers and briars in a search for blackberries.

Makes 6 to 8 servings.

Berry Sauce

The sauce is similar to hot blackberry jam.

> 1 cup blackberries
> ¾ cup sugar
> Juice of ½ lemon

Blend all ingredients and cook over medium heat, stirring, until clear like jam. Add a small amount of water if needed.

OVER THE CANNING KETTLE

All summer long, the kitchen was pungent with the tangy smell of pickling spices and vinegar heating in saucepans, alive with big kettles of jelly or preserves gently plopping as they cooked.

New England housewives fill their fruit closets with beach plum jelly, made from the fruit of bushes which bloom each year but bear fruit only once every three years. The sand plum is a favorite in the Midwest. The damson plum once grew abundantly in the South, where it is made into a deliciously tart preserve.

Jerusalem Artichoke Pickles

Approximately 2 gallons artichokes
Hot pepper to taste
1 gallon vinegar
3 cups sugar
½ cup noniodized salt
2 teaspoons tumeric
1½ teaspoons celery seed

Artichokes should never be dug until the stems are completely killed by cold weather. They can be left in the ground and dug at any time during the winter. If dug too early, pickles made from them may become soft.

Wash and scrub artichokes thoroughly. Cut into chunks. Pack into hot sterile jars, and add hot pepper to taste. Bring vinegar, sugar, salt, tumeric, and celery seed to a boil and simmer for 5 minutes. Pour liquid over artichokes. Seal jars. Place jars on rack in large kettle with water to cover. Bring water gently to a boil; simmer for 10 minutes. Makes about 8 quarts.

Mama called summer a failure if there weren't at least five hundred jars in rows of the pantry shelves by the time the last rose of summer faded.

In summer as we worked putting away food for winter, Mama reminded us of the story of the busy little ant and the lazy grasshopper. The ant gathered food in the summer to store away for winter, while the grasshopper played. The ant ate well in winter and the grasshopper starved.

Dilly Beans

3 pounds fresh green beans, washed
½ cup fresh dill, chopped
2 cloves garlic, peeled and halved
2 cups water
2 cups vinegar
4 tablespoons salt, noniodized
4 teaspoons sugar
½ teaspoon cayenne

Snip off ends of beans; drop a third of the beans at a time in boiling water for 5 minutes or just until tender and crisp. Lift beans out with slotted spoon; immediately pack upright in sterilized pint jars. Place 2 tablespoons dill and a half clove garlic in each jar. In a saucepan, bring water, vinegar, salt, sugar, and cayenne to a boil; pour hot over beans. Seal jars. Place jars on rack in large canning kettle. Add hot water to cover jars. Process by keeping water in kettle at simmering temperature for 10 minutes. Makes 4 pints.

Gooseberry Catsup

10 pounds ripe gooseberries
1 quart cider vinegar
5 pounds brown sugar
2 tablespoons pepper
2 tablespoons allspice
2 tablespoons cloves
2 tablespoons cinnamon

Beat gooseberries very fine. Boil in cider vinegar until reduced to a pulp. Add sugar and spices. Cook until thickened. Pour hot into hot sterilized jars. Seal. Makes about 12 quarts.

Chili Sauce

3 quarts ripe tomatoes, peeled and chopped
3 cups sweet red peppers, cut in strips
3 cups onions, chopped
3 tablespoons salt
4 cups cider vinegar
1 tablespoon stick cinnamon, broken
1 tablespoon whole cloves
1 tablespoon celery seed
2½ cups sugar

Put peppers and onions through fine blade of food grinder. Combine tomatoes, peppers, onions, salt, and vinegar; add spices tied in a bag; cook, stirring occasionally, until thick, about 3 hours. Add sugar; cook 30 minutes longer. Remove spice bag, discard; pour hot into hot sterilized jars. Seal jars. Makes about 5 pints.

Rhubarb Strawberry Jam

　　5 cups rhubarb, diced
　　4 cups sugar
　　1 8-ounce can crushed pineapple
　　1 6-ounce package strawberry gelatin

Combine rhubarb and sugar; let stand for 30 minutes. Add undrained pineapple; mix and cook for 30 minutes. Remove from heat; add gelatin, stir to dissolve. Pour hot into hot sterilized jars; seal jars. Makes about 3 half-pint jars.

Strawberry Conserve

　　3 pints strawberries, washed and capped
　　2 cups pineapple, chopped
　　1 orange, quartered and seeds removed
　　½ 15-ounce box raisins
　　Juice of lemon
　　Sugar

Crush strawberries slightly. Put pineapple, orange, and raisins through food chopper or blend in blender; combine with strawberries and lemon juice. Measure; add an equal measure of sugar. Cook until thick, stirring frequently. Pour hot into hot sterilized jars; seal. Place jars with water to cover on rack in large kettle. Bring gently to a boil; simmer for 10 minutes. Makes about 5 half pints.

Pear Conserve

　　15 cups pears, peeled, cored, and finely diced
　　10 cups sugar
　　1 15-ounce box raisins
　　Rind of 2 oranges, grated
　　Juice of 2 oranges
　　Juice of 2 lemons

In an enamel kettle pour sugar over pears; let stand overnight. Add raisins, orange rind, orange and lemon juice; simmer, stirring occasionally, for 30 to 35 minutes or until thick. Pour into jars and seal with paraffin. Makes about 16 half pints.

There is one thing that remains the same in this changing world—the rhubarb plant. For over half a century the same plant with its floppy leaves resembling elephants ears and deep pink stalks has made an annual appearance.

Cranberry Conserve

    1 1-pound box fresh cranberries
    1 No. 2 can crushed pineapple
    1 6-ounce can frozen orange juice concentrate
    Water
    1½ cups sugar
    ½ teaspoon cinnamon
    ½ teaspoon ginger
    ¼ teaspoon cloves
    1 cup raisins
    1 cup whole blanched almonds
    1 cup broken pecan meats

Wash cranberries and discard faulty ones. Drain pineapple and combine drained juice with undiluted orange juice concentrate. Add water to juice mixture to make 2 cups liquid. In a saucepan, mix liquid and sugar. Stir to dissolve sugar. Add spices. Bring to a boil and simmer for 10 minutes. Add cranberries, bring to a boil again, and boil for 5 minutes, stirring frequently, or until cranberries begin to pop. Stir in raisins and pineapple and simmer 5 minutes longer, stirring several times. Cool slightly. Stir in nuts. Pack in jars and seal with paraffin. Makes 3 pints.

Dried Sweet Potatoes

Boil sweet potatoes until done but not soft enough to mash. Peel and slice on a clean white cloth. Put out in the sun to dry like apples. It takes 3 to 4 days in the hot sun. Store in a dry place. Eat as they are, soak in warm water and cook, or make into pies.

Maraschino Cherries

    4½ pounds firm, ripe Royal Anne Cherries
    Salt
    Alum
    Water
    9 cups sugar
    1 ounce red food coloring
    1 ounce almond extract
    Lemon juice to taste

Pit cherries. Make a brine of 2 tablespoons salt and 1 teaspoon alum for each quart of water needed to cover fruit. Let cherries sit overnight in brine. The next day, wash cherries until no trace of salt remains. Combine cherries, sugar, 3 cups water, and food coloring. Bring to a boil. Remove from heat; let stand for 24 hours. Again bring to boiling point; let stand 24 hours longer. Bring to a boil a third time; add almond extract and lemon juice. Seal in hot sterilized jars. Makes 10 half pints.

Chow-Chow

1 quart cabbage, chopped
1 pint white onions, finely chopped
1 pint sweet red peppers, finely chopped
1 pint sweet green peppers, finely chopped
½ cup salt
4 tablespoons mustard seed
2 tablespoons celery seed
1½ pounds granulated sugar
1 tablespoon whole allspice
1 stick cinnamon
1 quart vinegar

Place chopped vegetables in an enamel kettle or crock and sprinkle with the salt. Allow to stand for 5 to 6 hours or overnight. Squeeze in a cheesecloth to remove juice. Tie spices in a bag and add to vinegar and sugar in a kettle. Bring to a boil. Add vegetables and cook together for 10 minutes. Pour into hot sterilized jars and seal.

Tomato Juice

A version with zip.

1 gallon ripe tomatoes, unpeeled
16 whole cloves
2 bay leaves
4 onions, coarsely chopped
2 tablespoons salt
4 teaspoons sugar
½ teaspoon black pepper
¼ cup vinegar

Cut tomatoes into quarters and place with remaining ingredients, except vinegar, in a kettle. Bring to a boil, stirring gently, until juicy. Simmer for 1 hour. Strain and reheat to boiling after adding vinegar. Pour hot into hot sterilized jars; seal jars. Process by placing jars on racks in large kettle with hot water to cover; bring water gently to a boil; simmer pints for 10 minutes, quarts for 15 minutes. Serve juice chilled or hot like bouillon.

The cranberry, that bittersweet little fruit, is as much a part of New England as the little farms against the snow and the dark, forested hills.

Just before the first frost in autumn, we picked the last green tomatoes on the vines in the garden. Often when icy winds were blowing through the naked stalks, there were fresh tomatoes for the table.

49

Potpourri or Rumtopf (Brandied Fruits)

    1 pint fresh sweet cherries, pitted
    Peel of 1 orange, cut in a spiral
    1 tablespoon whole cloves
    1 cinnamon stick
    1 teaspoon whole allspice
    1 bottle (4/5 quart) rum, brandy, or bourbon
    1 pint fresh peach halves, peeled and pitted
    1 pint apricot halves, peeled and pitted
    1 pint plum halves, peeled and pitted
    1 pint seeded or seedless grapes
    1 pint fresh pineapple chunks
    1 pint fresh raspberries
    1 pint fresh strawberries
    8 cups granulated sugar

Scald a 6-quart stone crock with boiling water and dry it. Put cherries in it with 1 cup sugar. Add orange peel, spices, and rum. Cover crock. Add other fruits, each with a cup of sugar, as they come in season, stirring well after each addition. You may need to add more rum, brandy, or bourbon if the fruit has absorbed original amount. Leave crock in a dark place to ripen for 2 to 3 months. Serve as a dessert on its own, as a sauce over ice cream, or with poundcake.

The Dill Crock

    ¾ cup whole mixed pickle spices
    6 fresh dill heads or 4 teaspoons dried dill
    40 to 50 medium-size cucumbers, washed
    3 cups vinegar
    1½ cups salt, noniodized
    2 gallons water
    3 cloves garlic, sliced, if desired

Place ½ cup spices and 3 heads or 2 teaspoons dill in a 5-gallon crock. Fill crock with cucumbers to within 4 or 5 inches of top. Mix 2 cups vinegar, salt, and water; pour over vegetables. Place 3 dill heads, remaining spices, and garlic, if used, over the top. Cover with a heavy plate; weight it to hold cucumbers under the brine. Keep crock at room temperature; each day discard scum that forms over the top. Let cucumbers ferment for 2 to 3 weeks or until well flavored with dill. Serve within a few days, or pack cured pickles in hot, sterilized quart jars. Strain brine; add remaining vinegar and bring to a boil, pour over pickles to top of jar. Seal jars. Place jars on rack in large kettle filled with water to the top of the jars. Bring water gently to a boil; simmer for 10 minutes. Makes about 6 quarts.

String beans, green tomatoes, small onions and cauliflowerets can be added to the crock. Cook string beans 3 minutes in boiling water before adding.

Delicatessen Pickles

A recipe from the owner of a Deli.

Wash freshly gathered cucumbers and place in gallon jars. To each jar, add 2 cut cloves of garlic and 2 to 3 heads of fresh dill.

Combine 1 cup cider vinegar, ½ cup plain (noniodized) salt, and 1 gallon of water, and bring to a boil. Pour hot mixture over cucumbers. Screw on lid and let stand in the refrigerator for 5 to 6 weeks before eating. Store pickles in the refrigerator as long as they last.

JELLY

Sugar sacks were often used as jelly bags. The juice of the fruit—apple, grape, blackberry, dewberry—was strained through the sack into the jelly kettle, and a cup of sugar was added for each cup of juice. After hours of simmering and skimming, a small amount of the hot liquid was poured into a saucer and allowed to cool. When the cooled liquid became firm like jelly, it was done.

Before the last century ended, Charles B. Knox, a salesman in Johnstown, N.Y., watched his wife making calf's foot jelly. Deciding the process took entirely too much time, he hit upon the idea of packaging powdered gelatin in an easy-to-use form. Mrs. Knox helped to train salesmen to demonstrate the product in the home, and also developed recipes for its use. Early in the century, Golden Glow salad and Perfection salad loomed into popularity. Golden Glow is made of grated raw carrots and pineapple in gelatin. Perfection is made of raw cabbage, pepper, and pimiento in gelatin.

A pleasant memory from childhood is that of fishing in the fragrant brine of the dill crock for dilled green beans, cauliflower, tiny pickled onions, and tangy, dilled green tomatoes.

Supper on the day devoted to making apple jelly was ham and eggs and cheese biscuits to serve with some of the freshly made jelly.

Calf's Foot Jelly

Boil 2 well-cleaned calves feet in a gallon of water until the water is reduced to a quart. Pour the liquid into a pan. When it is cold, skim off all the fat. Remove the jelly, but leave what may have settled at the bottom. Put the jelly into a saucepan with a pint of mountain wine, half a pound of loaf sugar, and the juice of 4 lemons. (Loaf sugar is a compact mass of refined sugar in a cone shape.) Add well-beaten whites of 6 or 8 eggs, stir the mixture well, put on the fire, and let boil for a few minutes. Put some thinly cut lemon peel into a large china basin. Pour jelly through a large flannel bag into the basin. Repeat pouring until jelly runs clear. The lemon peel will provide a pleasing color and flavor. Pour into jelly glasses and seal with paraffin.

Grape Jelly

> 1 6-ounce can frozen grape juice concentrate
> 1 1¾-ounce box commercial pectin
> 2 cups water
> 3¾ cups sugar

In large saucepan, combine undiluted juice, pectin, and water; cook rapidly over high heat until mixture bubbles around the edge. Remove from heat; stir in sugar. Return to heat; cook until mixture bubbles thoroughly. Remove from heat; skim, discard scum. Pour hot into hot jelly glasses. When cold, seal top with paraffin. Makes 5 to 6 jars.

Isinglass Jelly

Isinglass, according to Artemus Ward in *The Grocer's Encyclopedia* (1911), was prepared from the air or swim bladder of the sturgeon, cod, and similar fish.

> 5 ounces isinglass
> 3 quarts water
> Rind and juice of 4 lemons
> 2¼ pounds loaf sugar
> 6 egg whites and shells, beaten
> 3 pints sherry

Place all ingredients in a kettle and boil until perfectly clear; this will take about 45 minutes. Strain through a flannel bag. Pour into jelly glasses and allow to cool. Seal with paraffin.

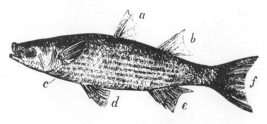

THE APPLE

A man named John Chapman was born in Massachusetts in 1774. He grew up to become an itinerant peddler who planted apple seeds as he roamed the countryside. He carried a sack of apple seeds gathered from cider press refuse. John Chapman, known as the legendary Johnny Appleseed, did his work well until his death at the age of seventy-one in 1845. At his birthplace a granite memorial stands bearing this inscription: "He planted seeds that others might enjoy fruit." It is said New England could scarcely have survived without the apple. That is no doubt true of other parts of the country.

America has enjoyed Johnny Appleseed's fruit raw, candied, baked, dried (the schnitz of the Pennsylvania Dutch); in sauce, dumplings, turnovers, and pies; and have used it to make cider and brandy.

By 1900 the McIntosh was fairly well known throughout the Northeast. In Vermont, it was first called the "chimney apple," its fresh pleasant aroma lending fragrance to any room. The Rome Beauty apple traces its origin to Rome Township, Lawrence County, Ohio, about 1816. Many of the old varieties have nearly vanished: Roxbury Russett, Chenango Strawberry, Smoke House, Gillflower, Snow, Spitzenburg, Jeniton, Limbertwig, Albemarle, Pippin (a favorite of Queen Victoria), Magnum Bonum.

One of the gala food celebrations in apple-producing Michigan occurs in Kent County in autumn. The wives of apple growers stage an apple smorgasbord. A spread of fifty or more apple dishes is set up on outdoor tables covered with apple-green cloths. In addition to the apple offerings, there is baked ham and coffee. The meal starter is chilled, pasteurized apple juice, which was developed at Michigan State College.

In autumn the custom was to grind apples in a hand-turned cider press to make cider. Putting yeast in cider turns the liquid into "hard" cider, a beverage with a "kick." Cider is distilled to make brandy.

Big pots filled with apple butter and set over open fires scents the air with a spicy aroma at the Fourth of July Festival in Kutztown, Pa. A big wooden paddle, sometimes called a horse's head, is used for stirring, and it takes a special big brass pot and hours to make apple butter properly. Sometimes neighbors join to "make together." Molasses is used for sweetening; oil of cinnamon and oil of cloves will lighten the color, while powdered spices will produce a darker shade.

A whole apple peel, all in one piece like a big corkscrew, was a little feat grandfather performed when he peeled apples with his pocket knife.

Baked Apple Butter

    2 quarts apples, peeled, cored, and finely chopped
    2 quarts apple cider
    4 cups sugar
    1 teaspoon cinnamon
    ¼ teaspoon allspice
    ¼ teaspoon cloves
    ¼ teaspoon ginger
    ¼ teaspoon nutmeg or mace
    ½ teaspoon salt

Cook apples and cider in roaster, covered, in a
300-degree oven for 2 to 3 hours or until thick and
mushy. Put through a food mill or mash thoroughly;
pour back into roaster, add sugar, spices, and salt.
Stir to blend in sugar. Return roaster to oven, and
continue cooking; stir occasionally, until butter is as
thick as desired. Pour hot butter into hot sterilized jars,
filling to ⅛ inch of top. Seal jars. Place jars in large
kettle with water to cover jars; bring water to a boil.
Keep water at simmering point for 5 minutes. Makes
about 6 pints.

Apple Preserves

An old recipe from an apple grower.

Pare apples. If small, cut into quarters. If large, cut into
eights. Cover HEAVILY with sugar. Cover and let
stand in a cool place overnight. The sugar will slowly
dissolve. When ready to cook, place over lowest heat on
the stove. Stir occasionally. Increase heat and watch
closely to prevent burning. Add a dash of ginger or
cinnamon. Cook until apples are clear and thoroughly
done. Pour into jars. Pour syrup over apples and seal.

Apple Pandowdy

    6 apples
    1 cup light brown sugar, firmly packed
    ½ teaspoon nutmeg
    1 teaspoon cinnamon
    1 cup warm water
    Margarine
    Biscuit dough

Peel, core, and slice apples into a baking dish. Mix
together brown sugar, nutmeg, and cinnamon; sprinkle
over apples. Add water and dot generously with
margarine. Make biscuit dough (recipe below) and
place over apples. Crimp edges around outside of
baking dish. Bake at 300 degrees for 1½ hours. Serve
hot with cream sweetened with sugar and flavored
with nutmeg. Makes 6 servings.

Under one of the apple trees in the
back of our house, I made a play
house with rooms marked off like
hopscotch on the dirt with a stick.
My brother had a special seat on a
curved branch of the tree. On
summer afternoons he crawled up
to sit and read a book.

Days we'd make apple butter, Ma'd
make gingerbread muffins to
spread it on for supper, with
chicken corn soup and coleslaw.

Biscuit Dough

2 cups flour, sifted
1 tablespoon sugar
3 teaspoons baking powder
1 teaspoon salt
⅓ cup shortening
½ cup milk

Sift together flour, sugar, baking powder, and salt.
Cut in shortening until mixture resembles coarse meal.
Add milk, mixing until flour is dampened. Turn out on
floured pastry cloth and knead lightly. Roll to a scant
½-inch thick. Cut a decorative design in center. Place
over apples.

Bean Pot Applesauce

5 pounds apples
1 cup brown sugar, firmly packed
1 cup apple cider
2 tablespoons lemon juice
½ teaspoon nutmeg

Pare and core apples; slice into eighths. Place in 3-quart
bean pot. In a saucepan, heat sugar and cider, stirring,
until sugar dissolves. Remove from heat; add lemon
juice and nutmeg; pour over apples. Cover and bake at
350 degrees for about 1 hour, or until apples are soft,
removing cover and stirring twice. Break up with a
fork to desired consistency. Makes about 2 quarts.

Apple Brown Betty

2 tablespoons butter
2 cups soft bread crumbs
½ cup sugar
¼ teaspoon cinnamon
¼ teaspoon nutmeg
Rind and juice of 1 lemon
3 cups apples, peeled and chopped
¼ cup water
Heavy cream

Melt butter and add the crumbs. Mix the sugar, spices,
and grated lemon rind. Put one-quarter of the crumbs
in the bottom of a buttered baking dish. Cover with
half the apples. Sprinkle with half the sugar mixture;
then add another quarter of the crumbs, the remainder
of the apples, and the rest of the sugar mixture. Add the
lemon juice and the water, and put the rest of the
crumbs over the top. Cover and bake for 45 minutes in
a 375-degree oven; uncover and brown. Serve with
cream.

Drying Apples

Apples peeled and sliced and put outdoors on clean cloths were dried in the hot sun. A bushel of apples dried down to four pounds, and it was not unusual for a farm family to dry up to four hundred pounds in a year.

Fumigated Apples

Peel, core, cut apples into eighths, filling a metal or wooden tub with them. Make a hole or well in the center of the apples. Place a plate in the hole. Put several thicknesses of white cloth over plate. Pour ½ cup of sulphur on the cloth. Ignite the cloth and immediately cover the tub tightly with oil cloth and an old quilt, else the fumes will smother you. Leave covered half a day or more because the apples have to be thoroughly fumigated to keep. Store apples in jars. They will keep for months.

Another way of fumigating is to hang a basket of apples in a barrel or box containing a fire of little sticks sprinkled with sulphur.

Peanut Butter

The old way was to grind peanuts several times in the meat grinder. This way should prove faster.

> **2 cups peanuts, roasted and salted**
> **2 to 3 tablespoons peanut oil**

Combine peanuts and oil in electric blender. Blend until smooth. Makes 1 cup.

I recall the delight I felt when Mother started making fumigated apples, for we knew we were going to have something good. They tasted like fresh apples and we used them all winter.

The lunch we carried to school which did not have a lunch room was two or three cold sausage biscuits. They were made from the sausage cakes and biscuits left from breakfast.

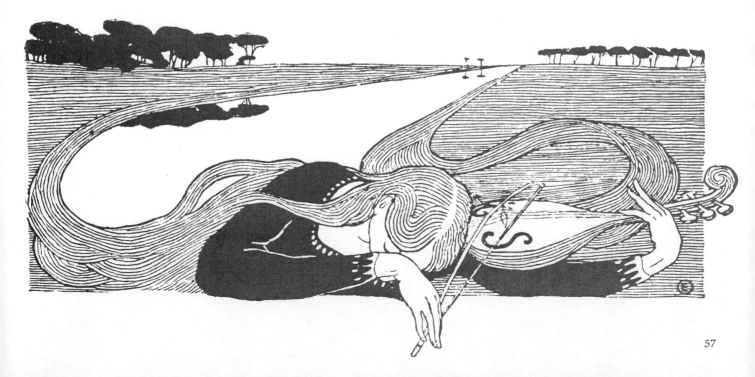

CHAPTER 2

The Livin' Wasn't Easy but It Was Cheap

At the beginning of the century the average worker earned twenty-two cents an hour. A 1905 source states that a family of two lived well on ten dollars a week and this sum included house rent and wages for one servant. Until the Depression a live-in servant who had one afternoon off each week could be hired for a weekly salary of two dollars.

1910 PRICES

Groceries

Spring chickens	7¢ per pound
Beef	10¢ per pound
Sausage	12½¢ per pound
Rooster	15¢ each
Hens	7¢ per pound
Pork	10¢ per pound
Turkey	10¢ per pound
Duck	6¢ per pound
Duck, dressed	10¢ per pound
Veal	10¢ per pound
Breakfast bacon	12½¢ per pound
Goose	5¢ per pound
Red apples	30¢ per peck
Seed potatoes	35¢ per bushel
Onion sets	25¢ for 3 quarts
Oranges	20¢ per dozen
Lemons	15¢ per dozen
Eggs	12¢ per dozen
Butter	18¢ per pound
Lye	5¢ per can
Garden seed	5¢ for 2 packages
Sugar	$5.80 for 100 pounds
Coffee	15¢ per pound

Household Items

Wood stove	$17.48
Cherry stoner	.70
Bread toaster	.20
Ice cream freezer	1.26
Wooden icebox	8.92
Coffee grinder	.49
Enameled teapot	.58

A 1934 FAMILY BUDGET

The man worked on a CWA (Civilian Works Administration) government work project, and earned eighteen dollars a week. He was head of a household of three adults and three children.

Weekly Expenditures

Rent for 5 rooms	$ 4.60
¼ ton of coal	3.15
Electricity	.80
Gas	.90
Health needs	1.50
14 quarts of milk, @ 12¢	1.68
14 loaves of bread, @ 10¢	1.40
5 pounds of sugar	.25
5 pounds of rice	.25
Vegetables	.75
Meat	2.00
Fruits	.70
2½ dozen eggs	.90
1 pound butter	.25
Fats	.15
Cereals	.50
¾ pound of coffee	.20
Soap	.30
Clothing	2.00
Church	1.00
	$23.28

The family went into debt $5.28 each week.

From 1932 to 1934, a doctor earned $3382 per year; a school teacher, $1227; and a hired farm hand, $260.00.

A new Dodge automobile cost $595.

At a Dollar Day sale in the thirties, tables were heaped with dresses on sale for one dollar each.

DINNER IN A RESTAURANT, 1927

Fixed Price: One dollar

Caviar on Toast

Consommé or Cream of Chicken soup

Choice of

Boiled Halibut, Egg Sauce

Fried Chicken, Waffles

Braised Sweetbreads

Roast Ribs of Prime Beef au Jus

Asparagus with Cream Sauce or Steamed Rice

Mashed or Boiled Potatoes

Endive Salad

Diplomatic Pudding, Blueberry Pie, Preserved Pears, Lemon Sherbet, or Ice Cream and Cakes

Coffee, Milk, or Iced Tea

TWO BITS

Until World War II, the price of the neighborhood movie and the blueplate special lunch at a cafe was two bits, twenty-five cents. The lunch included bread, butter, beverage, and dessert, but allowed no substitutions. Popcorn at the two-bit movie was five cents a box. The cost of a seat to see *Oliver* in a New Jersey theater in 1970 is three dollars, a box of popcorn, thirty-five cents.

WITH MORE TASTE THAN EXPENSE

Pigtail Stew Supper

5 pounds pigtails, pigs feet, pigs ears,
   hog liver, and back ribs, mixed
Water
Salt and pepper to taste
2 pods red pepper, sliced
5 pounds collard greens
½ pound salt pork, sliced
8 to 10 baked sweet potatoes

Place meat with water to cover, salt and pepper to taste, and 1 pepper pod in kettle; simmer for 2 to 3 hours. Wash collard greens; remove large ribs, discard. Meanwhile, in skillet fry salt pork until crisp; remove from skillet; drain. Place collards with 1 cup water, salt and pepper to taste, and remaining pepper pod in large pot; simmer for 30 minutes or until collards are tender, adding water if needed. To serve, place 2 to 3 large spoonsful each of meat stew and collards on dinner plate; garnish collards with salt pork, place a sweet potato on each plate. Serves 8 to 10.

Braised Rabbit

1 teaspoon salt
⅛ teaspoon pepper
1 cup flour
1 rabbit, dressed and cut into pieces
1 egg, beaten
1⅓ cups plus 1 tablespoon water
¾ cup dry bread crumbs
4 to 6 tablespoons lard or bacon drippings

Mix salt, pepper, and flour; use to coat pieces of rabbit.
Dip pieces in mixture of egg and 1 tablespoon water,
then coat in bread crumbs; brown in hot lard in skillet.
Add 1 cup water slowly; cover tightly and simmer
1 hour or until tender, adding remaining water as
needed. Makes 6 servings.

Old-Fashioned Beef Hash

From the days when the hash was a lot better than
the roast.

3 tablespoons bacon drippings or shortening
2 cups beef, cooked and diced
3 medium potatoes, boiled and diced
2 onions, diced
1 teaspoon salt
¼ teaspoon pepper
Hot water or beef bouillon

Heat drippings or shortening in skillet; add beef,
potatoes, onions, salt, and pepper. Cook, stirring
occasionally, until mixture begins to brown. Moisten
lightly as it cooks with water or bouillon. Serves 6.

Red Flannel Hash

6 slices salt pork
1 cup corned beef, cooked and chopped
¼ cup milk
3 cups boiled potatoes, chopped
1 cup beets, cooked and chopped
1 onion, chopped

Fry salt pork until crisp. Remove pieces and retain as
garnish. Combine meat, milk, and vegetables. Spread
mixture smoothly over the bottom of skillet in which
salt pork was fried. Brown slowly. When a crust forms,
turn as an omelet. Serve on a hot plate garnished with
crisp pork. Makes 6 servings.

Texas Hash

3 large onions, sliced
1 large green pepper, minced
3 tablespoons fat or meat drippings
1 pound ground beef
1 1-pound can tomatoes
1 cup raw regular rice
2 teaspoons Worcestershire sauce
2 teaspoons salt

Cook onions and green pepper in fat until onions are
golden. Add meat; cook and stir until it falls apart.
Add remaining ingredients and turn into a greased
2-quart casserole. Cover and bake in a 350-degree oven
for 1 hour, removing cover for the last 15 minutes.

Individual Meat Loaves

1 cup dry bread crumbs
1 medium onion, chopped
2 teaspoons salt
¼ teaspoon pepper
1 teaspoon dry mustard
1 teaspoon Worcestershire sauce
¼ cup catsup
2 eggs
2 pounds ground beef

Combine all ingredients; blend, shape into 6 loaves.
Place on lightly greased baking pan; bake, basting with
sauce (recipe below), in a 350-degree oven for 45
minutes or until done. Serves 6.

Meat Loaf Sauce

1 cup catsup
1 small onion, chopped
¼ cup vinegar
1 tablespoon sugar
½ teaspoon dry mustard

Combine all ingredients; use to baste loaves.

Chicken Vegetable Soup

1 3- to 3½-pound fryer
Water
2 cups corn kernels
2 cups lima beans
1 28-ounce can tomatoes
1 large onion, chopped
2 medium potatoes, peeled and cubed
1 tablespoon salt
½ teaspoon pepper

Cook chicken in water to cover in kettle for 1 hour or until done; lift chicken from broth. Remove chicken from bones, discard bones and skin; shred meat and return to broth. Add vegetables, salt, and pepper; simmer for 1 hour. Taste to check seasonings. Makes 8 servings.

Corn Chowder

4 cups potatoes, peeled and diced
2 cups water
2 tablespoons salt pork, diced
3 tablespoons onion, chopped
2 cups corn kernels, fresh or canned
2 cups milk
2 teaspoons salt
½ teaspoon pepper

Cook potatoes in water for 15 minutes. In skillet, cook salt pork and onions until browned; add with corn, milk, and seasonings to potatoes and water. Heat, but do not boil. Makes 6 servings.

Parsnip Stew

Follow recipe for corn chowder, substituting 2 cups cooked cubes of parsnip for corn.

Turnip Stew

Follow recipe for corn chowder, substituting 2 cups cooked cubes of turnip for corn.

Ham Hock Dinner

4 ham hocks
Water
4 medium carrots
4 medium onions
4 medium potatoes, halved
½ medium head cabbage, cut into 4 wedges
Salt
Pepper

Cover hocks with water, and simmer for 1½ hours or until meat is tender. Add carrots, onions, and potatoes; cook for 15 minutes. Add cabbage with salt and pepper to taste; simmer 10 minutes longer or until cabbage is done. Serves 4.

Salmon Croquettes

> 1 pound salmon
> ¼ cup soft bread crumbs
> 2 eggs
> 1 tablespoon water
> Fine dry bread crumbs
> Shortening

Flake salmon, add soft bread crumbs and 1 egg, and mix well. Shape into 5 or 6 croquettes. Beat remaining egg and water; coat croquettes in egg mixture, roll in fine crumbs. Brown on all sides in a small amount of shortening in a heavy skillet. Makes 5 or 6.

Baked Macaroni and Cheese

> 3 quarts water, boiling
> 1¼ teaspoons salt
> 1½ cups macaroni, broken
> 2 cups milk
> 3 eggs, beaten
> ½ teaspoon prepared mustard
> ½ pound process American cheese, sliced

In 3 quarts boiling water and 1 teaspoon salt, cook macaroni for 7 minutes; drain. Meanwhile, heat milk to boiling point; blend with beaten eggs, ¼ teaspoon salt, and mustard. Place half the macaroni in baking dish; top with half the cheese. Repeat layers. Pour in milk mixture; bake, covered, in a 350-degree oven for 45 minutes or until bubbly, remove lid the last 10 minutes of baking. Makes 6 servings.

Noodles

> 1 large egg
> ¾ cup flour
> Water, salted

Mix egg and flour; knead until it holds together and is smooth. Place in bowl; cover, let stand for 1 hour. Roll out thinly; cut into thin strips, and drop into boiling salted water. Cook for 5 minutes—do not overcook. Makes 2 to 3 servings.

Noodle Fritters

4 ounces thin egg noodles
2 eggs, beaten
½ cup flour
½ cup milk
½ teaspoon salt
Shortening for frying
Sugar

Cook noodles by package directions; drain. Add to eggs mixed with flour, milk, and salt. Drop by rounded tablespoons to make fritters the size of plump oysters in a small amount of hot shortening in a heavy skillet; cook slowly, turning once, until brown on both sides. Sprinkle with sugar. Makes 18. Good served with sausage and applesauce.

Poor Boys

When supplies of meat and fat were exhausted, Confederate soldiers cooked potatoes this way.

3 or more small, new potatoes per serving
Salt

Place washed, unpeeled potatoes in saucepan; add salted water to cover. Boil; sprinkle with additional salt as potatoes cook. Cook until water is cooked away; the "poor boys" have a coating of salt.

Fried Mush

As suggested by Fannie Farmer in 1916.

Pack mush (oatmeal) leftover from breakfast into a greased, 1-pound baking powder box. Cover to prevent crust from forming. The next morning remove from the box; slice thinly, dip in flour, and sauté. Serve with syrup.

French Toast

For breakfast and also for lunch or supper when meat was scarce. Before World War I, it was called German toast.

2 eggs
⅛ teaspoon salt
1 cup milk
6 slices bread
3 tablespoons shortening, drippings, or margarine
Syrup or sugar

Beat together eggs, salt, and milk; dip bread in mixture, coating both sides. Cook until brown on both sides in fat in heavy skillet. Serve with syrup or sprinkled with sugar.

Homemade Syrup

    2 cups brown sugar
    1 cup water

Combine sugar and water in saucepan; simmer for
10 minutes or until syrupy. Serve hot. Makes about
1½ cups.

Milk Toast

    1 pint milk
    ½ teaspoon salt
    6 slices dry toast
    2 tablespoons butter

Scald milk and salt. Spread toast with butter and place
each slice in a bowl. Pour hot milk over toast and serve.
Makes 6 servings.

Hard Times Rolls

1 2-pound bag flour (about 7½ cups)
1 tablespoon salt
4 heaping tablespoons sugar
1 package dry yeast
2½ cups warm water
Shortening

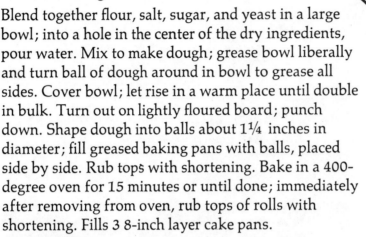

Blend together flour, salt, sugar, and yeast in a large bowl; into a hole in the center of the dry ingredients, pour water. Mix to make dough; grease bowl liberally and turn ball of dough around in bowl to grease all sides. Cover bowl; let rise in a warm place until double in bulk. Turn out on lightly floured board; punch down. Shape dough into balls about 1¼ inches in diameter; fill greased baking pans with balls, placed side by side. Rub tops with shortening. Bake in a 400-degree oven for 15 minutes or until done; immediately after removing from oven, rub tops of rolls with shortening. Fills 3 8-inch layer cake pans.

Popovers

6 to 8 teaspoons shortening
2 eggs
1 cup milk
½ cup flour
½ teaspoon salt

Place 1 teaspoon shortening in each of 6 to 8 straight-sided custard cups. Place cups in oven; turn on heat to 475 degrees. Combine eggs, milk, flour, and salt; beat with egg beater until well blended. Pour batter into sizzling hot cups, filling each half full. Bake for 15 minutes at 475 degrees; reduce heat to 350 degrees, and bake 10 to 15 minutes longer or until browned and firm. A few minutes before removing from oven, prick each with a fork to allow steam to escape. Turn off oven, leave popovers in oven for about 3 minutes to dry and get crisp. Makes 6 to 8.

Communion Bread

4 tablespoons shortening
1½ cups flour
3 tablespoons ice water, approximate

Cut shortening into flour to make fine crumbs. Add water to make a mixture that clings together. Roll dough out as for pie crust. Prick with a fork and cut into small squares. Place squares on baking sheet lined with wax paper. Bake in a 250-degree oven for 1½ hours or until crisp but not brown. Makes 30 to 40 pieces.

Another way of baking this bread was to make a thin batter of flour and water. The batter was then poured, one tablespoon at a time, on a hot flat iron (the iron heated on the kitchen stove and used for ironing fabric). A second hot iron was pressed down hard on the batter to cook it, the result was a thin wafer.

Fried Peach Pies

Also called half moon pies.

> **1 11-ounce package dried peaches**
> **Water**
> **½ cup sugar**
> **1 9½-ounce carton ready-to-bake biscuits**
> **Lard**

Place peaches with water to cover in saucepan; simmer for 30 minutes or until soft. Drain off excess liquid; discard. Mash peaches with potato masher; add sugar, cool thoroughly. Roll out biscuits on lightly floured board to make thin circles about 6 inches in diameter. Place portion of peach mixture on one half of each circle; fold over other half, seal edges tightly with a fork. Brown on each side in about ¼ inch hot lard in a heavy skillet. Makes 10.

Hypocrite Pie

When eggs were plentiful, cooks made egg custard pie, a favorite in many families. When eggs were scarce, cooks made a hypocrite pie with a base of sweetened plentiful fruit and a thin topping of egg custard to camouflage the fruit.

Hypocrite Pie

> **2½ cups dried apple or peach pulp, mashed**
> **¾ cup sugar**
> **1 egg, beaten**
> **⅛ teaspoon salt**
> **⅔ cup milk**
> **½ teaspoon vanilla**
> **1 8-inch pastry shell, unbaked**

To pulp, add ½ cup sugar; blend and spread in bottom of pie shell. Combine remaining sugar, egg, salt, milk, and vanilla; pour over fruit in pastry. Bake in a 350-degree oven for 40 minutes or until the custard topping is firm.

Stale bread was used to make a hearty, economical dessert. This version is adapted to modern supplies.

Bread Pudding

    1 1-pound loaf bread or equivalent, coarsely
        broken
    1 quart milk, hot
    3 eggs, beaten
    2 cups sugar
    2 tablespoons vanilla
    1 cup golden raisins
    3 tablespoons margarine

Pour hot milk over bread in bowl. Blend eggs, sugar
and vanilla; add to bread and mix well. Add raisins. In
9- by 13-inch baking pan, melt margarine; pour
mixture into pan. Bake in a 350-degree oven for 40
minutes or until firm and golden brown. Makes 24
servings. Serve warm or cold with nutmeg or lemon
sauce (recipes below).

Nutmeg Sauce

    1 tablespoon flour
    ½ cup sugar
    1 cup water, boiling
    1 egg, beaten
    ½ teaspoon nutmeg

In saucepan, blend flour and sugar; add boiling water.
Cook, stirring, until smooth and thick. Pour a small
amount of hot liquid into egg; beat together and add
remaining hot liquid. Return to heat; cook 1 minute
longer. Remove from heat; add nutmeg. Serve warm.
Makes about 1 cup.

Lemon Sauce

    ½ cup sugar
    1 tablespoon cornstarch or 2 tablespoons flour
    1 teaspoon lemon rind, grated
    1 cup water
    2 tablespoons butter or margarine
    2 tablespoons lemon juice

In saucepan, blend sugar, cornstarch, and lemon rind;
stir in cold water and cook until clear and thick, stirring
constantly. Remove from heat; stir in butter and lemon
juice until butter is melted. Serve hot or cold. Makes
about 1 cup.

Hard Times Cake

This cake was baked when eggs, milk, and butter were scarce. It was also called economy cake, poverty cake, poor's man cake, and mother's minus cake.

    2 cups sugar
    2 cups water
    1 pound raisins, chopped
    ¼ cup lard
    3 cups flour, sifted
    1 teaspoon salt
    2 teaspoons cinnamon
    2 teaspoons ground cloves
    2 teaspoons baking soda

Simmer together sugar, water, raisins, and lard for 5 minutes; set aside to cool. Sift together dry ingredients; add to raisin mixture, beat until smooth. Pour into 2 greased and floured loaf pans, 9 by 5 inches; bake in a 325-degree oven for 1 hour and 30 minutes or until done. Makes 2 loaves.

Jelly Doughnuts

    ½ cup butter or margarine
    ½ cup sugar
    2 eggs
    1 package dry yeast
    ¼ cup lukewarm water
    ¼ cup sour cream
    7 cups flour, sifted, approximate
    1 teaspoon salt
    1⅓ cups milk
    ½ 10-ounce jar jelly
    Oil for frying
    Confectioners' sugar

Cream butter and sugar; blend in eggs. Dissolve yeast in water; add to creamed mixture with sour cream. Sift together flour and salt; add to creamed mixture alternately with milk. Cover and let rise in a warm place for 1 to 1½ hours until double in bulk. Punch down; turn out on floured board, cut in half and roll each half to ¼-inch thickness. Cut with 2-inch-round cutter; place half of circles on floured baking sheets, place about 1 teaspoon jelly in the center of each. Top with remaining circles; press with a fork to seal edges tightly. Cover and let rise until light to the touch. Fry until well browned on both sides in deep hot fat at 375°F. Lift out with slotted spoon; roll in confectioners' sugar. Makes about 4 dozen.

Persimmon Pudding

2½ cups persimmon pulp
4 cups flour
2 cups milk
1 teaspoon baking soda
1 teaspoon baking powder
½ teaspoon salt
1 teaspoon cinnamon
3 eggs, beaten
6 tablespoons butter, melted
1 cup granulated sugar
1 cup brown sugar

Combine all ingredients thoroughly; pour into greased 11- by 13-inch baking dish 2 inches deep. Bake in 300-degree oven for 1 hour or until firm. Serve hot or cold. Makes 18 servings.

THE FREE LUNCH COUNTER

The institution called the Free Lunch Counter reached its zenith between 1890 and 1910, when saloons offered free food, usually an assortment of salty edibles to stimulate thirst, and lunch was free with a drink or two. The practice was a boon to the bachelor, college student, and junior executive.

Following is a menu from the grandiose free lunch counter of San Francisco's Palace of Art.

Radishes   Crab Salad   Celery
Clam Juice
Pig's Head   Bolinas Bay Clams   Headcheese
Homemade Sausage, Country Style
Beef à la Chili Colorado
Chili Con Carne   Honolulu Beans
Chicken Croquettes   Veal Croquettes
Terrapin Stew
Fried Clams   Sardines   Baked Ham
Saratoga Chips   Corned Beef
Tongue in Spicy Aspic   Beef Stew
Boston Baked Beans
Frizzled Beef   Smoked Salmon
Cheese   Crackers
Cracked Crab   Holland Herring
Almonds   Popcorn   Apples

Pickled Eggs

12 to 16 hard-cooked eggs
2 tablespoons sugar
1 teaspoon mixed pickling spices
2 cups cider vinegar
⅔ cup liquid drained from canned beets

Peel eggs and place in jar. In saucepan, combine sugar, salt, spices, vinegar, and beet juice and bring to a boil. Simmer for 3 minutes. Strain and pour over eggs. Put lid on jar and store in refrigerator for 2 days before serving. They will keep in refrigerator for several days.

CHAPTER 3
When the Day Started with Breakfast

The Autocrat of the Breakfast Table, a book by
Oliver Wendell Holmes, was still widely read in the
early part of this century. The day certainly started
with breakfast, although for most people it was
usually much less lavish than the one given by
Justice Holmes. This is his menu.

Littleneck Clams

Grilled Trout   Cucumbers, Sautéed

Omelette with Mushrooms in Cream   Grilled Plover

Filet Mignon   Potatoes

Asparagus with Hollandaise Sauce

Tomato and Lettuce Salad

Ice Cream   Strawberries   Cakes   Coffee

A plover, according to Artemus Ward in *The Grocer's
Encyclopedia* of 1911, is a genus of birds of many
varieties, from some no bigger than a sparrow to the
field or grey plover which is generally a little larger than
the woodcock. The most esteemed type is the golden
plover, principally imported from Europe. Plovers were
broiled or roasted like quail, and where their use is not
prohibited by law, plover's eggs are considered a
great delicacy.

Thomas Wolfe's characters woke up in the morning
"in a house pungent with breakfast cookery," and came
to a breakfast table loaded with brains and eggs, ham,
hot biscuits, fried apples seething in gummed syrups,
honey, golden butter, fried steak, and scalding coffee.
Or there were "stacked batter-cakes, rum-colored
molasses, fragrant brown sausages, a bowl of wet
cherries, plums, fat juicy bacon, jam."

Breakfast for Diamond Jim Brady began with a full
gallon of orange juice, followed by eggs, chops,
beefsteak, potatoes, hominy, corn bread, muffins, and
flapjacks.

Beefsteak was often served for breakfast early in the
century, but as the century progressed, bacon, ham, or
sausage with eggs became the more usual fare.
By the end of World War II, breakfast had changed to a
smaller and quicker meal. With weight problems,
cholesterol fears, kids in a hurry to get to school, and
adults in a hurry to get to work, breakfast now often
consists of a glass of juice, a cup of coffee, and a
doughnut, or it is a roll and coffee at the morning coffee
break in the factory or office. This change has come
gradually, and although breakfast specialties continue
to appear on tables all over the country, there are
indications that the breakfast habit may soon
disappear completely.

BREAKFAST MENUS AND SPECIALTIES
Shartlesville Breakfast

The traveler who "put up" at the hotel in Shartlesville, Pa., had this breakfast for many years.

Fruit Juices
Dried Peaches and Prunes
Pancakes
Bacon   Sausage   Eggs
Scrapple in Season
Fried Potatoes
Toast   Sugar Cakes
Butter   Jam
Coffee   Milk

Sugar Cakes

½ cup lard
1¾ cups sugar
3 eggs, beaten
3 cups flour
1 teaspoon baking soda
1 teaspoon cream of tartar
1 cup thick sour milk or cream
Additional sugar

Cream together lard and sugar until light and fluffy. Blend in eggs. Sift together dry ingredients and add alternately with milk to creamed mixture. Pour into 3 greased 8-inch pie tins. Sprinkle top of each with 1 tablespoon sugar. Bake in a 325-degree oven for 25 minutes or until done. Serve for breakfast or with coffee or lemonade to afternoon callers.

Sugar cake, another Pennsylvania Dutch favorite, is different from sugar cakes. Sugar cake is a coffee cake made of slightly sweet yeast dough. It is baked in sheets and, when finished, is an inch or more thick.

The top is covered with "puddles" of brown sugar and butter baked in little wells made in the dough. The stingy or frugal cook makes the holes in the dough for the butter and sugar with her forefinger, the generous cook makes them with her thumb.

Light cake with "buttons or dollars" appears on Pennsylvania Dutch tables. It is a yeast bread topped, before baking, with a mixture similar to hard sauce with the addition of flour, and shaped like silver dollars or buttons. Butter semmel, or butter rolls, and strickle sheets are other specialties of the Pennsylvania Dutch country. To make strickle sheets, yeast dough is rolled out and cut into small rounds and placed in a baking pan. Before baking, a syrup of sugar, water, butter, and cornstarch is poured in the pan.

Lemon Booder

Lemon butter, sometimes called lemon cheese, is a breakfast favorite and is also taken on picnics.

4 eggs
1½ cups sugar
¾ teaspoon ground mace
Grated rind and juice of 2 lemons

Beat eggs and combine with sugar, mace, and lemon rind and juice. Place in top of double boiler over hot water and cook until thick, about 20 minutes, stirring constantly. Store, covered, in refrigerator. Makes 1 pint.

Mrs. Rorer's Everyday Menus

Menus from Mrs. Rorer's *Everyday Menu Book* of 1905 give an idea of what families ate when gathered around the breakfast tables. These are menus from that book.

Baked Apples   Granose
Minced Beef   Toast
Coffee

Oranges
Oatmeal with Cream
Chops   Stewed Potatoes
Toast   Coffee

Chopped Dates in Hot Wheatlet with Cream
Hashed Duck
Toast   Coffee

Iced Currants
Foamy Omelet   Sautéed Potatoes
Twin Mountain Muffins
Coffee

Deluxe Oatmeal

4 cups milk
1 teaspoon salt
2 cups rolled oats

The night before serving, combine in the top of the double boiler milk, salt, and oats; cover and place in the refrigerator. The next morning, place top of double boiler over boiling water; cook for 30 minutes or until done, stirring occasionally. Serves 6.

Potatoes and Grits on the Side

In the West and the North, bacon and eggs are usually served with fried potatoes on the side. In the South, one is served grits. Grits are also called South Carolina and Georgia ice cream, hominy, and hominy grits. Some cooks slice sweet potatoes thinly, fry them in deep fat, and serve them sprinkled with sugar as a side dish for ham and brown gravy.

Breakfast for cowboys, the kind who work on ranches rather than in movies and television, is "dealt out" as early as 4 A.M. A ranch breakfast might include tomato juice, oatmeal, chicken fried steak, hot biscuits, brown gravy, fried eggs, cow salve (butter), lick (syrup), and java (coffee) with canned cow (evaporated milk). (Chicken fried steak is sliced round steak, cut into individual portions, coated in flour seasoned with salt and pepper, and fried in fat like fried chicken.)

In the Southwest, where a pungent taste is favored, the custom is to sprinkle chili powder in the bacon drippings before breaking in eggs to fry.

Codfish and Apple Pie

It is an old New England custom to serve codfish cakes and apple pie for breakfast, especially on Sunday. The codfish cakes or balls are dropped into the pan with a fork so that they have "whiskers." Old New Englanders scorn the smooth-shaven ball.

Another Sunday brunch favorite in New England is open-face baked bean sandwiches topped with rippled ribbons of crisp bacon.

Kidney Stew

>   3 beef kidneys
>   Salted water
>   3 tablespoons butter
>   ¼ cup flour
>   2 cups beef bouillon
>   2 teaspoons onion, minced
>   ¾ teaspoon salt
>   ⅛ teaspoon pepper
>   6 slices toast, crusts removed

Split kidneys; remove core and hard membrane, and discard. Cut kidneys into slices; cover slices with cold salted water and soak for 1 hour; drain well and dry on paper towels. Sauté slices in butter until lightly browned; add flour and continue to cook, stirring, until well browned. Add bouillon, onion, and seasonings. Stir to blend; cover and simmer for 15 minutes. Serve over toast. Makes 6 servings.

Breakfast Stew of Beef

    2 tablespoons butter
    1 medium onion, chopped
    2 pounds lean beef, cubed
    2 tablespoons flour
    1 cup beef broth
    ¾ teaspoon salt
    ¼ teaspoon pepper
    ½ teaspoon savory
    ½ teaspoon marjoram
    1 teaspoon prepared mustard
    Juice of ½ lemon
    Parsley, chopped

Melt butter in a saucepan. Add onion and cook until golden. Coat cubes of beef with flour. Add to onion and brown on all sides. Stir in broth, salt, pepper, savory, and marjoram. Cover and cook over a low heat for about 1½ hours or until very tender. Before serving, add mustard and lemon juice. Serve over toast, grits, or steamed rice, or with boiled potatoes. Sprinkle with chopped parsley. Serves 6.

Creamed Dried Beef

Creamed dried beef was a breakfast favorite also served for supper and lunch. Dried beef was once just that, not minced meat pressed together, cured in some fashion, and called dried beef. A round of beef was treated with salt the same way a ham is and then hung to dry and cure. Dried beef came to the grocery store in chunks which the grocer shaved into thin slices on the slicing machine. Because it was quite salty some cooks covered the beef briefly with boiling water before adding it to a cream sauce and serving it on toast or split biscuits. New Englanders call this dish red flannel stew.

Calf's Brains with Browned Butter

Remove the fine skin from the calf's brain and rinse the brain in water. Boil the brain in water, adding salt, the juice of a lemon, a few slices of carrots and ½ of a bay leaf. Boil for 10 minutes. Take out carefully with a skimmer. Split in two. Heat 2 ounces of butter until it turns dark brown, then add a dash of tarragon vinegar and pour over the brain. Sprinkle with chopped parsley, and serve with scrambled eggs.

Fish Roe Patties

1 egg
1 scant cup soft fresh bread crumbs
1 9-ounce fish roe, drained
½ teaspoon salt
¼ teaspoon pepper
Bacon drippings

Beat egg and add bread crumbs, roe, salt, and pepper. Blend with a fork, breaking up roe. Shape into 6 oblong patties. Brown on each side, turning once, in a small amount of drippings in a heavy skillet. Serve with scrambled eggs.

Roe and Scrambled Eggs

An old handwritten recipe.

For each serving, brown 2 tablespoons herring, or other fish, roe lightly in bacon fat in skillet. Add 2 beaten eggs and scramble eggs with roe. Season with salt and pepper.

Salt Fish

Soak fish in cold water overnight. Before cooking, drain well. Place fish on broiler rack, dot with butter and broil 4 inches from source of heat for 10 minutes or until fish flakes when touched with a fork.

Sauteed Oysters on Smithfield Ham

3 tablespoons butter
1 cup (½ pint) oysters
1 teaspoon flour
¼ teaspoon celery salt
¼ teaspoon pepper
1 teaspoon lemon juice
3 servings Smithfield ham, sliced and baked
Parsley, chopped

Melt butter in skillet over moderate heat, add oysters and cook until the edges begin to curl. Sprinkle with flour and blend in; add celery salt, pepper, and lemon juice; heat gently. Place ham on serving dish; spoon oysters over ham, and sprinkle with parsley. Serve with spoon bread and broiled tomato halves. Makes 3 servings.

Spoon Bread

2 cups milk
¾ cup cornmeal
3 tablespoons butter
1 teaspoon salt
3 eggs, separated

Heat milk; add cornmeal and cook, stirring, until smooth and thick. Remove from heat; add butter and salt; allow to cool slightly. Blend in egg yolks; beat egg whites until stiff, fold in. Pour into greased 9-inch baking dish; bake in a 350-degree oven for 35 minutes or until firm and lightly browned. Serves 6.

Creamed Chicken

2 cups cooked chicken, diced
¼ cup butter or margarine
¼ cup flour
2 cups milk
½ teaspoon salt or to taste
½ teaspoon celery salt
⅛ teaspoon pepper
6 biscuits, English muffins, slices of toast, or waffle sections
6 slices bacon, crisp

If cooked chicken is roasted or fried, portions of crisp skin may be included. Over moderate heat, melt butter in saucepan. Blend flour into butter; add milk, salt, celery salt, and pepper, stirring until smooth and thickened. A wire whisk is good for this purpose. Add chicken to sauce and heat. Serve over split hot biscuits, toasted English muffins, toast, or waffle sections. Sprinkle with crisp crumbled bacon. Makes 6 servings.

Chicken Livers Supreme

½ pound chicken livers
6 tablespoons flour
4 slices bacon
1 cup chicken broth
½ teaspoon salt
⅛ teaspoon pepper
½ cup mushrooms, sliced
Buttered toast

Coat chicken livers in 4 tablespoons flour. Fry bacon until crisp. Remove bacon to absorbent paper. Add chicken livers to bacon drippings and brown lightly, turning with a spatula to avoid breaking. Remove livers. Add 2 tablespoons flour, stir, and brown well. Add chicken broth slowly, stirring and cooking, until smooth and thick. Season with salt and pepper. Add livers and mushrooms to sauce and heat. Serve on hot buttered toast and sprinkle with crisp crumbled bacon. Makes 4 servings.

Crumbed Bacon

    2 eggs, beaten
    1 cup milk
    ¼ teaspoon salt
    ¼ teaspoon pepper
    ½ teaspoon prepared mustard
    12 thick slices bacon
    2 cups coarse cracker crumbs, approximate

To eggs, add milk, salt, pepper, and mustard; blend with egg beater. Dip bacon slices in egg mixture, coating thoroughly; place on cracker crumbs on wax paper. Coat bacon on both sides with crumbs. Place coated slices on rack in shallow baking pan; bake in a 375-degree oven for 15 minutes or until crisp. Makes 12 slices. Good with scrambled eggs and broiled tomatoes.

Eggs Brouilli

A dish prepared earlier in the century. Beat 4 eggs until well mixed; add ¼ cup stock (beef presumably) and ¼ cup cream. Blend and cook over boiling water. Add 1 "saltspoonful" of salt and ½ "saltspoonful" of pepper. Serve on squares of toasted bread.

Eggs a la Goldenrod

3 hard-cooked eggs
1½ tablespoons butter or margarine
1½ tablespoons flour
1 cup milk
½ teaspoon salt
⅛ teaspoon pepper
4 slices toast, crusts removed
Parsley

Cut eggs in half and separate the whites from the yolks.
Chop whites finely. Over low heat, melt butter or
margarine and blend in flour, milk, salt, and pepper
to make a cream sauce. Stir until smooth and thick;
add chopped egg whites and heat. Spoon mixture over
toast slices. Force egg yolks through a ricer or strainer
and sprinkle over the top. Garnish with parsley. Makes
4 servings.

Fried Eggs on Skillet Toast

⅓ cup butter, approximate
2 slices bread, crusts removed
2 eggs
Salt and pepper to taste

Melt butter in skillet over moderate heat; sauté bread
in butter until toasted and crisp on both sides. Remove
toast to serving plate and keep hot. Reduce heat under
skillet to low; break eggs into remaining butter and
fry gently to desired degree of doneness, adding
additional butter if needed. Place eggs on toast; sprinkle
with salt and pepper. Makes 1 serving.

Eggs au Beurre Noir

4 eggs
2½ tablespoons butter or margarine
4 slices toast, crusts removed
Salt and pepper to taste
1 tablespoon vinegar or lemon juice

Break eggs into 1½ tablespoons butter melted in a
heavy skillet. Cook eggs over low heat to desired
degree of doneness. Remove eggs to toast on hot platter
and sprinkle with salt and pepper. Keep hot. Add
remaining tablespoon butter to skillet and let cook
over low heat until lightly browned; watch to prevent
burning. Stir in vinegar or lemon juice; heat and spoon
over eggs. Makes 4 servings.

Superb Scrambled Eggs

    5 tablespoons butter
    2 tablespoons flour
    1 teaspoon green onion, minced
    1½ teaspoons salt
    ½ teaspoon pepper
    ⅛ teaspoon paprika
    1⅓ cups milk
    ¾ cup Cheddar cheese, grated
    1 large firm tomato
    8 eggs, slightly beaten
    4 slices bacon, fried crisp, crumbled

For sauce, melt 2 tablespoons butter in a heavy pan;
blend in flour, onion, ½ teaspoon salt, ¼ teaspoon
pepper, and paprika. Gradually add 1 cup milk; cook,
stirring constantly, until smooth and thick. Stir in
cheese; blend until melted. Cut tomato into four slices;
sauté in 1 tablespoon butter. Combine eggs, ⅓ cup
milk, 1 teaspoon salt, and ¼ teaspoon pepper. Melt
2 tablespoons butter in large heavy skillet; add eggs,
cook and stir, lifting cooked portions, until as firm as
desired. Serve eggs in 4 mounds; top each with tomato
slice. Spoon sauce over the top; sprinkle with bacon.
Makes 4 servings.

Scrambled Eggs and Brains

1 set calves' brains, boiled (recipe below)
4 eggs
½ teaspoon salt
⅛ teaspoon pepper
¼ cup milk
2 tablespoons butter

Cut or break cooked brains into small pieces. Beat eggs with a fork; add salt, pepper, milk, and brains. Melt butter in skillet over low to moderate heat. Pour in egg mixture; cook, stirring gently, until creamy and done. Serve plain or with crisp bacon. Makes 4 servings.

Boiled Brains

1 set calves' brains
Cold water, salted
Water, boiling
1 teaspoon salt
1 tablespoon vinegar or lemon juice

Wash brains; remove excess membrane and discard. Cover brains with cold salted water and soak for 30 minutes. Drain, rinse, and cover with boiling water. Add salt and vinegar or lemon juice; boil gently for 15 to 20 minutes. Drain.

Strawberry Omelet

3 eggs
1 tablespoon light cream or undiluted evaporated milk
¼ teaspoon salt
2 tablespoons butter or margarine
¼ cup sour cream
½ cup strawberries, sliced
2 tablespoons confectioners' sugar

To eggs, add cream or milk and salt; beat with a fork. In 10-inch skillet with rounded sides, melt butter over moderate heat; just as butter starts to brown, pour in eggs. Stir once or twice with a fork; lift edges to allow uncooked portion to run underneath. Shake pan back and forth to keep omelet free; when eggs are cooked but soft, top with half of sour cream and half the strawberries. Fold over; slide omelet out onto heated plate. Top with remaining sour cream and strawberries; sprinkle with sugar. Makes 2 servings.

Cream Waffles

  1 cup flour, sifted
  1½ teaspoons baking powder
  ½ teaspoon salt
  2 teaspoons sugar
  2 eggs, separated
  1 cup heavy cream
  2 tablespoons butter or margarine, melted

Sift together flour, baking powder, salt, and sugar. Stir egg yolks with a fork; add cream and blend. Add dry ingredients and beat only until smooth. Add melted butter. Beat egg whites until stiff and fold in. The resulting batter should be thick. Bake on hot waffle iron until steam no longer escapes. Serve with melted butter and heated syrup. Makes 4 to 5 average waffles.

Strawberry Hard Sauce

A fluff of pink to serve on waffles, as prepared in a plantation home in the Mississippi Delta.

Cream ½ cup butter with 3 cups confectioners' sugar until light and fluffy. Mix in 1 cup crushed strawberries.

Elderberry Blossom Pancakes

Cooks in Nebraska prepare ordinary pancake batter and add a few finely chopped blossoms from the elderberry bush. The blooms make the cakes lighter and add a delicate flavor.

Angel Wing Hot Cakes

  1 cup flour, sifted
  1 teaspoon baking soda
  1 teaspoon salt
  1 egg
  1 cup buttermilk
  2 tablespoons shortening, melted

Sift together flour, baking soda, and salt. Break egg over dry ingredients. Add buttermilk and melted shortening. Stir together until flour is dampened. The batter will be lumpy; leave it that way.
Drop by tablespoonfuls on lightly greased hot griddle. Spread out batter thinly on griddle and cook until bubbly. Turn and brown on the other side. Serve at once. Enough for 2 hearty eaters, or 3 moderate ones.

The first sound of morning was the crackling of logs when my father uncovered the coals and started a fire in the big fireplace. Next came the smell of sausage and coffee to awaken all of the body at once.

President Taft loved waffles; at one sitting he ate seven complete waffles or twenty-eight quarters before getting on with breakfast.

Of course, we ate a big breakfast, because there was work to be done on the farm before breakfast. Sometimes before I went to school, Papa had me plow for an hour.

Buckwheat Cakes

½ package dry yeast
2½ cups water, lukewarm
½ teaspoon sugar
2¾ cups buckwheat flour
½ teaspoon salt
¼ cup all-purpose flour
1 tablespoon molasses
½ teaspoon baking soda
1 teaspoon butter, melted
Cold water

The night before cooking, dissolve yeast in ½ cup lukewarm water; add sugar. Combine buckwheat flour, salt, all-purpose flour, and 2 cups water. Blend until smooth; mix in yeast. Cover; let stand in a cool place overnight. The next morning, stir in molasses, baking soda, butter, and sufficient cold water to make batter the desired consistency. Bake cakes, turning once, on lightly greased hot griddle. Serves 6.

German Apple Pancakes

2 eggs
½ cup flour
½ teaspoon salt
½ cup milk
2 tablespoons margarine, melted
2 tablespoons confectioners' sugar
1 20-ounce can apple pie filling
2 tablespoons brown sugar
¼ teaspoon cinnamon

Beat eggs until blended, add flour, salt, and milk; beat until smooth. Stir in margarine. Pour batter into buttered 10-inch glass pie pan or black iron skillet heated until sizzling in oven. Bake on bottom shelf of a 450-degree oven for 20 minutes. Prick pancake with a fork; reduce heat to 350 degrees and bake 10 minutes longer or until done. Sprinkle with confectioners' sugar. Spread apple pie filling over the top; sprinkle with brown sugar and cinnamon. Serve at once. Makes 6 servings.

Baked Bacon Pancakes

¾ cup flour, sifted
½ teaspoon salt
2 eggs, beaten
¾ cup milk
¼ pound bacon

To prepare for breakfast, make the batter the night before. Sift together flour and salt. Add beaten eggs and milk; beat until smooth with egg beater. Cover tightly and chill overnight. For breakfast, cook bacon until crisp. Drain slices on paper towels; reserve 2 tablespoons drippings. Pour drippings into 8-inch heavy baking pan and place pan into oven. Heat oven to 450 degrees; allow drippings to heat. When drippings are hot, beat batter with egg beater; add crumbled bacon and turn batter into hot drippings. Bake pancake for 10 to 15 minutes at 450 degrees or until it puffs up; reduce temperature to 300 degrees and continue baking for 10 minutes or until crisp and brown. Serve at once. Makes 4 servings. The pancake is good with scrambled eggs and applesauce.

At night when I go to bed hungry, I dream of a stack of Mama's buckwheat cakes drenched in butter and syrup. The hunger comes from being on a low cholesterol diet.

Philadelphia Sticky Buns

These are not just any cinnamon buns. They are fragrant with cinnamon and are the epitome of stickiness.

1¼ cups milk
1 package dry yeast
¼ cup warm water
About 5 cups flour, sifted
1½ teaspoons salt
2 tablespoons plus ¾ cup sugar
½ cup shortening
2 eggs
¼ cup butter or margarine, softened
½ cup brown sugar
2 teaspoons cinnamon
½ cup walnuts, chopped
½ cup raisins or currants
1 cup dark corn syrup

Scald milk; cool to lukewarm. Dissolve yeast in water and combine with milk. Blend in 2 cups of the flour, salt, and 2 tablespoons sugar. Set aside in a warm place to become bubbly.

Cream shortening with ¾ cup sugar. Add eggs, one at a time, beating well after each is added. Add bubbly mixture. Stir in enough flour (about 3 cups) to make a soft dough. Cover and let rise in a warm place until doubled in bulk. Knead dough on lightly floured board; divide dough in half and roll out each part to ¼-inch thickness. Spread with softened butter. Sprinkle with mixture of brown sugar and cinnamon. Scatter the nuts and raisins on top. Roll up like a jelly roll and cut into 1½-inch lengths. Butter and coat the bottoms of two deep 9-inch layer pans with syrup. Place the dough slices in the pans. Cover and let rise until doubled in bulk. Bake in a 350-degree oven for 45 minutes or until done. Turn out upside down immediately. Makes 24.

Stickies

Roll out biscuit dough very thinly. Spread with soft butter and cover with brown sugar. Sprinkle with cinnamon. Roll up like a jelly roll. Cut roll into slices about ¼-inch thick. Place in well-buttered shallow baking pan. Sprinkle with brown sugar and cinnamon. Bake in a 450-degree oven until golden brown. Remove from pan while hot.

Beaten Biscuits

    2 cups flour, sifted
    1 teaspoon salt, scant
    ½ teaspoon sugar
    ⅓ cup lard
    ⅓ cup milk
    ⅓ cup water, approximate
    Butter

Sift together flour, salt, and sugar; cut in lard with 2
knives to make coarse crumbs. Add milk and water to
make a stiff dough; knead until dough holds together.
Place on a sturdy surface; beat with mallet or edge of
heavy saucer until dough becomes smooth and satiny
and forms blisters. Shape into small biscuits by hand or
roll out and cut with a small cutter. Bake in a 350-
degree oven for 20 minutes or until golden brown.
Split open while hot; fill with butter. Makes about 18.

Fried Apples

    6 medium or 8 small tart apples
    ⅓ cup bacon drippings or mixture of salad
        oil and margarine
    ½ to ¾ cup sugar

An ideal apple for frying is a green apple called the
June apple, which ripens in early summer. The Rambo,
which ripens in midsummer, and the Stayman Winesap
are also good. The June apple and the Rambo tend to
become mushy when cooked.

To prepare, core unpeeled apples and cut into slices
¼ inch thick. Heat drippings or oil and margarine in
heavy skillet; add apple rings. Cook over moderate
heat, lifting apple slices as they brown lightly to the
top. Continue to cook, until all the apple slices are
almost soft. If needed to prevent sticking, add more
drippings or margarine and oil. Sprinkle with sugar,
reduce heat to low and cook for about 15 minutes
more or until done. Makes 6 servings.

Creamed Tomatoes

A breakfast favorite in Maryland.

Coat tomato slices with seasoned flour. Brown on
both sides. Add a bit of sugar and stir. Cook gently
to allow liquid to evaporate. Stir in a little sweet or
sour cream and serve with bacon, scrambled eggs,
and toast.

I prize memories of the delightful
beaten biscuits a lady in Sardis,
Miss., made for me and brought
to a scrumptious "Befo' the Wah"
breakfast given in my honor.

In the thirties when I was in med
school at the University of
Pennsylvania, my breakfast cost
five cents. It was a sticky cinnamon
bun as big as a saucer from Horn &
Hardart, the automat.

91

Fried Syrup

Fried syrup is made by gradually mixing cane syrup into fried ham drippings and heating and blending until the mixture boils. Serve over hot biscuits.

Cheese Strata

> **12 slices day-old bread, crusts removed**
> **½ pound process American cheese, sliced**
> **4 eggs**
> **2½ cups milk**
> **1 teaspoon salt**
> **¼ teaspoon pepper**
> **Apple jelly**

Arrange 6 slices bread in bottom of baking dish, fitting them so that the entire surface of dish is covered; cover bread with cheese. Cover cheese with remaining bread. Beat together eggs, milk, salt, and pepper; pour over bread. Let stand in refrigerator for several hours or overnight. Bake in a 325-degree oven for 40 minutes or until puffed up and lightly browned. Serve with apple jelly. Serves 6.

Apple Cheese Bake

½ pound bacon
8 slices firm white bread, crusts removed
2 cups applesauce
2 cups Cheddar cheese, grated
6 eggs
2 cups milk
1 teaspoon celery salt
½ teaspoon dry mustard
Dash pepper
Additional bacon for garnish, if desired

Cook bacon until crisp; drain and crumble. Place half
the bread slices in bottom of greased baking dish,
about 8 inches square. Cover bread with applesauce,
cheese, and bacon; top with remaining bread slices.
Beat eggs; stir in milk, celery salt, mustard, and pepper.
Pour egg mixture over ingredients in baking dish; let
stand in refrigerator for at least 1 hour or overnight.
Bake in a 325-degree oven for 50 to 55 minutes or
until top is puffy and golden. If desired, garnish with
additional crisp bacon strips. Serve immediately.
Serves 6.

CHAPTER 4

Lunch, Luncheons, and Supper

Lunch ranged from the dinner pail contents of the workingman to the fancy luncheons for guests in the home.

The workingman's dinner pail was a simple tin bucket with a lid before the black box with a hinged lid to hold a Thermos appeared. Lunch boxes for school children were of tin, often colorfully painted, sized to hold two sandwiches, an apple, and cookies.

Before drive-ins and quick lunch restaurants, some workmen ate lunch at the country store. Their lunch consisted of crackers from the cracker barrel, pickles from the pickle barrel, and hoop cheese. Later, fare was more varied when sardines, deviled ham, and baked beans reached the shelves.

A THING ABOUT COLOR

Thomas Alva Edison (1848–1931) in 1879 gave the world the incandescent lamp. Color television may, at that time, have been a glint in the incandescent lamp bulb but its appearance was most of a century away. Color, however, was not lacking when hostesses entertained in the first decades of this century. Luncheons which followed color schemes were especially favored. Cookbooks of the period abound with "color" menus. These are some suggestions from *The Century Cook Book* (1904).

For green, ferns make a light and dainty centerpiece. Spinach can be used for a soup, a vegetable, and as coloring for sauces. Green salads, angelica for decoration, and pistachio nuts fit the scheme. Yellow is sunny in effect. For a yellow meal, use yellow flowers, gilt compotiers, gilded china, and light diffused through yellow shades. The yolks of eggs render important service for coloring, covering, and garnishing, and oranges furnish many delicious dishes.

For a white meal use white flowers, silver, a profusion of cut glass, lace shades, white grapes, spun sugar, whipped cream, white sauces, white meats, whites of eggs, celery, and snow scenes. At one white meal, the dining room was strung with white muslin and the gaslight from a crystal chandelier filtered down on the table through huge silk tissue moths that spread their silvery white wings. The table was decorated with clusters of bridal roses, white carnations, and white poppies, and food was served on pure white porcelain. The hostess, a blonde, was dressed in white from top to toe.

TEAROOMS

Tearooms came into existence for the same reason as boarding houses. They were a means of earning a living for a woman who owned her own home. The name derives from the practice of serving afternoon tea with fancy sandwiches and cookies. Tearooms also served lunch, popular with the ladies, and a few offered an evening meal. Tearoom food is different in character from hotel and restaurant food. Prepared in smaller quantities, it is like the specialties from a fine home kitchen.

From the *Wellesley Alumnae Magazine* of 1966:

"The names Alice and Grace Coombs conjure up fragrant memories to Wellesley alumnae who were fortunate enough to patronize the Wellesley Tea Room between 1912–1922. No one really regretted the hours spent sitting on the stairs, waiting one's turn for space in a very simple second-floor dining room. The proprietress had the good sense to serve a few delicious specialties rather than a wide selection of mediocre dishes. Among the most popular items were chicken à la king, a crisp, fresh fruit salad, and her famous Wellesley Special, a delectable concoction of fudge layer cake, ice cream, whipped cream, and thick chocolate sauce.

"Hundreds of the latter were consumed each week. In those days, no one seemed particularly concerned over her figure. Girls were heard to say that they wanted Wellesley fudge cake or maybe a Wellesley Special when they returned to their fiftieth reunion. No one could imagine a greater treat."

Bows of ribbon tied to the stem of a sherbet dish, the handle of a cup, or to a toothpick stuck into food helped carry out the color scheme; for example, a bow of red ribbon was tied to the stem of a dish of raspberry sherbet for a red luncheon. Candied violets were considered an essential garnish for a lavender luncheon.

Elsie De Wolfe, Lady Mendl, was one of the century's best-known hostesses, both here and in Europe, where she once lived in the Trianon at Versailles. She was also a well-known interior decorator. This is from her book, *Recipes for Successful Dining*, dated 1934.

"A very successful decoration I have used in Paris is a cloth of silver (lamé) with a lovely crystal ship, all its glass sails and its pennants set and flying, mirrored in a sheet of glass which forms the center. Added to this are two rock-crystal birds and four rock-crystal candlesticks.

"In the year 1929, I used two rock-crystal vases in which were branches of white orchids, but those days are gone, I fear, forever, and a few white carnations have to suffice now. Enfin, perhaps the orchids will bloom again."

A Golf Luncheon

As suggested early in century.

Chicken Salad
Brown Bread and Butter Sandwiches
Ripe Olives
Deviled Eggs
Peach Ice Cream
Rolled Wafers

For the table decoration, cover the center with a square of canvas. Cover the canvas with short rock moss, which nicely resembles grass. Press some silver paper into the moss to represent a little stream of water. Use slightly dried dough to make the golf balls, and for small golf clubs use doll's toys.

Wellesley Fudge Cake

½ cup butter
2 cups light brown sugar, packed
1 teaspoon vanilla
2 eggs
2 cups flour, sifted
1 teaspoon baking powder
¼ teaspoon salt
½ cup sour milk
½ cup cold water
4 1-ounce squares unsweetened chocolate, melted and
cooled slightly

Cream butter and sugar together until light and fluffy. Add vanilla and eggs, one at a time, beating well after each is added. Sift together dry ingredients and add to creamed mixture alternately with sour milk and water, beginning and ending with flour mixture; blend in chocolate. Turn into 2 greased and floured 9-inch layer cake pans. Bake in a 350-degree oven for 25 to 30 minutes or until cake tests done. Turn out, cool, and frost with chocolate frosting. For the Wellesley Special, cut cake and top slices with ice cream, chocolate sauce (recipe below), and whipped cream.

Chocolate Sauce

2 squares unsweetened chocolate
1 cup sugar
⅓ cup water
½ teaspoon vanilla

In saucepan, combine chocolate and sugar; cook, stirring, over medium heat until chocolate is melted and blended. Add water and heat to the boiling point; remove from heat, add vanilla. Serve hot or cold. Makes about ¾ cup.

In the days of eight-course dinners, chicken croquettes appeared as an entrée and became a stock offering at tearooms.

Chicken Croquettes

   2 cups cooked chicken, diced
   ½ teaspoon salt
   ¼ teaspoon celery salt
   ½ teaspoon paprika
   1 teaspoon onion juice
   1 tablespoon lemon juice
   Fine bread crumbs
   1 egg
   1 tablespoon water
   1 cup thick white sauce (recipe below)

Blend all ingredients except crumbs, egg, water, and sauce. Cover mixture and chill thoroughly. Shape into 8 cone-shaped croquettes. Coat first in crumbs, then in egg slightly beaten with water, then again in crumbs. Fry until golden brown in hot, deep fat heated to 350 degrees in an electric skillet. Serve plain, with cream sauce, or with cream sauce mixed with cooked green peas.

Thick White Sauce

   3 tablespoons butter or margarine
   ⅓ cup flour
   1 teaspoon salt
   1 cup milk

Combine all ingredients, and make into a smooth sauce over medium heat.

Chicken Luncheon Squares

   3 cups cooked chicken, diced
   1 8-ounce can cream style corn
   1 cup fresh bread crumbs
   1 cup chicken broth
   ½ cup celery, minced
   ¼ cup green onions with some tops, thinly sliced
   3 eggs, beaten
   1 teaspoon salt
   ½ teaspoon poultry seasoning

Blend all ingredients; turn into a greased 8-inch-square baking pan. Bake at 350-degrees for 50 minutes or until firm and golden brown. Cut into squares. Makes 9 squares.

Cranberry Casserole

3 cups apples, chopped and unpeeled
2 cups raw cranberries
1¼ cups granulated sugar
1½ cups quick-cooking oats, uncooked
½ cup brown sugar, packed
⅓ cup flour
⅓ cup pecans, chopped
½ cup margarine or butter, melted

In 2-quart casserole, combine apples, cranberries, and granulated sugar; top with mixture of remaining ingredients. Bake in a 350-degree oven for 1 hour or until bubbly and lightly brown. Serve hot. Good with chicken and turkey. Makes 8 servings.

Deviled Crab

2 cups crab meat
2 hard-cooked eggs, chopped
1 teaspoon onion, grated
⅛ teaspoon lemon rind, grated
2 teaspoons lemon juice
1 teaspoon parsley, minced
½ teaspoon Worcestershire sauce
½ teaspoon prepared mustard
1 cup bread crumbs, buttered
2 tablespoons mayonnaise

Combine crab, eggs, onion, lemon rind and juice, parsley, Worcestershire, mustard, half the crumbs, and mayonnaise. Pile mixture into 6 individual baking shells. Sprinkle with remaining crumbs. Bake in a 400-degree oven for 15 minutes or until hot and crumbs are lightly browned. Serves 6.

THE CHAFING DISH

Early in the century the chafing dish had a renaissance. It was favored for informal meals such as Sunday night supper and was at its best at the midnight hour. It heated food quickly and was entirely mobile.

Specialties for the chafing dish included panned oysters, oyster stew, creamed oysters and clams, creamed dishes, terrapin from a can, chicken livers with madeira, welsh rarebit, and golden buck.

When our cook made croquettes all golden brown, they looked like a village of tepees. She served them in a puddle of cream sauce and there was always something mysterious about cutting into a croquette.

Pineapple Canapes

From *The Century Cook Book* of 1904.

Split some square sponge cakes, which can be bought at the baker's for 2 cents each. Melt a little butter in the chafing dish. When it is hot, put in the slices of cake, and brown them a little on both sides. Lay the slices on a plate and spread each one with a layer of canned chopped pineapple. Thicken the pineapple juice with arrowroot and spoon over the cake.

Strawberries, raspberries, and peaches also make good sweet canapés.

BETWEEN TWO PIECES OF BREAD AND IN A BUN

Americans put more ingredients between pieces of bread and in buns than do any other people in the world. The sandwich is like the umbrella in the old minstrel show joke. Someone asked: What was born in Baltimore and raised all over the world? The answer was the umbrella. The sandwich was born in England, but it has been raised in America.

The Hamburger

The ubiquitous hamburger in a bun belongs to this century and this country. The century managed to turn without benefit of a hamburger in a bun, which first appeared in 1904 at the International Exposition in St. Louis. The flourishing days came after World War II when hamburger house after identical hamburger house appeared as if the father of the franchise flew from coast to coast dropping them one by one from a plane.

Hot Dogs

Coney Island is generally credited as the place where wieners or frankfurters were first served in this country. Charles Feltmann, a German immigrant and butcher, in the last century helped create a popular beer garden and amusement spot along the boardwalk. It was there he served an all-beef frankfurter.

Just who was the first to put a frank in a bun to make a hot dog has been debated. One story credits Antoine Ludwig Feuchtwanger, a Bavarian sausage peddler at the St. Louis Exposition of 1904. It seems that Herr Feuchtwanger provided white mitts for his customers to protect their hands from the hot wiener. Customers failed to return the mitts, which ate into the profits, so he conceived the idea of a bun to fit the sausage.

Chili for Hot Dogs

As prepared by a Greek cafe owner named Spiro who came from the old country.

1 medium-size onion, chopped
1 pound ground beef
¼ pound good-quality bulk pork sausage
1 6-ounce can tomato paste
1 8-ounce can tomato sauce
1 tablespoon Worcestershire sauce
1 tablespoon chili powder or to taste
Liquid hot pepper sauce to taste

In a skillet, cook onion, beef, and sausage together, stirring, until lightly browned. Drain off excess fat and discard. Add remaining ingredients and simmer for 10 to 15 minutes, adding small amounts of water as needed to prevent dryness.

THE DAGWOOD

Dagwood is the bumbling, fumbling partner of Blondie who has represented the modern American woman—emancipated, capable, and superior—in the comics since the thirties.

To satisfy his appetite, Dagwood builds great stacked sandwiches of everything he can find in the refrigerator. His compulsive eating is no doubt a psychological defense of sorts against Blondie. His sandwich is known as the Dagwood.

THE CLUB SANDWICH

Who invented, discovered, or concocted the club sandwich is not clear. One story contends that a man came home late one night from his club. He was hungry so he raided the icebox and made himself a super-sandwich which he dubbed "club." Another account gives credit to the chef of some club who composed a sandwich in "stories." Regardless, millions of Americans have lunched on clubs and, no doubt, a portion of America has been built over clubs.

Marshall Field Special

This sandwich, of tearoom origin, is one of the country's best. It is an open-face sandwich which fills a dinner plate. The base is two slices of buttered rye bread, one in the center of the plate and the second cut in half and arranged on each side.

The bread is topped with a ½ inch thick slice of lettuce, 1 slice of baked ham, 1 slice of Swiss cheese and 1 slice of roast turkey or chicken, followed by tomato slices, hard-cooked egg slices, sliced stuffed olives, and crisp bacon strips. The sandwich is served with small cups of Russian dressing.

PEANUT BUTTER

Without peanut butter, a mother is hard pushed to raise children. A St. Louis physician developed peanut butter in 1890 for the benefit of patients who needed an easily digested form of protein. It was not common on grocery shelves for a while, but once it was, peanut butter became a staple in households with children.

Ham Biscuits

Thin slices of baked or fried ham between buttered biscuits have been served by the thousands at tea parties, luncheons, and receptions.

The Reuben

The Reuben has become almost as American as apple pie. It has made a hit even in Hawaii, where it introduced the flavor of sauerkraut for the first time to the predominantly Oriental palate of the islanders. Conceived by Mrs. Fern Snider, lady chef of the Rose Bowl Restaurant of Omaha, Neb., it was the winner of one of the annual National Sandwich contests.

The Reuben is made by spreading Russian rye bread with Thousand Island dressing. This is topped with 1 slice of Swiss cheese, sauerkraut, and 2 slices of corned beef, and closed with a second slice of bread. The outside surface is spread with butter or margarine and the sandwich is grilled until the cheese is melted.

SUPPER

In homes where dinner was served in the middle of the day, supper consisted of dinner leftovers warmed up and "set out." In other homes, supper was a simple meal.

In New England, Saturday's supper is baked beans and brown bread. The custom began when the early settlers enforced a twenty-four hour cooking ban that started at sundown on Saturday, marking the beginning of their Sabbath.

In Milwaukee we used to stop at a stand on the shore of Lake Michigan for a bratwurst sandwich, a cooked sausage larger than a wiener, browned on a grill and plunked between a long split bun.

Bean Supper

Boston Baked Beans
Brown Bread   Hot Rolls
Pepper Relish   Mustard Pickles
Chili Sauce
Coleslaw
Apple Pie   Coffee

Boston Brown Bread

    1 cup cornmeal
    2 teaspoons baking soda
    1 teaspoon salt
    2 cups whole wheat flour
    ½ cup raisins
    ¾ cup molasses
    2 cups buttermilk

Sift together cornmeal, baking soda, and salt; mix with flour, raisins, molasses, and buttermilk. Fill molds or tin cans about ⅔ full; cover tightly. Foil tied tightly with string is a way to cover tin cans. Place on a rack in a deep kettle with 2 to 3 inches of boiling water. Cover kettle and steam by allowing water to simmer for 3 hours. Uncover molds, and allow loaves to dry in a 250-degree oven for 15 to 20 minutes. Makes 2 or 3 loaves.

On days when Mother made brown bread we rushed home after school, scorning chocolate sundaes in the drugstore as something we could have any day, whereas brown bread was infrequent and of short duration. We put butter, and nothing but butter, on it.

Italian Spaghetti Sauce

1½ pounds ground beef
1 medium green pepper, chopped
1 medium onion, chopped
3 tablespoons salad oil
2 tablespoons Worcestershire sauce
1 heaping tablespoon Italian seasoning
1 teaspoon dehydrated parsley
Pinch each of cinnamon, ginger, allspice, and cloves
¼ teaspoon sugar
A generous amount of salt
2 bay leaves
4 8-ounce cans tomato sauce
3 6-ounce cans tomato paste
1 1-pound can tomatoes
1 10¾-ounce can tomato soup
1 6-ounce can tomato purée
1 4-ounce can sliced mushrooms, undrained
Hot pepper sauce to taste

Cook meat, green pepper, and onion in oil in a skillet or large heavy pot, stirring, until red color leaves meat. Add remaining ingredients and stir to blend. Cover tightly and simmer for 1 hour, stirring often to prevent sticking. Serves 8 to 10.

Superb Swiss Steak

1½ pounds round steak, cut 1 inch thick
½ cup flour
1 tablespoon dry mustard
Salt and pepper to taste
2 tablespoons fat
1 1-pound can tomatoes
1 tablespoon lemon juice
1 large onion, sliced
½ cup celery, diced
2 to 3 carrots, diced
2 tablespoons Worcestershire sauce
1 tablespoon brown sugar

Sprinkle meat with mixture of flour, mustard, salt, and pepper, and pound with a meat pounder or edge of a saucer. Cut meat into individual portions and brown lightly in fat in heavy skillet. Lift meat into a casserole if skillet is not ovenworthy. Add remaining ingredients. Cover and bake in a 300-degree oven for 2½ hours or until the meat is fork tender. Do not overcook as this will cause the meat to dry out. Serves 6.

CHAPTER 5   Dinner Time

THE ERA OF THE FIFTEEN-COURSE DINNER

The trend which was to produce the TV dinner with food neatly compartmentalized had started, slowly but surely, by the turn of the century.

When Ulysses S. Grant was President in the previous century, guests at the White House sat down to a dinner of twenty-nine courses and six wines. Some sources claim there were thirty-six courses.

The number of courses dropped to fifteen by the time of Diamond Jim Brady (1856-1917), a gourmet the likes of which the world will probably never have again.

The late restaurateur George Rector said that Diamond Jim was the best twenty-five customers he had.

For dinner, Diamond Jim started with two or three dozen oysters, each measuring six inches from tip to tail. Next came half a dozen crabs, followed by green turtle soup and six or seven large lobsters. After that he consumed two portions of terrapin, two whole ducks, and a steak and vegetables. The meal was topped off with a variety of desserts. Rector recalled that when Brady pointed to a tray of French pastries, he meant the whole tray, not just one piece. After dinner, he ate a two-pound box of candy. A regular at first nights, he arrived at the theater with a box of candy under his arm. It was discovered at Johns Hopkins that his stomach was six times as large as a normal stomach.

By 1904, according to the following menu from *The Century Cook Book* hostesses were serving only twelve courses:

1. Canapes of caviar, small bits of anchovy toast, or muskmelons (in season) but ordinarily oysters or clams on the half shell with a quarter of a lemon is the first dish presented. Cayenne pepper and grated horseradish are served and also very thin slices of brown bread buttered and folded together, then cut into small squares or triangles.

2. Soup. It is better to serve a clear soup as heavy soups are too hearty. One ladleful of soup is sufficient. Hors d'oeuvre, radishes, celery, olives, are passed after the soup. Salted almonds are taken at any time during the dinner.

3. Fish. If boiled or fried, fish is served upon a napkin. If baked, no napkin is used. Boiled potatoes are served with boiled fish, and are more attractive when cut with a potato scoop into small balls. Cucumbers dressed with oil and vinegar are also served.

4. Entrées. The list includes croquettes, timbales, quenelles, sweetbreads, calf's brains, calf's head à la vinaigrette, chicken livers, stuffed mushrooms, frogs' legs and false terrapin. False terrapin is calf's head meat and brains in a brown sauce.

5. Vegetables. A vegetable, such as asparagus, artichokes, or cauliflower, is served at this time, although the French reserve the vegetable until after the joint (the roast). Only one vegetable besides potato is permitted with a meat course, and if more are wanted they are served as a separate course.

6. The joint with one green vegetable and potato.

7. Frozen punch. It is not passed, but a glassful, standing on a plate with a coffee spoon beside it, is placed before each person. If preferred, a cheese omelet or soufflé may be served instead of punch.

8. Game and salad or poultry and salad. Cheese and crackers may be served immediately afterward as a separate course, or they may be passed after the dessert.

9. Sweet puddings, soufflés, Bavarian cream.

10. Ice cream or any frozen dessert. Cakes and brandied peaches, preserved ginger, or wine jellies may be passed with ice cream.

11. Fruit, fresh or glacé, and bonbons.

12. Coffee, liqueurs.

A young lady learned the art of playing hostess. The custom was to have the printed menu in front of her at the table. She announced each course the way the chairman of the board conducts a board meeting.

She was thoroughly informed about the two kinds of meal service—English and Russian. In English service, food is placed on the table to be served by host and hostess or for guests to help themselves. It was customary for the host, seated in front of fowl or roast, to carve and serve it and pass the dinner plate to the hostess who served the vegetables. Casters on the table held condiments.

In Russian service, food is served on platters and held for guests to help themselves. The meat is carved in the kitchen. For more formal service, heated plates are filled in the kitchen. In Russian service, condiments are on the sideboard, now known as the buffet.

With many-course dinners came the finger bowl, a glass bowl filled with tepid water on a lace doily and with a slice of lemon or a leaf of rose geranium floating in it.

Between courses, crumbs were removed from the table with a silver table crumber. Waiters wore white cotton gloves.

A lady wore her gloves as she was escorted to the table at a formal dinner, also called a repast, by an escort in white tie and tails. During the meal, she deposited her gloves and her fan in her lap.

A butler presided in the dining room and served no one. He directed the other servants. *The Century Cook Book* (1904) suggested this attire: "The butler wears a dress suit with white tie. The footman, or second man, wears the livery of the family, or, in default of that, a coat of dark color, with brass buttons, and a bright-striped waistcoat. First-class butlers and footmen do not wear mustaches.

"The dining room maid wears a plain black dress, a white apron, and a small white cap but no crown."

It was all very genteel.

Henry Barnard, a northerner and graduate of Yale University, took a tour of the South during the last century. From Tidewater Virginia he wrote to his sister, describing a succession of feasts at which he was a guest. For one, he wrote, the hostess was at one end of the table, with a large dish of rich soup; the host at the other end, with "a saddle of fine mutton, buttressed by ham, beef, turkey, duck, and innumerable vegetables."

When the dinner is finished, the gentlemen return to the drawing room with the ladies, and then withdraw to the smoking room for half an hour. Shortly after their return to the drawing room the guests take their leave.

The butler keeps count of the arrival of expected guests, and announces dinner shortly after all are in the drawing room. He then enters the room, and, looking at the hostess, says, "Dinner is served," or he simply bows to the hostess.

Footstools placed under the dining table for the ladies add much to their comfort during a meal.

At large dinners a gentleman finds in the dressing room, or a servant passes to him before he enters the drawing room, a tray holding small addressed envelopes. He selects the one bearing his own name, and finds on an inclosed card the name of the lady he is to take to the table.

That part of the meal was followed by sparkling champagne. The "upper table cloth" was removed and on the next one was "placed the dessert, consisting of fine plum pudding, pies, tarts, etc. etc.—after this comes ice cream, West India preserves, peaches conserved in brandy, etc. When you have eaten this, off goes the second table cloth, and then upon the bare mahogany table is set the figs, raisins, and almonds . . . Madeira, Port, and a sweet wine for the ladies . . . after the first and second glass the ladies retire, and the gentlemen begin to circulate the bottle pretty briskly."

A similar pattern of dining continued into this century and is still followed, with a reduction in the number of foods on the menu, in some homes. Only one cloth is used, a decrease from the two, but certainly that cloth is of the finest damask with large matching monogrammed napkins. The number of hostesses able to manage dining on damask is gradually decreasing; and eventually, few will attempt the ways of the past.

IT WASN'T ALL OPULENT

All men who sat down to dinner during what was called the Age of Opulence did not do so wearing white ties and tails, or even white shirts. The majority sat down in their work clothes, in their blue shirts—the mark of the working man. They often sat down to a meal of grub. Grub is a plate of food, frequently only one kind, served with bread. Grub is a plate of beans, thick soup, fish, rabbit stew, chicken stew, pork ribs, boiled or mashed potatoes.

The middle class or the well-to-do class lived on vittles (victuals). Vittles consist of offerings from the farm, garden, fields and streams. In the hands of a good manager, the vittles were superb in quality and abundant in quantity.

Marjorie Kinnan Rawlings told it the way it was in the book, *The Yearling*. The family lived off the land and once, when away from home, the boy in the book dreamed "of one of Ma's dinners of ham slices, steaming, brown and dripping in their own juice; tawny biscuits, corn bread, bowls of cowpeas with squares of white bacon floating among them, and fried squirrel." "Ma" made a stew called sandbuggers with potatoes, onions and cooters. (A cooter is a variety of turtle.) Ma who had neither cook stove nor running water cooked on an open fire.

Dinner was on the table punctually at noon when the hands came from the fields in warm weather. The men stopped by the well to wash their hands in a tin bowl and dry them on the towel on a roller. They drank cool well water from a dipper.

Fresh cakes of butter and buttermilk from the spring house went to the table along with a basket of hot corn muffins at just the moment everyone was seated.

Dishes which are typically American, ranging from vittles to repasts, appear in a list made by Mark Twain. While on a tour of Europe during the last century, Mark Twain found the food not to his liking. While still in Europe, he wrote: "It has been many months, at the present writing, since I have had a nourishing meal, but I shall soon have a modest, private affair, all to myself. I have selected a few dishes, and made out a little bill of fare, which will go home in the steamer that precedes me, and be hot when I arrive—as follows:

Radishes. Baked apples, with cream.
Fried oysters; stewed oysters. Frogs.
American coffee, with real cream. American butter.
Hot biscuits, Southern style.
Porter-house steak.
Saratoga potatoes.
Broiled chicken, American style.
Hot biscuits, Southern style.
Hot buckwheat cakes.
American toast. Clear maple syrup.
Virginia bacon, broiled.
Blue points, on the half shell.
Cherry-stone clams.
San Francisco mussels, steamed.
Oyster soup. Clam soup.
Philadelphia Terrapin soup.
Oysters roasted in the shell—Northern style.
Soft-shell crabs. Connecticut shad.
Brook trout, from Sierra Nevadas.
Lake trout, from Tahoe.
Sheep-head and croakers, from New Orleans.
Black bass from the Mississippi.
American roast beef.
Roast turkey, Thanksgiving style.
Cranberry sauce. Celery. Roast wild turkey.
Woodcock.
Canvas-back-duck, from Baltimore.
Prairie hens, from Illinois.
Missouri partridges, broiled.
'Possum. Coon.
Boston bacon and beans.
Bacon and greens, Southern style.
Hominy. Boiled onions. Turnips.
Pumpkin. Squash. Asparagus.
Butter beans. Sweet potatoes.
Lettuce. Succotash. String beans.
Mashed potatoes. Catsup.
Boiled potatoes, in their skins.

Dinner at the cattle spread, the ranch, never had anything fancy like a radish rose on the grub and nobody pampered kids to eat the way city kids got pampered.

When all the dishes were on it, the dinner table looked like an old-fashioned flower garden in full bloom; you ate first with the eyes.

The hostess must use much tact in placing guests at the table. If one is a great talker let the other be a good listener.

New potatoes, minus the skins.
Early potatoes, roasted in the ashes, Southern
style, served hot.
Sliced tomatoes, with sugar or vinegar.
Stewed tomatoes.
Green corn, cut from the ear and served with
butter and pepper.
Green corn, on the ear.
Hot corn-pone, with chitlings, Southern style.
Hot hoe-cake, Southern style.
Hot egg-bread, Southern style.
Hot light-bread, Southern style.
Buttermilk. Iced sweet milk.
Apple dumplings, with real cream.
Apple pie. Apple fritters.
Apple puffs, Southern style.
Peach cobbler, Southern style.
Peach pie. American mince pie.
Pumpkin pie. Squash pie.
All sorts of American pastry.

Fresh American fruits of all sorts, including
strawberries which are not to be doled out as if they
were jewelry, but in a more liberal way. Ice-Water—not
prepared in the ineffectual tumbler, but in the sincere
and capable refrigerator."

In the Pennsylvania Dutch country, the heavily laden
dinner table is still seen at the Fourth of July festival
held in Kutztown. In costume, women of the area cook
all the Pennsylvania Dutch (Pennsylvania German is a
more descriptive term) favorites and set them out
family style on big tables in tents. The dishes are then
passed up and down the table with each person filling
his own plate.

H. J. Heinz II was host a few years ago at a Pennsylvania Dutch dinner sponsored by his company which is based in Pittsburgh. The meal was for the newspaper food editors of the country and was held at the Waldorf-Astoria Hotel in New York City. The menu consisted of sauerbraten in rich brown gravy, *gschmelzte* nudle, oven-baked beans, tomatoes, fried eggplant, sweets and sours, shoo-fly pie, cheesecake, cider, and coffee. *(Gschmelzte nudle* is the dialect name for noodles drenched in browned butter and coated with bread crumbs.)

Here is another Pennsylvania Dutch dinner.

Corn Chowder

Chicken Potpie

Red Cabbage   Scalloped Potatoes

Seven Sweets: sweet pickled peaches, apple butter, quince honey, ginger pears, grape conserve, rhubarb jam, tomato preserves

Seven Sours: red-beet eggs, Jerusalem artichoke, pickles, pickled wax beans, cantaloupe pickle, piccalilli, corn relish, carrot pickles

Homemade Bread

Shoo-fly Pie   Applesauce Cake

Coffee

In 1950 the Shartlesville Hotel in Shartlesville, Pa., was still serving the following at one sitting. The price was $1.75. Up, no doubt, from previous years.

Each member of the family had his own silver napkin ring. Once or twice a week the napkins were laundered. Guests were given fresh napkins.

The rules for dining were rigid. When children were allowed to eat with adults, they were seen and not heard, and each sat at the table until permission was granted for leaving.

THE MEAL

Platter of brown-roasted, milk-fed young tom turkey
An equally large dish of soft-stewed chicken
Huge slabs of smoking hot roast beef
Country-style sausages, 1½ inches in diameter
Cold summer sausage, made of beef and pork
Chicken potpie
Chicken salad
Chicken patties
Red kidney beans with slivers of beef
Golden candied sweet potatoes
Mashed white potatoes
Plump dried lima beans,
crisp green string beans, stewed dried corn,
noodles, green garden peas, chick peas
Pepper cabbage and cream coleslaw
Pickled beets
Homemade cucumber pickles
Cold string beans in sweet-hot mustard sauce
Cider-colored applesauce,
aromatic with a trace of cinnamon
Crabapple jelly, strawberry jam, blackberry preserves
Yellow potato salad, made with homemade mayonnaise
Stewed dried peaches and prunes
Fluffy, lump, old-fashioned tapioca pudding
Cherry gelatin dessert
Shoo-fly pie
Mashed potato doughnuts
White, rye, and whole wheat bread
with chunks of butter
Chocolate and vanilla ice cream
coffee, tea, and milk

In New England, Friday's dinner is cod fish, also called
"Cape Cod Turkey." If a boiled dinner is scheduled,
it frequently appears on Monday or Thursday with red
flannel hash the next day. A boiled dinner consists of
corned beef, potatoes, carrots, onions, beets, white
turnips, and cabbage. Traditionally the beef is brown
rather than reddish, due to the absence of saltpeter
in curing.

EVERYDAY DINNERS

The dinner put on the table of the moderate income family has followed the meat-and-potato pattern for most of the century. This is a menu suggested by Fannie Farmer in 1914.

Cream of Celery Soup
Roast Beef
Franconia Potatoes   Yorkshire Pudding
Macaroni and Cheese
Tomato and Lettuce Salad
Chocolate Cream

This is an everyday dinner menu suggested in 1927.
Oysters on Half-Shell   Celery
Mock Turtle Soup   Crackers
Steak   Mashed Potatoes
Spinach Garnished with Hard-Boiled Eggs
Caramel Ice Cream

Mrs. Sarah Rorer suggested this dinner menu in her book of menus.

Soup Soubise, Croutons
Egyptian Cylinders
Brown Sauce
Pea Patties
Lettuce and Celery Salad
Wafers   Parmesan Balls
Mock Charlotte

Egyptian Cylinders are rolls about four-inches long of chopped meat, mixed cooked vegetables, and nuts. The rolls are cooked in butter.

Shore Dinner
Lobster Stew   Crackers
Steamed Clams   Fried Clams
Boiled Lobster
French Fried Potatoes
French Fried Onion Rings
Tomato and Cucumber Salad
Hot Rolls

Beef Steak and Kidney Pie

  ¾ pound calf kidney
  2 tablespoons flour
  1 teaspoon salt
  ¾ teaspoon black pepper, freshly ground
  4 tablespoons butter
  4 shallots, finely chopped
  2 pounds beef steak, cut into bite-size pieces
  1 cup beef bouillon
  1 bay leaf
  1 teaspoon parsley, chopped
  A pinch each of ground cloves and marjoram
  ½ pound mushrooms, sliced and sautéed
  Splash of dry sherry or madeira
  1 tablespoon Worcestershire sauce

Clean and split kidney, remove fat and large tubes, and soak in salted water for 1 hour. Dry and cut into ¼-inch slices. Mix flour, salt, and pepper; roll kidney and beef in mixture. Melt butter in heavy pot and sauté shallots. When shallots have taken on a little color, add beef and kidneys and brown lightly, turning. Add bouillon, bay leaf, parsley, cloves, and marjoram. Stir, cover, and simmer for 1 to 1¼ hours or until meat is tender. Add mushrooms, sherry, and Worcestershire. If liquid is too thin, thicken with a smooth paste of flour and water.

Grease a deep baking dish. Place a pie funnel in the center. Add meat mixture and allow to cool. In the meantime, make pastry (recipe below); then place over meat. Make vents in the pastry to allow steam to escape and bake in a 450-degree oven for 8 to 10 minutes. Lower heat to 375 degrees, and continue baking for 15 minutes or until crust is golden.

Calves or beef liver may be very satisfactorily substituted for kidney if kidney is not available. Another substitution is two 12-ounce cans of roast beef for the beef.

Pastry

  1½ cups flour, sifted
  ½ teaspoon salt
  ¼ teaspoon baking powder
  ¼ pound (½ cup) lard
  1 egg
  ½ teaspoon lemon juice
  2½ tablespoons ice water

Sift flour with salt and baking powder. Cut lard into flour mixture until crumbs form. Beat egg lightly and add half the egg (use other half for another purpose or discard). Add lemon juice and water. Stir with a fork until blended, then shape into a ball. Roll out on lightly floured board.

Cassoulet

    1 pound dried small white beans
    2 teaspoons salt
    Pinch each: basil, marjoram, thyme, oregano, mace, savory
    1 pound smoked sausage links, thinly sliced
    ¾ cup onions, chopped
    2½ cups cooked beef, turkey, chicken, or lamb, diced
    3 cups dry white wine
    1 8-ounce can tomato sauce
    ½ cup fresh parsley, minced
    5 tablespoons butter, melted
    ¾ cup fine dry bread crumbs

Cover beans with cold water and bring to a boil; remove from heat and soak for 3 to 4 hours. Add salt and herbs; cook beans until almost tender—about 1 hour— adding small amounts of water as needed if beans become dry. In a large casserole arrange layers of drained beans, onions, sausage, and meat or poultry. Blend wine and tomato sauce; pour into casserole. Mix parsley, butter, and bread crumbs; spread over top of casserole. Bake at 325 degrees uncovered for 2 hours. Makes 8 to 10 servings.

Fresh and Pickled Honeycomb Tripe

Fresh tripe is coated in beaten egg and pan-fried; or it can be broiled and stewed. Pickled tripe is parboiled a few minutes, dried and cut into pieces before being cooked in the same ways as fresh tripe. Tripe is an old favorite either by itself or in Philadelphia pepper-pot soup.

Mountain Oysters

Also called Rocky Mountain oysters and Lamb fries, Mountain oysters are the testicles of virgin lambs bred in the sheep-grazing states of Colorado, Wyoming, Utah, and Idaho. They are also the testicles removed from bull calves to convert them into steers. Ranchers, who fry them in the same manner as oysters, think they rival sweetbreads.

When we had floating island for dessert, Mama told us stories about faraway places. We dreamed of sailing away on a sailing ship to an exotic island.

The etched glass punch cups used for serving apple float and prune whip were heirlooms Mama insisted on washing with her own hands. As a child I thought that breaking one of those cups meant instant banishment to Siberia.

Eels

Cooks cut them into three-inch pieces, roll them in seasoned cornmeal, and pan-fry.

In New England, eel stifle, made with eels, onions, potatoes, and salt pork, was popular when eels were available. Stifle is a stew made with either meat or fish.

Crab Imperial

Moisten lump crab meat with mayonnaise. Season with salt and white pepper to taste, and add several dashes of Worcestershire sauce. Lift the crab meat gently up and down in the air the way a child lifts soap suds to play with them. This motion aerates the mixture in such a way that, when served, it has the quality of a soufflé. Pile gently and amply into buttered individual baking shells. Brush top with melted butter. Heat in a 375-degree oven for 15 to 20 minutes or until lightly browned. Serve with lemon wedges.

Fisheye Tapioca

Susan Staver, a boarding-house proprietress in Boston, is credited with introducing quick-cooking tapioca at the end of the last century. A sailor rooming at her house complained that her tapioca pudding was lumpy, so she tried grinding "fisheye" tapioca in the coffee grinder before making the pudding again. It worked. The pudding was less lumpy and it cooked much faster. Miss Staver peddled bags of her ground tapioca from door to door to her neighbors. This became known as today's quick-cooking tapioca. Pearl Tapioca is available in food specialty shops.

Cream Tapioca Pudding

Soak 3 tablespoonfuls of tapioca in a little water till transparent. Add to 1 quart of boiling milk, and boil for 15 minutes. Beat well the yolks of 2 eggs with 1 cup of sugar, and stir in a little cornstarch and flavoring. Add the boiled milk. Put the whole mixture in a baking dish. Make a meringue from the egg whites and spread over mixture. Top with grated coconut and bake until meringue browns.

Pearl Tapioca Pudding

1 cup pearl tapioca
3½ cups water
1¾ cups brown sugar
2 tablespoons butter, melted
1 teaspoon vanilla
Cream

Add 1½ cups water to tapioca and allow to soak overnight. The next day, add sugar, 2 cups water, butter, and vanilla to tapioca. Pour into a baking dish. Bake in a 350-degree oven for 1 hour or until clear. Serve warm or cold with thick cream. Serves 6.

Apple Float

1 pint applesauce sweetened to taste
2 egg whites
6 tablespoons sugar
Nutmeg
Sweet cream or milk

The applesauce should be free from lumps. Beat egg whites until stiff, adding sugar gradually. Fold beaten egg whites into applesauce. Sprinkle with nutmeg. Serve chilled with cream. Makes 4 to 6 servings.

Floating Island

4 egg yolks or 2 whole eggs, beaten
⅓ cup plus 1 tablespoon sugar
¼ teaspoon salt
2 cups milk
½ teaspoon vanilla
1 egg white

In top of double boiler, combine egg yolks or eggs, ⅓ cup sugar, and salt; place over simmering water. Cook, stirring constantly, until mixture coats a spoon thinly. Overcooking causes curdling. Pour immediately into a bowl; add vanilla, chill. Meanwhile, beat egg white, gradually adding 1 tablespoon sugar, until it forms a light meringue. Fill 4 muffin tins ½ full of water; spoon meringue on top of water to make peaked mounds. Bake in a 325-degree oven for 10 minutes or until mounds are lightly brown. Cool; lift mounds from water with slotted spoon. Place atop custard. Makes 4 servings.

SUNDAY DINNER

Once in America the whole weekly tempo of the household culminated when the family, relatives, friends, and guests, invited and uninvited, sat down to Sunday dinner. It was the day for wearing the Sunday suit, Sunday dress, Sunday hat, and going to church. After church, the table was filled with the best the household had to offer.

The way it was still is, at this writing, at the Krebs, a restaurant in Skaneateles, N.Y. The Krebs, which opened in 1899, offers home cooking which disregards calories and capacity. The atmosphere is homey, like going to Aunt Jenny's on a Sunday long ago. There is no menu and all the guests sit shoulder to shoulder, bonded in a companionship shared by those who like to eat and eat and eat.

At the Krebs, there are six courses. First comes shrimp cocktail, melon, or fruit cup, followed by a choice of three soups and an indiscriminate array of pickles and relishes. Waitresses with filled trays appear like the chorus coming in on cue in a musical comedy. One has a vast platter divided equally with fried chicken and sliced steak or roast beef. Another carries mashed white potatoes with gravy, and candied sweet potatoes. Creamed mushrooms are offered as if they cost no more than popcorn. Fresh vegetables are endless in their season. There are home-baked brown bread, rolls, and sticky cinnamon buns. There is an assortment of salads and desserts, including ice cream, pie, strawberry pie in June, melon in summer, and heaps of brownies and angel food cake in all seasons.

In 1915, the book *Fifty-two Sunday Dinners* was published. It included menus offering variations on the chicken-every-Sunday theme. Here is an example:

Noodle Soup
Boiled Beef with Horseradish Sauce
Baked Potatoes
Macaroni with Tomato Sauce
Chiffonade Salad
Steamed Cottage Pudding, Banana Sauce
Coffee

Be certain the dinner is sufficiently good and abundant to accommodate the visitor who may unexpectedly come. The knowledge that the dinner is more than adequate, and that the linen is clean, will banish anxiety from the breasts of the master and mistress.

In our little village 'setting a good table' was a status symbol. Town wags had certain tones of voice used to pass along bits of gossip. The tone for a woman of means who 'set' a poor table was similar to the tone used for a girl who had a child out of wedlock.

Sunday dinner in New England might offer some treatment of "lamb fores," lamb shoulders which are boned and stuffed with dressing and roasted. Yankee pot roast, tender and succulent from slow, leisurely cooking, is another favorite. A flavor secret is browning the meat in salt pork drippings. Potatoes, onions, and carrots are cooked with the meat and in some homes, a sliced white turnip is added.

Cod Dinner

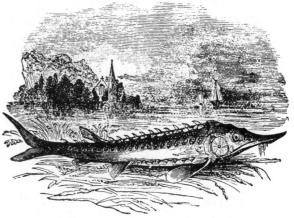

3 pounds salt cod fillets
18 white onions, boiled
8 small beets, cooked
8 carrots, cooked
8 medium size potatoes, cooked
Butter or margarine to taste
Parsley, finely minced
½ pound salt pork, diced
Egg sauce (recipe below)
2 lemons, sliced
¼ teaspoon paprika

Cover fillets with cold water and soak for 8 hours, changing water twice. When ready to cook, drain cod and cover with fresh cold water. Bring to a boil, reduce heat, and simmer for 20 minutes. Drain, add fresh boiling water, and boil 5 minutes. Season vegetables to taste with butter or margarine. Sprinkle potatoes with parsley. Fry salt pork until crisp and brown.

Place fish in center of a large hot platter. At one end arrange hot sliced beets and boiled onions. At the opposite end place carrots and potatoes. Pour the egg sauce over the fish. Garnish with lemon slices sprinkled with minced parsley. Dust sauce with paprika. Serve crisp pork in pork drippings in gravy boat. Serves 8.

Egg Sauce

½ cup butter or margarine
½ cup flour
4 cups milk
6 hard-cooked eggs
2 teaspoons salt
½ teaspoon pepper

Melt butter and blend in flour. Add milk gradually, stirring constantly, and cook until thick and smooth. Chop eggs, reserving 1 yolk for garnish. Add chopped eggs and seasonings. Sieve reserved egg yolk over sauce. Makes about 4 cups sauce.

Salt Pork Milk Gravy

A favorite in New England

1 cup salt pork, cubed
3 tablespoons flour
2 cups milk
Salt to taste

In a heavy skillet, cook cubes of pork slowly until crusty and brown or until "crackly and brittle." Remove; drain. Discard all but ¼ cup drippings. Into drippings in pan, blend flour; stir in milk and cook until thickened. Season to taste—little or no salt is needed because of the saltiness of the pork. Add browned cubes; serve over baked or boiled potatoes, or hot biscuits. Makes about 2 cups.

Sauerbraten

1 4-pound beef chuck roast
2 teaspoons salt
¼ teaspoon black pepper
2 cups water
2 cups cider or wine vinegar
1 medium onion, chopped
¼ cup celery, chopped
3 bay leaves
12 peppercorns
6 whole cloves
¼ teaspoon thyme
1 teaspoon mustard seed
1 large carrot, sliced
¼ cup sugar
Flour
2 tablespoons oil
¼ cup raisins, plumped
18 gingersnaps, crushed

Rub beef with salt and pepper; place in large bowl or crock with water, vinegar, onion, celery, bay leaves, peppercorns, cloves, thyme, mustard seed, carrot, and sugar. Cover and marinate in refrigerator for 3 days. Turn several times. When ready to cook, remove meat from marinade. Dry and dust with flour, brown on all sides in hot oil in heavy kettle. Cover and simmer slowly 3 hours or until tender. Lift meat onto hot platter. Strain stock. Add raisins and gingersnaps; cook, stirring, until smooth and thickened. Serve gravy with meat. Serves 4 to 6.

Times there wasn't anything for dinner but a dinner plate piled high with tiny new boiled potatoes with salt pork cream gravy. It tasted like Heaven to a hungry boy.

We never knew ahead of time how many there would be for Sunday dinner. There were often two and three sittings at the table, the way meals are served on ocean liners. Children had to wait for the third sitting; we called it the third table.

Fish came from the fish market or fishmonger wrapped in newspaper tied with a string. It was my job to scale it and clean the insides. I made the scales fly on a wooden table in the backyard.

THANKSGIVING

A proper New England Thanksgiving dinner consists of roast stuffed turkey, cranberry sauce or jelly, mashed potatoes with giblet gravy, creamed onions, mashed turnips, and possibly Hubbard squash, with Indian pudding as one of the desserts.

In Maryland a typical menu starts with oyster stew and includes roast stuffed turkey and baked old ham, mashed potatoes, green limas, candied sweet potatoes, sauerkraut, dried sweet corn, scalloped oysters, and white potato pie in addition to the familiar pumpkin, mince, and apple pies. (Old ham is a country ham which has cured a year or more.)

For Thanksgiving in the Midwest, there were usually two kinds of pies, mince and pumpkin. In the East, there was a sliver each of cranberry, mince, and pumpkin. Boston cooks made four kinds—mince, cranberry, pumpkin, and Marlborough. Marlborough is a glorified apple pie made of applesauce and lemon juice in a custard-like mixture. Wine jelly was on the menu in the area of Charleston, S. C. In the Southwest it is traditional to pack Thanksgiving dinner in the car, drive to the desert and spread out the food.

Scalloped Oysters

½ cup plus 1 tablespoon butter
⅓ cup flour
1 teaspoon paprika
¾ teaspoon salt
½ teaspoon celery salt
⅛ teaspoon black pepper
Dash of cayenne
1 tablespoon lemon juice
1 quart oysters
2 teaspoons Worcestershire sauce
2 cups Ritz crackers, coarsely broken

Melt ½ cup butter. Blend in flour, paprika, salt, celery salt, pepper, and cayenne. Remove from heat. Add lemon juice, Worcestershire, undrained oysters, and half the crackers. Pour into baking dish. Top with remaining crackers, dot with 1 tablespoon butter. Bake at 375 degrees for 25 minutes or until bubbly. Makes 5 to 6 servings.

Oyster Patties

Serve for breakfast on Thanksgiving and Christmas
1 cup buttermilk
2 cups coarse fresh bread crumbs, made from ends of bread and crusts
2 eggs
½ cup pancake mix
1 tablespoon sugar
½ teaspoon celery salt
¼ cup salad oil or butter, melted
1 pint oysters
Shortening

Pour buttermilk over crumbs; soak, covered, overnight in the refrigerator. The next day, mash and blend soaked crumbs with a fork; blend in eggs, pancake mix, sugar, celery salt, and oil or butter. Add oysters. Heat griddle as for pancakes, using only enough shortening to prevent sticking. Bake, rather than fry, small patties each with one oyster, until brown on both sides. If desired, cook patties ahead of time; reheat in a single layer on a baking sheet in a 350-degree oven for about five minutes. Good served with crisp bacon. Makes about 36.

Plantation Sweet Potato Pone

4 large sweet potatoes
Rind of 1 lemon, grated
Rind of ½ orange, grated
2 eggs, beaten
½ cup brown sugar
½ teaspoon cinnamon
½ teaspoon nutmeg
½ teaspoon ground cloves
½ cup molasses
⅔ cup milk
⅓ cup bourbon
½ cup (1 stick) butter, melted

Peel sweet potatoes and grate them. Add lemon and orange rinds. Beat eggs and sugar together, and stir into potato mixture. Add spices, molasses, milk, bourbon, and butter. Mix thoroughly and bake in a 325-degree oven for 1 hour to an hour and 15 minutes. Serve hot as a vegetable. Makes 12 or more servings.

Vintage Salad

1 red apple
2 cups Tokay grapes
½ cup pitted dates, sliced
2 cups celery, thinly sliced
1 tablespoon candied ginger, chopped
½ pint sour cream
¼ teaspoon lemon rind, grated
2 teaspoons lemon juice
½ teaspoon salt
⅛ teaspoon curry powder
¼ cup toasted almonds, chopped
Salad greens

Dice unpeeled red apple. Cut grapes in half and remove seeds. Combine apple, grapes, dates, celery, and ginger. Combine sour cream, lemon rind and juice, salt, and curry powder. Toss lightly with apple mixture. Chill. Serve on beds of salad greens. Sprinkle with almonds. Makes 5 to 6 servings.

Favorite Thanksgiving Salad

1 3-ounce package lemon gelatin
¾ cup boiling water
1 8-ounce bottle ginger ale
1 cup pitted dates, chopped
1 rib celery, chopped
½ cup pecans, chopped
1 apple, peeled and chopped

Use hot water to dissolve gelatin. Cool to room temperature. Add remaining ingredients. Pour into mold or molds and chill until firm. Makes 6 servings.

Drawn Butter Sauce

A Thanksgiving steamed pudding was popular with this sauce.

⅓ cup butter
3 tablespoons flour
1¼ cups boiling water
⅓ teaspoon salt
1 cup sugar
¼ cup brandy
⅛ teaspoon nutmeg

Melt half the butter in a saucepan. Blend in flour; add boiling water and let mixture come to a boil, stirring. Remove from heat and add remaining butter in small bits; continue stirring. Add salt, sugar, brandy, and nutmeg. Beat and serve hot over pudding (recipe below).

At Thanksgiving dinner, a fleet of sauceboats filled the spaces around the main dishes, with sweet-and-sour pickles, jelly, and spiced fruits of which I recall particularly spiced whole crab apples and peach pickles.

Before the last rose of summer faded, anticipation of the Thanksgiving turkey began to mount. The turkey's debut on the big china platter was as regal as a baron of beef for a medieval king. After the feast we ate turkey for days and days.

At Thanksgiving Grandmother directed her kitchen full of womenfolk the way a symphony conductor conducts. My job was whipping the cream and she'd tell me the exact beat on which to stop whipping.

Steamed Pudding

¾ cup flour, sifted
1 teaspoon baking powder
1 teaspoon baking soda
½ teaspoon salt
½ teaspoon cinnamon
¼ teaspoon ground cloves
½ teaspoon nutmeg
½ teaspoon allspice
1 cup brown sugar
½ cup molasses
1 cup raw sweet potatoes, peeled and grated
1 cup raw carrots, scraped and grated
½ cup bread crumbs, soft
1 teaspoon orange rind, grated
½ cup orange juice
½ cup beef suet, ground or finely chopped

Sift together flour, baking powder, baking soda, salt, sugar, and spices; add remaining ingredients, mix thoroughly. Pour into two 2-quart pudding molds or cans. Cover molds or cans tightly; lacking lids, use foil tied with string. Place molds on rack in 3 to 4 inches hot water in large kettle; cover kettle and steam by simmering 3 hours. Replace water as needed with boiling water. Serve with butter brandy sauce or hard sauce. Makes 16 to 18 servings.

Mincemeat

Mincemeat used to come, not in compressed packages wrapped in cellophane and not in vacuum-sealed jars, but in crocks, and it often contained meat. This recipe came from a woman who lived in Salem, Mass. In her younger days, she worked in Fanny Farmer's kitchen.

5 pounds lean beef
1 pound beef suet, finely chopped
5 pounds apples, peeled and finely chopped
4 pounds raisins
2 pounds currants
1 pound preserved citron, thinly sliced
¼ pound each candied orange and lemon rinds, thinly sliced
2 tablespoons mace
2 tablespoons cinnamon
2 tablespoons salt
1 tablespoon each ground cloves, allspice, nutmeg
1 pint molasses
3 pounds brown sugar
2 quarts apple cider
1 pint brandy
1 pint sherry

Cook beef in enough water to cover until tender. Drain and cool. When cold, cut into fine pieces. Cook beef with remaining ingredients except brandy and sherry. When cold, add brandy and sherry. Store in a crock in a cold place.

Meatless Mincemeat

This older recipe for mincemeat is meatless. One whiff should ease the pains of preparation.

The aromatic smell of the plum puddings steaming away in boiling water permeated our white frame house scrubbed scrupulously clean for Christmas.

½ gallon cherry preserves
½ gallon plum preserves
6 pounds raisins, stoned and chopped
6 pounds currants, washed and dried
3 pounds citron, sliced
1 dozen large apples, peeled and chopped
Rind of 2 oranges, finely cut
8 pounds suet, chopped
2 pounds brown sugar
½ gallon sweet cider
6 nutmegs, grated
1 tablespoon ground allspice
1 tablespoon ground cloves
1½ gallons whiskey

Mix together all ingredients except whiskey. Bring to a boil for a few minutes, then add whiskey. When pies are made add a little more whiskey and some sugar if mixture is not sweet enough.

Wine Jelly

2 envelopes unflavored gelatin
½ cup cold water
1½ cups boiling water
1 cup sugar
Pinch of salt
3 tablespoons lemon juice, strained
¾ cup orange juice, strained
¾ cup sherry
Whipped cream

Soften gelatin in cold water. Dissolve in boiling water. Add sugar, salt, lemon juice, orange juice, and sherry. Stir to blend. Pour into a mold and chill until firm. Serve topped with whipped cream. Serves 6.

CHRISTMAS

Christmas was a lot of little things:
an Advent wreath with a tiny gift and message
        for each of the twelve months
lighting a bayberry candle and watching it flicker
        on the faces of those gathered around
a bowl of white narcissuses set to bloom on cue
        cookie rolling, baking, and decorating, with
women working as hard on cookies as Santa's gnomes
        worked on toys at the North Pole
keeping the huge woodbox in the kitchen filled
        with neat lengths of wood so Mom could bake
Julekake (Norwegian Christmas bread) with lots
        and lots of raisins
rolling and cutting cookies to the rhythm of
        Christmas carols
searching for holly and mistletoe
        going in the homemade sleigh drawn by the old
gray horse to select a tree to chop down
        the smell of the tree in the house
trimming the tree with slightly tarnished tinsel,
        paper ropes, ornaments aged with a patina
etched over years of use, and strings of popcorn
        and cranberries
the children who gazed with upturned faces holding
        wonder like a cup
the Sunday school Christmas program with the tots
        performing uninhibited
being gently awakened in the night by the sound of
        carolers strolling down the street
the message in *Amahl and the Night Visitors*
        the church choir singing "Joy to the World"
trying to stay awake all night on Christmas Eve to hear
        Santa Claus and his reindeer land on the roof
a stocking full of candies, nuts, apples, oranges, and
        tangerines, and a new doll for the girls and an
erector set or a sweater for the boys
        Christmas dinner, the greatest meal of the whole
year, with everyone eating himself into near stupor
        Christmas was a good time, one which gathered
momentum from one year to the next.
Earlier in the century a little girl named Virginia wrote
a letter to a newspaper asking: "Is there a
Santa Claus?" The affirmative answer has become a
classic. It stated, in essence, that in the same way
beauty is in the eyes of the beholder, Santa Claus and
Christmas are in the heart.

The grocer in our little village had
a row of shiny lard cans filled with
Christmas candies—little round
pieces with a flower design, curled
ribbon shapes, and red raspberries.
Christmas was the only time he
had oranges and tangerines.

A goose was valuable not only for
Christmas dinner but for its fine
feathers for filling pillows.

To put us in the mood for
trimming the Christmas tree,
Father always put Christmas
records on our Victrola.

The Hostess was the name of a leaflet published monthly by the Randolph Confection Co. of St. Louis, Mo., subscription price twenty-five cents a year. The issue for December, 1905, gave a Christmas dinner menu. The accompanying article pointed out that the Christmas menu was traditional but it was "quite permissible to indulge in various little additions and innovations more in harmony with our modern ideas of feasting. The handsomest, heaviest available cloth should grace the Christmas table, with the finest glass and china the house affords. Hothouse flowers are out of place on a Christmas table and the centerpiece should be made of holly or other evergreens, surrounding a dish of richly colored seasonable fruits, nuts, and raisins."

This dinner "will be found very pleasing and not too difficult as a large portion of the cooking may be done a day or two before."

MENU FOR CHRISTMAS

Grapefruit Cocktail
Oyster Soup
Celery   Olives   Salted Almonds
Sweetbread Patties
Turkey with Chestnut Dressing
Cranberry Jelly
Riced Potatoes   Green Peas
Baked Squash
Apple, Celery, and Nut Salad with
Mayonnaise Dressing
Pumpkin Pie   Mince Pie   Plum Pudding
Angel Ice Cream   Assorted Cakes
Glacé Fruits   Mixed Nuts   Raisins
Small Black Coffee

Grapefruit Cocktail

Allow 1 large grapefruit for 4 guests. Remove the pulp and mix with it the pulp of 3 oranges, 1 diced banana, 4 Turkish figs cut in bits, 1 cup of seeded dessert raisins, and ½ cup of crystalized maraschino cherries. Sweeten with powdered sugar to taste and serve very cold in lemonade cups with orange spoons.

It is presumed that Turkish figs are the same as Smyrna figs, which set the quality standard for all fig-producing countries. Greek and Italian figs were inferior. Early in the century dried California figs were gaining "considerable importance." Southern figs went mainly into preserves.

Figs also figured in the Thanksgiving and Christmas festivities in the book *Look Homeward, Angel* by Thomas Wolfe (1900-1938). In the book Wolfe writes about his youth. The main character, Eugene Gant, is Wolfe.

For Thanksgiving and Christmas the Gants had four heavy turkeys. Eugene fattened them on shelled corn several times a day. Eliza baked for weeks in advance and "the whole energy of the family focused upon the great ritual of the feast."

"A day or two before, the auxiliary dainties arrived in piled grocer's boxes—the magic of strange foods and fruits was added to familiar fare; there were glossed sticky dates, cold rich figs, cramped belly to belly in small boxes, dusty raisins." The dainties included mixed nuts, sacks of assorted candies, piles of yellow Florida oranges and tangerines—all with "sharp, acrid, nostalgic odors."

Mrs. Rorer wrote in 1905 that "all sorts of novelties are looked for and the bills of fare are made as unique as possible. Not so with the Christmas dinner; it has remained unchanged for generations. Christmas would not be Christmas without turkey or goose, plum pudding and sugar-plums. The pudding for the feast should be made at least two months before the occasion, and put away to ripen and become mellow and rich." The turkey should be drawn and hung in a cold place for at least one day before roasting.

Mrs. Rorer felt dinner should not be beyond the capacity of the cook or the housewife to whom the preparation is assigned.

This is one of Mrs. Rorer's Chrismas menus.

The Christmas tree was trimmed with spools painted various colors and strung together, strings of popcorn and cranberries, and real candles in little metal holders which clipped to the branches.

In our mill village of fifty neat cottages, pot-bellied, pink-cheeked Santas visited every house on Christmas Eve, leaving for each child a "treat," a huge brown paper bag stuffed with candy, nuts, and fruits.

For Christmas dinner, we had not one turkey, but two, one wild one and one tame one, and sometimes also wild duck and ham.

Cherrystone Oysters in Beds of Cress
Consommé à la Royal
Broiled Salmon, Lobster Sauce
Parisienne Potatoes
Turkey, Chestnut Stuffing, Cranberry Sauce
Boiled Rice   Creamed Onions
Shaddock   Sherbet
Canvasback Duck   Fox Grape Jelly
Lettuce Salad, French Dressing
Mince Pie   Pumpkin Custard
Nuts   Raisins
Fruits
Coffee

Pepper Steak Old Heidelberg

Pepper Steak Old Heidelberg is a German Christmas dinner favorite.

3 6-ounce servings sirloin or rib eye steak
¼ teaspoon salt
½ teaspoon coarsely ground black pepper
⅛ teaspoon garlic powder
2 tablespoons butter or margarine
½ teaspoon thyme
½ teaspoon rosemary
½ teaspoon crushed red pepper
2 tablespoons onion, finely chopped
20 capers, drained
4 fresh mushrooms, finely chopped
2 teaspoons German mustard
1 teaspoon Worcestershire sauce
½ cup sour cream
¼ cup German white wine
1 teaspoon fresh lemon juice

Sprinkle steaks with salt, black pepper, and garlic powder; pound until about ¼ inch thick. Melt butter in heavy skillet; cook steaks in butter, browning lightly on each side, to desired degree of doneness. Remove from pan; keep warm. To butter in skillet, add thyme, rosemary, red pepper, onion, capers, mushrooms, mustard, and Worcestershire sauce; cook, stirring, a few minutes. Add sour cream, wine, and lemon juice; heat but do not boil. Spoon sauce over steaks; serve with roast potatoes and/or potato croquettes and asparagus.

Serves 3.

Roast Goose

12- to 14-pound young goose
Salt
Pepper
¼ teaspoon ginger
1 recipe mincemeat stuffing (recipe below)
Flour

Sprinkle cavity of goose with 1 teaspoon salt, ½ teaspoon pepper, and ginger. Stuff with mincemeat stuffing. Fasten cavity with wooden picks. Place goose on rack in roasting pan; roast in a 350-degree oven for 3 to 3½ hours or until done, basting with drippings. To test for doneness squeeze thigh. Serve with gravy made from fat drippings. For each tablespoon fat; add 2 tablespoons flour and cook, stirring, until golden. Add 1 cup water; continue to cook, stirring, until smooth and thick. Season to taste with salt and pepper. Use remaining drippings for seasoning vegetables or discard. Allow ¾ to 1 pound goose (dressed weight) per person.

Mincemeat Stuffing

½ cup butter
⅓ cup onion, chopped
¼ cup parsley, chopped
1 teaspoon salt
¼ teaspoon pepper
3½ cups soft bread crumbs
1⅓ cups mincemeat
½ cup orange juice
Melt butter in skillet; cook onion until golden.

Blend in remaining ingredients; stuff goose or duck and roast.

THE ART OF GOOSE NOODLING

Fattening a goose with noodles, which probably originated in ancient Egypt, is similar to the French practice of gorging a goose on grain. The practice came to this country from Germany. Germans who settled Watertown, Wis., a century ago brought the art to that community where it was continued by at least one man through the Christmas season of 1970. That man, Fred Rumler, has produced noodled geese for 30 years and sent two-thirds of his production to New York City where Luchow's was one of his customers. In the process, a healthy corn-fed goose in the 20-pound range is selected and fed on noodles made from a flour paste of wheat, barley, and rye. Feeding is done by hand every four hours, day and night. The feeding fosters a thirst which requires two gallons of water each day. In about three weeks of the regimen the goose's weight is almost doubled.

Red Cabbage, German Style

2 tablespoons butter or margarine
1 small onion, chopped
3 tablespoons sugar
6 cups red cabbage, shredded
½ cup red wine vinegar
1½ teapsoons salt
1 cup tart apple, peeled and diced
1 cup sour cream

In butter or margarine melted in a heavy skillet, cook onion until golden; sprinkle with 1 tablespoon sugar. Add cabbage, vinegar, and salt; cover and simmer gently for 15 minutes. Add apple and 2 tablespoons sugar; continue to cook 5 to 10 minutes longer. Meantime, bring sour cream to room temperature. Place cabbage in serving dish and spread sour cream over the top. Makes 8 servings.
Good served with roast goose.

The variety and quantities of food served for Christmas dinner were so tremendous it was as if the meal were to be the last on earth. After eating, everyone spent the afternoon in a near stupor.

Eggnog Christmas Salad

   1 No. 2 can crushed pineapple
   1 tablespoon plain gelatin
   3 tablespoons lemon juice
   1½ cups dairy eggnog
   ¾ cup celery, chopped
   1 3-ounce package raspberry gelatin
   1¾ cups boiling water
   1¼ cups raw cranberry-orange relish

Drain pineapple and heat juice to boiling. Use to
dissolve plain gelatin which has been soaked in lemon
juice. Cool to room temperature. Add eggnog,
pineapple, and celery. Pour into 5-cup mold and chill
until firm. Dissolve raspberry gelatin in boiling water.
To make cranberry-orange relish, run 1 pound raw
fresh cranberries and 2 oranges (minus seeds) through
food grinder or electric blender. Sweeten with 1 cup
sugar. Chill for several hours to allow flavors to blend.
Add relish and pour over portion already in mold.
Serves 10.

Christmas Cake

   1 pound butter or margarine
   2½ cups light brown sugar, packed
   6 eggs
   4 cups flour, sifted
   1 teaspoon baking powder
   2 tablespoons nutmeg
   ½ cup apricot brandy
   1 pound seedless golden raisins
   3 cups pecans, chopped

Cream butter and sugar together. Add eggs, one at a
time; beat well after each addition. Sift together flour,
baking powder, and nutmeg. Add gradually to creamed
mixture and beat until well blended. Stir in brandy.
Fold in raisins and pecans. Pour mixture into a greased
and floured 10-inch tube pan. Bake in a 300-degree
oven for 1 hour and 40 minutes, or until done.

The ritual of putting a meal on
the table started with the rapid
'taking up' of food in the kitchen
and, in warm weather, someone
was stationed to shoo away flies
with a fly bush in the dining room.
A fly bush is a stick with strips
of paper tied to one end.

Once everyone was seated at the
dinner table the passing of bowls
and platters started. Each person
filled his own plate. The process
was like a relay race with the
question 'Didja get' this or that
passed along with the food. The
moment the passing stopped
silence fell as the eating began.

Kentucky Bourbon Fruit Cake

1 pound candied cherries, red and green combined
½ pound dates pitted and chopped
1 pint bourbon whiskey
5 cups flour, sifted
¾ cups (3 sticks) butter
2 cups granulated sugar
1 cup light brown sugar, packed
6 eggs
1 pound shelled pecan halves
2 teaspoons nutmeg
1 teaspoon baking powder

Pour bourbon over cherries and dates. Cover and let stand overnight. Cream butter until light and fluffy. Add sugars gradually and continue creaming. Add eggs, one at a time, beating well after each addition. Use a portion of the flour to coat nuts. Add remaining flour to creamed mixture alternately with soaked fruit and the liquid in which it was soaked. Stir in nutmeg and baking powder. Add floured nuts. Blend well.

Grease a large tube pan. Line with brown paper cut to fit. Grease and flour paper. Pour in batter. Place foil over the top of the pan and squeeze tightly around edges. Place a pan of hot water in bottom of oven. Bake cake in a 275-degree oven for 4½ hours or until done. Remove foil about the last hour of baking time to allow top to dry. Remove from oven and let cool in pan. Makes about an 8-pound cake.

The Best of All Fruit Cakes

1 pound butter
1 pound sugar
12 eggs
4 cups plus 2 tablespoons plain flour
1 tablespoon lemon extract
1 teaspoon ground cinnamon
1 teaspoon ground cloves
½ teaspoon nutmeg
½ teaspoon ground ginger
¾ teaspoon ground mace
1 pound red candied pineapple
1 pound green candied pineapple
1½ pounds yellow candied pineapple
¾ pound candied citron
¼ pound crystalized ginger
1 pound dates
½ box dark raisins
½ box white raisins
1½ pounds red candied cherries
1 pound green candied cherries
½ pound candied lemon rind
½ pound candied orange rind
2 1-pound jars mixed candied fruit
½ pound black walnuts, shelled
½ pound English walnuts, shelled
1 pound pecans, shelled
1 cup sweet dessert wine such as muscadine or port

Reserve some pineapple, cherries, and whole nuts for decorating the tops of the cakes.

Dice all fruit and chop nuts. Mix well. Add just enough flour to the fruit mixture to coat fruit. Add spices to remaining flour and sift together. Cream butter and sugar. Beat eggs and add. Mix well. Add lemon extract and flour mixture. Mix well. Combine batter and fruit together. It is best to add a small amount of both at a time, until all is well blended. Blend in wine. Turn into 2 large tube pans and 2 meat-loaf pans that have been greased and lined with greased and floured brown paper. Bake at 225 degrees for 4 to 4½ hours. Decorate the cake tops before cake is done. Cake is moist and ready to eat the next day.

Chiefly I remember the aroma of the fruit cakes—a rich, dark, mahogany smell lurking in the side board which rose up at you like a genie out of a bottle when you opened the door.

Tipsy Squire

A version of trifle.

1 medium-size angel food cake
1 cup sherry
1 cup heavy cream, whipped
½ cup pecans, chopped
1 cup seeded Muscat raisins
1 cup fresh coconut, grated, optional
Boiled custard

Line the bottom of a large bowl with angel cake broken into small pieces. Sprinkle the cake with sherry. Add some raisins, nuts, and coconut, then add a layer of boiled custard. Sprinkle again with sherry and add a layer of whipped cream. Proceed with the layers until the bowl is full. Let chill 24 hours. Decorate top with additional whipped cream, maraschino cherries, and angelica or citron.

Boiled Custard

1 pint milk, scalded
3 eggs
½ cup sugar
Pinch of salt
2 tablespoons flour
1 teaspoon vanilla

Beat eggs. Add sugar, salt, and flour which have been mixed together. Add to the milk and cook in double boiler, stirring, until smooth and thick. Do not overcook, or the custard will curdle.

Rum Squares

2½ cups confectioners' sugar
1 cup flour, sifted
½ teaspoon salt
1 teaspoon baking powder
½ pound candied green pineapple, finely chopped
½ pound candied red cherries, finely chopped
1 pound dates, pitted and finely chopped
4 eggs
1 teaspoon vanilla
⅓ cup soft butter
1 teaspoon instant coffee powder
Rum

Sift together 1 cup confectioners' sugar, salt, flour, and baking powder. Add candied fruits and dates. Beat eggs with vanilla and pour over fruit mixture. Turn into a greased and floured pan about 11 by 7 inches. Bake in a 325-degree oven (300 degrees if pan is Pyrex) for 45 minutes or until done. Cool in pan and then cover with layer of frosting made by blending butter with 1½ cups confectioners' sugar and coffee powder. Add sufficient rum to make a mixture of proper spreading consistency. Cut into 1-inch squares. Make about three weeks before Christmas to allow the squares to mellow before serving.

Springerle

4 eggs
1 pound powdered sugar
3⅓ cups flour, sifted
A lump of soft butter about the size of a large egg
½ teaspoon anise oil
3 tablespoons anise seed

Beat eggs until blended, gradually add sugar, and continue beating. If using an electric mixer, beat at moderate speed for about 10 minutes. For hand beating, increase the time to 20 minutes. During the beating, add the butter, so that it will be well blended. The butter helps keep the cookies soft. Most springerles are rather hard. At the end of the beating time, add anise oil and anise seed, then gradually add flour. Mix well. Roll out dough, which will be rather soft, on a well-floured board. Keep the thickness at least ⅛ inch so the cookies will be plump. Use a well-floured springerle board or rolling pin to make designs on the dough. Cut apart with a sharp knife and gently place cookies on a large tray to dry. Allow them to remain overnight, or for at least 10 to 12 hours. Bake on greased and floured baking sheets in a 350-degree oven for 10 to 12 minutes. Do not allow them to brown, they should remain pale in color. The cookies will stay soft about 2 weeks.

Ambrosia

8 large oranges, peeled and sliced
½ fresh coconut, grated
½ cup confectioners' sugar

Arrange slices of orange in a cut-glass dish. Scatter coconut thickly over the orange layer. Sprinkle lightly with sugar. Repeat the layers until the dish is filled. Serve soon after it is prepared.

Another Ambrosia

6 large oranges
1 large coconut
1 large pineapple
¾ cup confectioners' sugar
¼ cup Cointreau

Peel and dice oranges, discarding white membrane. Shred coconut and pineapple; combine with oranges, sugar, and Cointreau. Chill.

Vermont Ambrosia

A woman who grew up on ambrosia in the South developed this version after moving to Vermont.

Peel oranges and cut into slices. Arrange slices in overlapping layers on dessert plate. Top with sour cream and over the sour cream, shave maple sugar.

Heavenly Hash

1 8-ounce package dates
1 cup nut meats
1 No. 2 can crushed pineapple
1 medium bottle maraschino cherries and juice
⅓ pound marshmallows
1 banana
1 pint heavy cream, whipped
Few grains salt
½ teaspoon vanilla
Sugar to taste

Chop fruits, nuts, and marshmallows. Fold into whipped cream with salt, vanilla, and sugar to taste. Chill for several hours or overnight.

The heavenly hash of the Northwest consists of layers of fruits—rhubarb preserves, gooseberry preserves tinted pale green, strawberries, apricots, red raspberries, boysenberries, peaches, pears, purple plums, and quinces.

Eggnog

12 eggs, separated
1 cup sugar
1 quart whiskey
¼ cup rum
1 quart light cream
1 quart heavy cream

Combine egg yolks and sugar and beat together until thick, smooth, light, and lemon colored. Add whiskey a little at a time, continuing to beat vigorously. Add rum and beat again. Add light cream. Whip heavy cream and fold in. Fold in stiffly beaten egg whites. Let stand a day or two to ripen.

Stollen

A beautiful offering for breakfast on Christmas morning.

- 1 cup milk
- ½ cup plus 2 tablespoons granulated sugar
- ½ teaspoon salt
- 1 package dry yeast
- ¼ cup warm water
- 5 cups flour, sifted
- ½ cup candied citron, diced
- ½ cup candied cherries, diced
- 1 cup slivered almonds
- Grated rind of 1 lemon
- 1 cup seedless raisins
- 2 eggs, beaten
- 1 cup soft butter or margarine
- ¼ teaspoon nutmeg
- ½ teaspoon cinnamon
- ⅔ cup confectioners' sugar

Scald milk. Remove from heat and add ½ cup sugar and salt. Cool to lukewarm. In the meanwhile, sprinkle yeast into water in small bowl and stir to dissolve. Add lukewarm milk with 1 cup flour. Beat with egg beater to remove lumps. Cover and let rise in a warm place until doubled in bulk, about 1½ hours.

Stir in citron, cherries, almonds, lemon rind, raisins, eggs, ¾ cup soft butter, nutmeg, and 3 cups flour. Turn out on lightly floured board and knead in 1 cup flour until dough is smooth and elastic. Divide dough into two parts. Roll out each part to make ½-inch thick oval. Brush with ¼ cup melted butter and sprinkle with mixture of cinnamon and 2 tablespoons sugar.

Make lengthwise crease down center of each oval. Fold over like pocketbook rolls. Place on a greased baking sheet. Shape to make two crescents. Cover with wax paper, then with a towel; let rise in warm place about 1 hour or until nearly doubled in bulk. Bake in a 350-degree oven 45 to 50 minutes or until done. While hot, pour a paste mixture of hot water stirred into about ⅔ cup confectioners' sugar over the stollen. Makes 2 stollen.

In 1905 a St. Louis candy company offered by mail a special five-dollar box of dainties for Christmas. It was prepaid east of the Rockies. This was "a superb gift for anyone, especially those living in the country, to whom such things are the treat of a lifetime."
The box contained the following bargain:

1 full pound assorted glacé fruits	$ .60
1 full pound pecan-dates	.30
1 full pound marshmallow dates	.35
1 full pound ginger dates	.35
1 full pound maple-pecan pralines	.75
1 full pound peppermint creams	.30
1 full pound salted almonds	.75
1 half-pound crystalized ginger	.30
1 full pound Turkish dessert figs	.30
1 full pound imperial dessert raisins	.40
1 full pound fresh pecan meats	.65
1 full pound shelled duchess almonds	.65
2 full pounds choicest mixed nuts	.55
13½ pounds Regular Price	$6.25

On Christmas morning after the chaos of opening the presents and turning out the contents of stockings, the adults left the children to enjoy their toys and sought a quiet place to enjoy stollen and coffee.

CHAPTER 6

Soups, Stews, and Chowders

An account of settlers of the Old Northwest in the *American Heritage Cookbook* describes the soup pot as it was, not only on the trail, but in many homes: "The tin kettle in which they cooked their food would hold eight to ten gallons. It was hung over the fire, nearly full of water, then nine quarts of peas, one quart per man, the daily allowance, were put in; and when they were well bursted, two or three pounds of pork, cut into strips, for seasoning, were added, and all allowed to boil or simmer until daylight, when the cook added four biscuits, broken up, to the mess, and invited all hands to breakfast. The swelling of the peas and biscuits had now filled the kettle to the brim, so thick that a stick would stand upright in it." (The peas were dried and were probably beans rather than peas.)

Soup prepared in an iron pot over the open hearth was a mainstay of most frontier families. The soup was left to simmer all day and was stirred only occasionally. Soups were hearty and often thick enough to support a wooden spoon stuck in the center. Ships' cooks called thick soups storm soup, meaning the soup stayed in a pot swaying on a stormy sea. Soup was also prepared in pots over an open fire outdoors. The outdoor soups provided food for groups gathered for special occasions. A favorite in Mississippi was called meadow stew. What goes into a kettle of soup depends on the cook. According to a legend which comes in a number of versions, cooks once made stone soup by boiling a well-scrubbed stone in water with the addition of whatever soup ingredients were available, thereby making a good soup minus or despite the stone.

There was a special kind of security on that autumn day when the windows were pulled down and the doors closed, shutting out the chill and leaving us inside in a cozy package with a pot boiling on the stove and steam on the windows.

The chubby little people who are known as the Campbell Soup kids first appeared in 1905 in Campbell Soup ads placed in streetcars. They were created by Grace Drayton, a Philadelphia artist. Mrs. Drayton, in an interview in 1926, said the kids were sketched from her own image as she saw it in the mirror. She claimed she was plump and "funny looking."

Succotash Stew

Citizens of Plymouth celebrated Forefathers' Day on December 21 with a three-dish meal—succotash stew, hot johnnycake, and Indian pudding—commemorating the landing of the Pilgrims. The stew is made of corned beef, chicken, dried white beans, hulled corn, a turnip, and potatoes. The meat and potatoes are served on a platter and the soup in a tureen.

Kentucky Burgoo

A thick soup cooked for long hours in iron kettles and served to celebrate the Kentucky Derby, election day, and other special events.

> 2 pounds pork shank
> 2 pounds veal shank
> 2 pounds beef shank
> 2 pounds breast of lamb
> 1 4-pound hen
> 8 quarts water
> 1½ pounds potatoes, diced
> 1½ pounds onions, diced
> 1 bunch carrots, diced
> 2 green peppers, diced
> 2 cups okra, sliced
> 1 cup celery, diced
> 2 cups cabbage, chopped
> 2 cups corn kernels
> 2 cups lima beans
> 2 pods red pepper
> 1 quart tomato purée
> Salt
> Cayenne
> Hot pepper sauce
> 2 tablespoons A-1 sauce
> 2 tablespoons Worcestershire sauce
> Parsley, chopped

Put all the meat in cold water and bring slowly to a boil. Simmer until meat is tender enough to fall from bones. Remove meat from stock. Cool and chop meat, discarding fat, skin, and bones. Return meat to stock. Add all the vegetables and the tomato purée. Simmer until thick, but still soupy. Season with remaining ingredients. Stir. Add parsley just before serving. Makes about 25 servings.

Cioppino

Pronounced cho-PEEN-o, this fish stew is a California dish similar to the bouillabaisse of Marseilles, France.

4 cloves garlic, minced
1 medium onion, finely diced
1 green pepper, finely diced
1 leek with leaves, finely diced
3 green onions, finely diced
Oil
1 pound, 4-ounce can solid pack tomatoes,
**   finely chopped**
1 8-ounce can tomato sauce
Pinch of thyme
1 bay leaf
Salt and pepper to taste
2 cups white wine
16 Little Neck clams in the shell, uncooked
4 medium oysters in the shell, uncooked
4 lobster claws, cooked
2 medium West Coast crabs, cooked
8 large shrimp, uncooked

Cook garlic, onion, green pepper, leek, and green onions in a small amount of oil until golden. Add tomatoes, tomato sauce, thyme, and bay leaf. Cover. Cook slowly for 2 to 3 hours, stirring frequently. Add salt and pepper to taste. Add wine; cook for 10 minutes.

Spoon soup over layered shellfish assortment in another pot. Simmer, covered, for 15 minutes, adding water if necessary. Serve in soup plates and garnish with fingers of garlic toast. Makes 4 generous servings.

Long before the days of mixes, we canned what we called soup mix— a mixture of corn, lima beans, okra, and tomatoes. Jars of the mix and turnips, potatoes, and onions from the root cellar went into the soup pot all winter long.

Bouillabaisse Florida Style

2 pounds red snapper, mullet, or redfish fillets,
fresh or frozen
1 pound raw shrimp, fresh or frozen
1 10-ounce can frozen oysters
½ cup butter, margarine, or olive oil
1 cup onion, coarsely chopped
1 clove garlic, finely chopped
3 tablespoons flour
1 cup fresh tomato, peeled and coarsely chopped
2 cups clam juice or water
1 cup tomato juice
½ cup dry sherry
½ lemon, sliced
2 teaspoons salt or to taste
⅛ teaspoon cayenne
⅛ teaspoon thyme
3 whole allspice
1 bay leaf

Thaw fish if frozen; remove skin, cut into chunks.
Thaw shrimp if frozen; peel, devein, and wash. Thaw
oysters. In butter or other fat in large heavy kettle,
cook onion and garlic until golden. Blend in flour; add
tomato, clam juice or water, tomato juice, sherry,
lemon, and seasonings. Simmer gently for 30 minutes.
Add fish, shrimp, and oysters; simmer gently for 10
minutes or until fish flakes easily. Remove bay leaf;
discard. Makes 8 servings.

Galveston Gumbo

Cooks in New Orleans and surrounding areas fill soup
pots with a variety of gumbos seasoned with filé
powder, powdered sassafras. If available, add 1 teaspoon
filé just before serving. Do not allow filé to cook.

2 pounds raw shrimp, fresh or frozen
2 10-ounce cans frozen oysters
1½ cups onion, chopped
1½ cups celery, sliced
1 cup green pepper, chopped
1 clove garlic, finely chopped
⅓ cup cooking oil
⅓ cup flour
1 28-ounce can tomatoes
1 13¾-ounce can chicken broth
1 tablespoon Worcestershire sauce
2½ teaspoons salt
¼ teaspoon pepper
2 to 3 dashes hot pepper sauce
1 bay leaf
1 10-ounce package frozen sliced okra
6 to 8 servings hot rice, cooked and seasoned

Thaw shrimp if frozen; peel, devein. Thaw oysters.
Cook onion, celery, green pepper, and garlic in oil in
large kettle until golden; blend in flour. Add tomatoes,
broth, Worcestershire, salt, pepper, hot pepper sauce,
and bay leaf. Cover; simmer gently for 30 minutes,
stirring occasionally. Add shrimp, oysters, and okra;
simmer for 10 minutes. Serve over hot rice. Makes
9 cups or 6 to 8 servings.

Pine Bark Stew

The name comes from the fuel used for cooking the stew in a pot over an open fire. Pine bark burns for hours, providing extremely slow heat. A few oak sticks add sparkle and crackle.

> 1 pound bacon
> 12 medium potatoes, peeled and sliced
> 12 medium onions, sliced
> Boiling salted water
> 12 servings bigmouth bass, bream, or red breast, cleaned
> 2 teaspoons curry powder
> Sauce (recipe below)

Cook bacon. Remove from pan and reserve. In bacon fat, place a layer of ⅓ of the potatoes and a layer of ⅓ of the onions in a large pot. Cover with boiling salted water. Simmer gently for 10 minutes. Add a layer of ½ of the fish; sprinkle with 1 teaspoon curry powder. Add a second layer of another ⅓ of the potatoes and onions, and the rest of the fish, and sprinkle with remaining curry powder. Add boiling salted water to cover. Top with a third layer of potatoes and onions. Cover. Cook very slowly until top layer of potatoes is cooked. Pour sauce over stew. Place bacon on top and serve with rice. Makes 12 servings.

Sauce

> ½ pound butter
> ⅓ cup Worcestershire sauce
> 1 cup tomato catsup
> ½ teaspoon red pepper
> ½ teaspoon black pepper

Mix all ingredients in saucepan; heat to blend and melt butter.

Brunswick Stew

A favorite in Virginia, North Carolina, and Georgia. When available, a rabbit and/or a squirrel is cooked with the chicken and meat.

> 1 large hen or stewing chicken
> 1 pound lean veal or beef
> Water
> 2 large potatoes, peeled and diced
> 1 large onion, diced
> 4 cups whole kernel corn
> 4 cups lima beans
> 2 8-ounce cans tomato sauce
> Salt, pepper, hot pepper sauce, Worcestershire sauce, butter

Cook chicken and veal or beef together in water to cover until meat is "shredding" tender. Cool. Shred chicken and meat with fingers, discarding skin, bones, and fat. Put meat back in broth, skim off excess fat, and continue to simmer.

In another pot, cook potatoes, onion, corn, lima beans, and tomato sauce with boiling salted water to cover until vegetables are done. Add meat and chicken. The mixture will be thin like soup.

Simmer for several hours until thickened. Cooked in a black iron pot outdoors the stew takes on the flavor of the burning wood. The secret is the long period of simmering. As it simmers, season to taste with salt, pepper, hot pepper sauce, Worcestershire sauce, and a liberal amount of butter. Serves 6 to 8. Serve with coleslaw and corn sticks.

Wash Pot Turtle Soup

7 pounds turtle meat
About 3½ gallons water
¼ medium-size head cabbage
6 carrots
1 pound fresh green beans
1 bunch celery
8 onions, each about 2½ inches in diameter
8 potatoes, about 3 inches in diameter
2 No. 2½ cans tomatoes
1 16-ounce can green peas
Kernels from 2 ears of corn
3 lemons
6 eggs, hard cooked
1 10-ounce can tomato purée
½ cup whole allspice
1 pod hot red pepper
Salt and pepper to taste
Claret
About 1 cup browned flour
1 14-ounce bottle catsup

Put turtle meat in cold water and bring slowly to a boil. Reduce heat and simmer gently until the meat is falling-apart tender. Allow 2½ to 3½ hours to cook the meat. Strain broth. Put meat, vegetables, including tomatoes, 5 of the eggs, and 2 of the lemons, through the meat chopper. Reserve 1 egg and 1 lemon for garnish. Place broth, ground meat, vegetables, and tomato purée in pot; add allspice and pepper pod tied in a small bag. Simmer for about 4 more hours. Stir often. Watch to prevent scorching, especially toward the end. Blend portion of claret with flour to make a paste; add to pot with catsup. Slice reserved egg and lemon over the top. Makes about 5 gallons.

Unexpected company was never a problem. Ma said that by watering the soup a little, there was always enough to feed a few more.

At the first sign of nippy weather Ma put the soup pot on active duty. Most of the winter the pot sat on the back of the stove purring like a kitten.

Green Turtle Soup

1½ pounds turtle meat
1 teaspoon salt
Water
1 tablespoon flour
1 tablespoon shortening
1 medium onion, chopped
2 tablespoons butter
1 8-ounce can tomato sauce
2 eggs, hard cooked
1 teaspoon ground cloves
½ teaspoon nutmeg
1 teaspoon cinnamon
¼ teaspoon pepper
½ lemon, thinly sliced
3 cloves garlic, peeled and crushed
½ cup sherry

Cut turtle meat into small pieces; place in pot with salt and water to cover, simmer slowly for 2 to 3 hours or until tender, adding water as needed. Drain, reserving stock. Blend flour into shortening to make roux. Sauté onion in butter in kettle; add roux, tomato sauce, egg yolks mashed with spices, turtle meat, and reserved stock. Simmer for 30 minutes; add lemon and garlic, and continue to simmer for 20 minutes. Add more salt if needed. Just before serving, add chopped egg whites and sherry. Makes 6 servings.

Clam Chowder

¼ cup salt pork or bacon, diced
1 cup onions, diced
1 cup celery, diced
1 tablespoon flour
1 cup potatoes, diced
1 quart water
1 teaspoon salt or to taste
½ teaspoon pepper
1 tablespoon Worcestershire sauce
1 quart clams, ground or coarsely chopped

In skillet, fry salt pork or bacon until crisp; drain. In drippings, cook onions and celery until golden; sprinkle in flour, blend. Add potatoes, water, salt, pepper, and Worcestershire; simmer for 20 minutes or until potatoes are tender. Add clams and salt pork or bacon; taste to check seasonings; heat and serve. Makes about 2 quarts.

Oyster Stew

Nowhere is the oyster better presented than in the raw bar down in the bowels of Grand Central Station in New York City. The chefs who shuffle along on their tired feet and turn out bowl after bowl of the best oyster stew in the world appear to have been doing just that since the station first opened. They work with chafing dishes which tilt in full view of the stool seats around the bar. This recipe was developed after watching the chefs at Grand Central prepare the stew a number of times.

>1 tablespoon plus 1 small pat butter
>1/16 teaspoon salt
>Dash of pepper
>4 to 5 drops Worcestershire sauce
>Dash of paprika
>7 plump oysters, shucked
>½ cup clam juice
>1 cup milk or ½ cup milk and ½ cup cream

To butter melted in pan over moderate heat, add seasonings and oysters; cook until edges of oysters curl. Add clam juice and milk; heat to the boiling point, but do not allow to boil. Pour into a bowl; float pat of butter on top. Makes 1 serving.

Oyster Bisque

>4 tablespoons butter
>½ pint oysters, coarsely chopped
>¼ teaspoon salt
>⅛ teaspoon celery salt
>¼ teaspoon pepper
>Dash of paprika
>4 to 5 drops Worcestershire sauce
>2 tablespoons flour
>2 cups milk

To butter melted in pan over moderate heat, add oysters and seasonings; cook until oysters curl. Sprinkle with flour; blend in. Add milk; heat just to the boiling point, but do not allow to boil. Makes 2 servings.

Brown Oyster Stew

A favorite in Charleston, S.C.

>4 slices bacon
>1 large onion, sliced
>2 tablespoons flour
>1 pint oysters
>2 tablespoons benne (sesame) seed, crushed
>   or pounded
>Salt and pepper to taste

Pan-fry bacon; drain. In drippings, cook onion until golden; remove from pan. In drippings, brown flour. Drain oysters; to drained liquid, add water to make 1½ cups. Blend liquid into browned flour; cook, stirring, until smooth and thickened. Add oysters, benne seed, crumbled bacon, and onion; season with salt and pepper. Heat; serve over rice or hominy. Serves 4.

Black Bean Soup

2 cups dried black beans
12 cups water
¼ pound salt pork, ham, or bacon
½ pound lean beef, cubed
1 carrot, diced
3 small onions, minced
3 whole cloves
¼ teaspoon mace
Hot pepper sauce to taste
Salt and pepper to taste
¼ cup sherry
3 hard-cooked eggs, sliced
1 lemon, thinly sliced

Wash beans, pick them over, and soak overnight. In the morning, drain and add water, salt pork, beef, carrot, onions, and seasonings. Cover and cook slowly for 3 hours or until beans are very soft. Remove meat and run remaining mixture through sieve. Combine bean mixture, meat, and sherry in pot; heat. Place in tureen; add eggs and lemon. Serves 8 to 10.

A mention of oyster-corn soup or of creamed oysters atop crunchy buttered toast or split biscuits gives many Yankees hunger pains regardless of where they are.

Seven Bean Soup

3 smoked ham hocks
1 pound soup bones (beef)
Water
5 cups dried beans: 1 cup navy beans, and ⅔
  cup each pinto, cranberry, kidney, black,
  garbanzo, and lima beans
5 medium onions, chopped
5 medium carrots, finely chopped
5 ribs celery or 1 small bunch, chopped
1 28-ounce can tomatoes
Salt and pepper to taste
Smoked brown 'n' serve sausages, optional

Cover hocks and bones with water and half again as
much water as it takes to cover them. Simmer covered
for 2½ hours. Meanwhile, cook beans in 5 quarts of
water for 2 hours, or until tender. Lift meat from
broth. Skim off excess fat. Remove skin and bones
from meat. Dice meat and return to stock. Add beans
and bean liquid, chopped vegetables, and tomatoes.
Simmer 20 minutes longer, seasoning to taste with
salt and pepper and other seasonings if desired. Serve
in bowls topped with sliced brown 'n' serve sausages
which have been browned in a skillet. Makes about
20 servings.

Minestrone

1 pound navy or pinto beans, dried
4 quarts water
8 slices beef shank cut 1 inch thick
2 large onions, chopped
¼ cup olive oil
2 medium carrots, sliced
2 cups celery, sliced
1 28-ounce can tomatoes
2 teaspoons salt
1 teaspoon Italian seasoning
2 medium potatoes, peeled and diced
2 cups green beans, in 1 inch lengths
3 cups zucchini, sliced
2 cups cabbage, shredded
1 cup macaroni, in 1-inch lengths
¼ cup parsley, minced
1 clove garlic, crushed
1 teaspoon basil
Grated Parmesan cheese

Outside the kitchen door there was a little herb garden. Mama gathered little snippets of this one and that one—they made an ordinary pot of bean soup taste like a French chef's creation.

When a ham hanging in the smokehouse was cut, there was fried ham for supper every night until only the hock was left. Papa sawed off the hock and it went into a pot of lentil soup.

Cover beans with water; bring to a boil, cook for 5 minutes. Remove from heat; let stand for 1 hour, then add beef, and simmer for 2 hours or until meat is tender. Remove meat from kettle; cut into chunks, discard bones and gristle. Remove half the beans; mash and return to kettle with meat. In skillet, cook onion in 3 tablespoons oil until golden; add to meat mixture with carrots, celery, tomatoes, salt, Italian seasoning, potatoes, and green beans. Cook for 15 minutes; add zucchini, cabbage, and macaroni, and simmer 8 minutes longer. Sauté parsley, garlic, and basil in remaining oil. Add to soup; heat. Taste for salt. Serve sprinkled with cheese. Makes 6 quarts or 16 servings of 1½ cups each.

Hamburger Chowder

2 pounds ground beef
1 large onion, chopped
1 28-ounce can tomatoes
1 10½-ounce can consommé
Water
1 beef bouillon cube
1 cup celery and tops, diced
1 cup carrots, diced
1 10-ounce package frozen small lima beans
1 12-ounce can whole kernel corn, undrained
¼ cup pearl barley
½ teaspoon sugar
2 teaspoons salt or to taste
½ teaspoon pepper

In deep kettle, brown meat and onion, stirring; add tomatoes, consommé, 1 consommé can water, bouillon cube dissolved in 1 cup boiling water, celery, carrots, limas, corn, barley, and seasonings. Simmer, covered, for 1 hour. If mixture becomes too thick, add additional consommé, bouillon, or water. Taste for seasonings. Serves 6.

Beef Stew

2 pounds beef chuck, cut in 1½-inch cubes
2 tablespoons shortening
4 cups plus 2 tablespoons water
1 teaspoon lemon juice
1 teaspoon Worcestershire sauce
1 large onion, sliced
1 bay leaf
1 tablespoon salt
¼ teaspoon sugar
½ teaspoon pepper
½ teaspoon paprika
Dash each of allspice and cloves
4 carrots, scraped and sliced
1 10-ounce package frozen mixed vegetables
4 medium potatoes, peeled and diced
1½ tablespoons flour

In large heavy kettle, brown meat in hot shortening; add 4 cups water, lemon juice, Worcestershire, onion, bay leaf, and seasonings. Bring to a boil; cover tightly and simmer for 1½ hours, stirring occasionally. Add vegetables; continue cooking for 30 minutes. Make a paste of flour and 2 tablespoons of cold water; blend with some hot liquid from stew, then combine with stew. Heat; stir until smooth and thickened. Makes 6 to 8 servings.

Chicken Corn Soup

This recipe is adapted to the use of a young chicken in place of the customary stewing chicken.

1 broiler-fryer, about 2½ pounds
Water
2 teaspoons salt
½ teaspoon black pepper
4 medium-size potatoes, peeled and diced
2 cups whole kernel corn, fresh or canned
¼ cup flour
2 hard-cooked eggs
¼ cup parsley, chopped, if desired

Place whole chicken in a pot with water to cover. Add salt and pepper. Bring to a boil, reduce heat to simmer, and cook until chicken is easy to remove from bones. When done, lift chicken from broth and allow to cool enough so it can be handled. Meanwhile, boil broth vigorously to reduce volume by about one-third. Pull chicken from bones, discarding bones. Shred into pieces. Put skin in electric blender and twirl. Add chicken and skin to broth. Add potatoes and corn and cook for 15 minutes or until potatoes are done. Blend flour with a little cold water to make a paste. Add to soup. Stir until smooth and slightly thickened. Dice eggs and add. Add ¼ cup chopped parsley, if desired, just before serving. Makes 6 servings. Wilted lettuce and hot gingerbread muffins are excellent accompaniments.

Summer Soup

6 small new potatoes, peeled and halved
2 cups water
2 teaspoons salt
¼ teaspoon pepper
2 tablespoons butter
4 green onions, cut in 3-inch lengths
16 3-inch carrots (if not available, cut larger carrots)
2 cups fresh green beans, cut, or 1 10-ounce package frozen cut green beans
2 cups fresh green peas or 1 10-ounce package frozen green peas
2 cups fresh whole okra or 1 10-ounce package frozen whole okra
2 cups light cream
3 tablespoons flour

Cook potatoes in water for about 5 minutes; they should not become tender. Add salt, pepper, butter, onions, carrots, green beans, peas, and okra. Simmer 15 minutes longer or until vegetables reach desired degree of doneness. Blend together cream and flour until smooth. Blend into vegetables. Cook gently, stirring, until thickened. Makes 6 or more servings.

Vegetable Soup

    1 cup dried navy beans
    Water
    1 pound beef chuck, cubed
    4 teaspoons salt
    ½ teaspoon pepper
    3 medium potatoes, peeled and cubed
    4 carrots, scraped and diced
    1 10-ounce package frozen mixed vegetables
    1 10-ounce package frozen small lima beans
    1 10-ounce package frozen corn
    2 medium onions, diced
    1 28-ounce can tomatoes
    1 26-ounce can tomato soup
    1 teaspoon sugar
    1 teaspoon vinegar
    1 teaspoon celery salt

Wash beans, place in pot with 4 cups water. Bring to a boil; remove from heat and let stand, covered, for 1 hour. Simmer beans for 1 hour; add beef, 4 cups water, salt, and pepper, and simmer for 1 hour. Meanwhile, in separate pan cook potatoes and carrots in water to cover for 15 minutes. To pot of beef and beans; add potatoes, carrots, mixed vegetables, lima beans, corn, onions, tomatoes, tomato soup, 1 soup can of water, sugar, vinegar, and celery salt. Simmer for 1 hour. Makes 5 quarts.

Supper was often vegetable soup and biscuits. Sometimes there were graham biscuits. There was sorghum in a glass cruet with pewter lid and a glass compote of honey to eat with the biscuits.

When there was sickness in a home in the neighborhood, Mama put a jar of homemade soup and one of boiled custard in her market basket. With her shawl tied around her shoulders off she went to comfort with soup and custard.

Cream of Fresh Tomato Soup

    4 tablespoons butter
    1 medium onion, chopped
    1 rib celery, chopped
    1 bay leaf
    ¼ cup cooked ham, chopped
    4 black peppercorns
    2 tablespoons flour
    6 cups chicken stock
    8 medium-size fresh tomatoes, unpeeled
    2 cups heavy cream
    Salt and pepper to taste

Brown butter very lightly in a heavy pan. Add onion,
celery, bay leaf, ham, and peppercorns. Blend in flour.
Add chicken stock. Core tomatoes, quarter, and add.
Simmer, covered, for 1 hour. Strain. Heat cream in top
of double boiler over hot water and add to hot strained
mixture. Reheat over hot water. Add salt and pepper
to taste. Makes 8 servings.

Potato Soup

    10 medium-size new, red-skinned potatoes,
        peeled and diced
    2 onions, finely chopped
    Water
    1 quart Half and Half (half milk and half cream)
    2 teaspoons salt
    ½ teaspoon pepper

Place potatoes and onions in large saucepan with
just enough cold water to cover; cover and cook for
30 minutes. Break up potatoes with fork or potato
masher; add Half and Half, salt, and pepper; heat
but do not boil. Makes about 2 quarts or 12 servings.

Lentil Soup

    1 large lean ham hock
    2½ quarts water
    2 cups lentils
    2 tablespoons butter
    1 cup celery and leaves, chopped
    1 medium onion, chopped
    ½ cup carrots, chopped
    1 bay leaf
    ¼ teaspoon thyme
    1 teaspoon salt or to taste
    ½ teaspoon pepper
    ½ teaspoon sugar

Place ham hock in large kettle; cover with water and simmer for 1 to 2 hours or until ham is tender. Remove ham; discard fat and bone, shred meat. Skim fat from stock and discard; add shredded ham and lentils. In butter, sauté celery and leaves, onion, and carrots; add to kettle with seasonings. Simmer for 20 minutes or until lentils are done. Taste to check seasonings. Makes 8 to 10 servings.

French Onion Soup

5 small to medium onions, thinly sliced
5 tablespoons margarine
3 10½-ounce cans beef consommé
2 soup cans water
1 tablespoon Worcestershire sauce
½ teaspoon salt
⅛ teaspoon pepper
8 slices French bread, cut ¾ inch thick
⅓ cup grated Parmesan cheese

Separate onions into rings and cook in 2 tablespoons margarine in a deep heavy kettle until golden. Add consommé, water, Worcestershire sauce, salt, and pepper. Bring to a boil, cover tightly, and simmer for 15 minutes. Toast slices of bread on one side. Spread remaining 3 tablespoons margarine on untoasted side of each slice of bread. Sprinkle buttered bread with Parmesan cheese. Place slices under broiler until lightly browned. Serve soup in bowls and float a slice of toast on each serving. Makes 8 servings.

Haslet Stew

Haslet is pork liver, heart, and lights (lungs).

For the stew, cut liver and heart and only a small portion of the lights into small cubes. Wash well. Place in a heavy pot. Cover with cold water. Bring to a boil. Drain off water and discard. Cover with fresh water. Add 2 to 3 pounds backbones and spareribs cut into small pieces. Cover with water. Season with salt, black pepper, red pepper, and sage, and cook until tender. When the meat is done, add small cornmeal dumplings. Cover pot and cook until dumplings are done.

The big black pot in the back was used for boiling the laundry to make it nice and white. It was also used for cooking a stew for a crowd.

Camp Meeting Stew

A camp meeting is a church-sponsored event held annually for a period of time in the summer at a camp similar to a fish or logging camp. Services resembling revivals are held in a large hall or tent. Often "good eats were next to godliness and there were more pies than piety."
From Alabama.

   6 slices bacon or middling meat (salt pork)
   6 large onions, chopped
   2 green peppers, chopped
   4 pounds veal shoulder
   2 3 to 3½-pound chickens
   3 pounds boneless beef, cubed for stew
   Water
   2 quarts canned tomatoes
   1 cup catsup
   5 ribs celery, chopped
   1 tablespoon salt or to taste
   1 teaspoon pepper
   2 tablespoons Worcestershire sauce
   2 bay leaves
   1 teaspoon sugar
   ¼ teaspoon ground cloves
   ¼ teaspoon ground allspice
   ¼ teaspoon cayenne or to taste
   6 medium potatoes, cubed
   12 ears corn, cut from cob

In skillet, fry bacon until crisp; drain. In drippings, brown onions and peppers; place with veal, chickens, and beef in large pot with water to cover. Add tomatoes, catsup, celery, and seasonings; simmer for 4 to 5 hours adding more water as needed. Lift veal and chickens from pot; discard skin and bones, shred meat and return to pot. Skim off excess fat; discard. Add potatoes and corn; continue cooking 30 minutes longer. Taste for seasoning. Makes about 2 gallons.

Washday Stew

In many homes, a pot of stew was put on to cook early on Monday morning, universal washday. The stew varied from home to home. Along the Gulf coast in the region of New Orleans, red beans and rice were as traditional on Monday as baked beans and brown bread on Saturday in New England. To make red beans and rice, beans soaked overnight were cooked in the soaking liquid with pickled or smoked pork, preferably the shoulder, a minced onion, a clove of garlic, a chopped carrot, and herbs. The meat and vegetables were heaped on a platter with a border of rice.

Preaching Soup

The Amish meet in homes for religious services rather than in churches. For generations, Dutch bean soup, also called Amish preaching soup, has been served for Sunday dinner between preachings. It is made by simmering a ham bone with navy beans, chopped onion, celery, celery tops, and wisps of parsley. In spring the accompaniment is succulent young green onions freshly pulled from the earth and washed. Served with the soup are the traditional 7 sweets and 7 sours, homemade bread, and freshly churned butter.

Son-of-a-Bitch Stew

This stew, made with beef or venison, is a favorite of cowhands. It consists of heart, liver, tongue, kidneys, sweetbreads, and brains all cooked together with a little salt pork and an onion or two. Only a small quantity of water is used and seasonings are salt and pepper.

Son-of-a-Gun Stew

Son-of-a-Gun stew is similar to Son-of-a-Bitch stew, except it contains marrow gut, the long, slender tube that connects the two stomachs of cud-chewing animals, like cows, deer, sheep, and elk. Ranch chefs specify the amount of marrow gut by its length, such as twenty inches, two feet, or three feet.

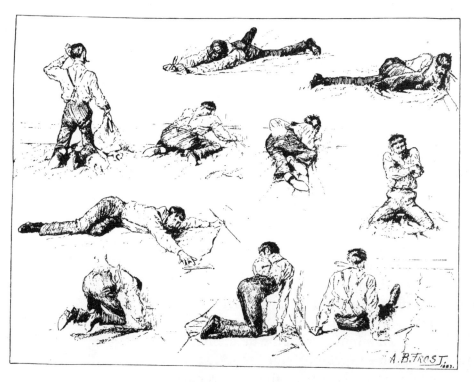

CHAPTER 7
From Garden & Farm

Early in the century, before modern refrigeration and freezing, fresh vegetables were available only during the growing season. They were gathered, picked, or dug from a home garden or purchased from a farm or peddler, but not from a grocery store except in cities with green grocers of the old European tradition. Ears of corn came in shucks, carrots came with tops, green peas and lima beans came in pods, and potatoes and other vegetables came covered with dirt or soil. A cook had to wash, peel, shell, scrape, shuck, slice, and dice before vegetables were ready to cook. The preparation moved gradually from home kitchen to factory. Improved varieties and upgraded shipping practices have brought a wide selection of fresh vegetables to the supermarket year round. Frozen vegetables, packed minutes from the field, offer more freshness than some vegetables shipped in the fresh form. According to a report from the U.S. Department of Agriculture, the trend of the seventies will be away from fresh vegetables. A decline in consumption started in the late thirties and early forties—first of fresh peas and lima beans, followed shortly by snap beans. In the fifties the demand for fresh cabbage dwindled. Next shoppers picked fewer bunches of carrots from produce bins and frozen broccoli outsold fresh. The present trend is towards frozen rather than fresh ears of corn. By 1969, canned or frozen items accounted for approximately 54 per cent of the total vegetable consumption. Why the trend? What encourages shoppers to switch to the frozen and canned lines and away from the familiar fresh-from-the-farm varieties? Convenience is the main factor. Today's busy homemaker, who cannot fit fresh spinach soufflé into her schedule, finds frozen spinach soufflé more suitable to her life style. And the fresh spinach found in supermarkets today is often limp and aging.

The switch is not limited to frozen and canned vegetables; other new forms appear in numbers. The potato, for instance, which was once available only in one form—fresh, unpeeled, unfried, and unmashed, now comes in almost one hundred different ways.

AMAZING MAIZE

Without corn, it is difficult to imagine how man and beast would have survived. The earliest American settlers were introduced to corn by the Indians who discovered it growing as a wild grass which they cultivated into one of the world's finest foods and most valuable crops. The Pilgrims, ravished after their trip on the *Mayflower*, discovered upon landing baskets of corn buried by Indians to provide a winter supply and seed for spring planting. When France owned Louisiana, French women who came to live there had to learn to use cornmeal as a replacement for the wheat flour they had used in France. One French woman, sensing a need, set about to learn culinary secrets from the Choctaw Indians who cooked with cornmeal and corn. She subsequently set up a cooking school and the Creole cuisine was born. Cornmeal mush, called *polenta*, is a staple in Italian cookery.

Corn Pudding

    1 17-ounce can whole kernel corn, drained
    1 cup milk
    2 eggs, beaten
    ¼ cup sugar
    ¼ teaspoon salt
    2 tablespoons margarine, melted

Mix all ingredients together, and turn into greased baking dish. Bake in a 350-degree oven for 40 minutes or until firm. Makes 6 servings. Serve as a vegetable.

Early in the spring grandmother went walking in the fields where she stooped to gather edible wild greens in her apron. She claimed that after winter meals of dried beans, the "system" needed something green.

It took almost all the dishes in the house to serve the vegetables when the garden was bearing. For one meal, the offerings were boiled new potatoes, mashed potatoes with a chunk of butter melting in the center, little potatoes cooked on top of green beans, stewed corn, corn-on-the-cob, squash cooked with onions, buttered okra, cucumbers sliced in vinegar, and sliced tomatoes.

THE POTATO

How lonesome a steak without a baked potato drooling butter or sour cream. How naked the hamburger from the drive-in without French fries. These are some of the joys of the potato:

Potatoes Grandmother mashed with the potato masher and whipped into fluffy whirls to be made into miniature forts to hold wells of gravy on the dinner plate.

Hot, crisp French fries fresh from a kettle of fat.

The sight of steam rising out of a mealy baked potato which is too hot to handle.

The first "mess" of new potatoes served with butter or cream gravy, or combined with the first of the green peas.

A Fourth of July celebration in New England is not a celebration without green peas and small boiled new potatoes served with broiled salmon steak or poached salmon with egg sauce, Indian pudding, and apple pandowdy or watermelon.

The yam, the golden sweet potato, also has its moments of glory, baked slowly in the jacket, candied, or whipped and put under a bed of marshmallows to toast and melt.

Mashed Potatoes

6 medium potatoes
1 teaspoon salt
¼ teaspoon pepper, preferably white
¼ cup butter or margarine
½ cup milk, approximate

Place unpeeled potatoes in saucepan; cover with water. Bring to a boil; simmer for 30 minutes or until potatoes are soft when pierced with a knife. Pour off cooking liquid immediately and discard; break open potatoes to allow steam to escape. Peel; mash thoroughly with potato masher. Add salt and pepper. Meanwhile, in saucepan heat butter or margarine in milk until melted and milk is hot; pour over potatoes. Beat with wooden spoon until light and fluffy, adding more hot milk, if needed, to produce desired consistency. If potatoes are not served at once, keep hot in top of double boiler over boiling water. Makes 6 to 8 servings.

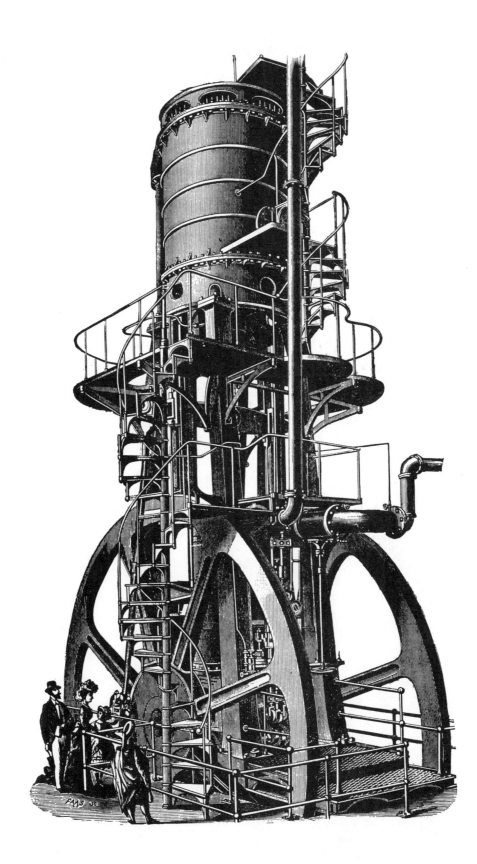

Beans

Without beans—green beans, string beans with strings and without strings, kidney, lima, wax, fava, marrow, speckled, cranberry, October, black, chili, pinto, shellies, hullies—all the beans before the boil-in-the-bag beans, this country may not have made it.

Kids even filled little cloth bags with dried beans and tossed the beanbags like balls.

In John Steinbeck's *Tortilla Flat*, Señora Teresina Cortez, her eight children, and her ancient mother lived in a cottage near a place called Tortilla Flat. The señora knew about beans, which with tortillas she fed to the children three times a day.

She obtained the beans from a nearby bean ranch. After the bean threshing, big piles of bean chaff remained. When the chaff was tossed on a blanket, the wind blew away the chaff leaving twenty or more pounds of beans in an afternoon. It was a bad year when the señora failed to gather three or four hundred pounds.

She felt that beans were a roof over the stomach and a warm cloak against economic cold. One year the bean crop failed. Kind friends stole food for her— crates of cantaloupes, celery, abalone steaks, lettuce. The children became sick after eating the new foods for a few weeks. The señora explained to her thieving friends the children needed beans. They stole beans for her and all was well once again with the children.

Pinto Beans

    1 pound dried pinto beans
    1½ quarts water
    ¼ pound salt pork or streak-of-lean pork

Wash beans and place in large kettle. Cover with cold water. Allow to stand overnight, or for 12 to 15 hours. (A quicker soaking procedure is as follows: Cover beans with cold water early in the morning. Place over high heat. Bring water to boiling point. Boil briskly for 2 minutes. Remove from heat. Cover and allow to soak for 1 hour.) To cook, drain off soaking liquid into another pot. Add salt pork, gashed almost to the skin at ¼-inch intervals, to the liquid. Bring to a boil and simmer for about 1 hour. Add beans. Return to a boil. Reduce to simmer. Cover and let simmer for 2 hours or until done. Add small quantities of hot water as needed. Serves 6 to 8. Slow cooking prevents the skins from bursting. Smooth skins are an indication of a good bean cook.

Other kinds of dried beans are cooked the same way. In the West and Southwest, cooks add garlic and chili powder.

Chef Louis Szathmary, proprietor of The Bakery, a Chicago restaurant, says that beans must be cooked gently so "every bean has a personality."

Baked Beans

    1 pound dried white navy beans
    2 quarts water, boiling
    2 8-ounce cans tomato sauce
    ⅓ cup molasses
    2 teaspoons prepared mustard
    1 tablespoon salt
    ½ teaspoon black pepper
    2 tablespoons brown sugar
    4 teaspoons vinegar
    ⅓ cup catsup
    2 teaspoons Worcestershire sauce
    1 onion, chopped
    1 chunk (approximately ¼ pound) salt pork
      or bacon slices

Wash and pick over beans. Add beans to boiling water in a pot slowly so the water does not stop boiling. Simmer for 2 to 3 hours or until the beans are tender, adding more hot water as needed.

In a large bean pot or casserole, make sauce by combining all ingredients except onion and pork. Drain beans reserving cooking liquid. Add beans to sauce with onion. Gash pork and stick into the center or top with bacon slices. Cover and bake in a 250-degree oven for 5 hours. Remove cover occasionally and add reserved bean liquid if mixture seems dry. Serves 6 to 8.

In the South, "salat" means cooked greens, most often turnip greens, or the tops of turnips. It also means cressy greens, mustard greens, and wild edible greens.

Schnitzel Beans

1 pound green beans
4 strips bacon
2 medium-size onions, finely chopped
3 medium-size fresh ripe tomatoes, peeled and diced
1 teaspoon salt
¼ teaspoon pepper
¼ cup water

Cut beans diagonally into short lengths. Fry bacon until crisp and drain. In bacon drippings, cook onions until golden. Add beans, tomatoes, seasonings, and water. Cover, bring to a boil, lower heat, and simmer for 20 minutes. Add crumbled bacon and serve. Makes 6 servings.

Gumbo Vegetables

In the original recipe, all fresh vegetables were used.

1 large onion, peeled and diced
¼ cup green pepper, diced
2 tablespoons butter or margarine
1 8-ounce can tomato sauce
1 No. 2½ can tomatoes
3 medium-size potatoes, peeled and diced
1 bay leaf
1 teaspoon thyme
1 teaspoon Worcestershire sauce
1 10-ounce package frozen whole okra
1 10-ounce package frozen whole kernel corn
Salt, pepper, seasoned salt to taste

Sauté onion and green pepper in butter in a large skillet until golden. Add tomato sauce, tomatoes, potatoes, bay leaf, thyme, and Worcestershire sauce. Cover and simmer for about 15 minutes. Add okra and corn. Season to taste with salt, pepper, and seasoned salt. Continue cooking, while stirring, about 15 minutes longer or until done. Makes 8 or more servings.

Turnip Greens with Garden Sass

After a long winter with no fresh greens in the diet, the "system" yearned for the first tender greens of spring.

> **4 pounds young turnip greens**
> **1 quart water**
> **1 2-inch-square salt pork**
> **1 teaspoon salt**
> **1 pod red pepper or pinch of cayenne**

Wash and pick over greens, discarding coarse stalks. Put water in heavy pan. Bring to a boil. Add pork and pepper pod and simmer for 30 minutes. Add greens and salt. Simmer for about 1 hour. Drain and serve pot liquor in a cup to sip with the meal. Cut through the greens several times with a knife. Pass garden sass (recipe below) to spoon over the top. Makes 6 servings.

Garden Sass

> **2 tomatoes, diced**
> **¾ cup celery, diced**
> **1 large cucumber, peeled and diced**
> **1 green pepper, chopped**
> **2 tablespoons onion, finely chopped**
> **1 tablespoon French dressing**
> **2 to 3 tablespoons cider vinegar**
> **Salt and pepper to taste**

Mix all ingredients and chill for 2 hours. Makes 2 cups.

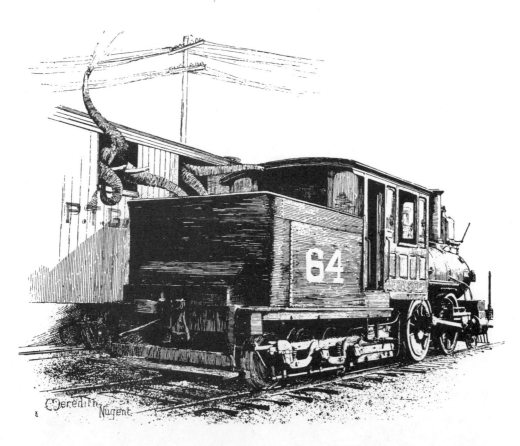

Garden Abundance

A fine accompaniment for fried or broiled chicken
2 large onions, peeled and sliced
2 large green peppers, with membranes and seeds
    removed and sliced
¼ cup salad oil or margarine
3 medium-size yellow summer squash, coarsely
    cubed
1 cup celery, sliced
2 chicken bouillon cubes
6 medium-size ripe tomatoes, peeled and
    coarsely cubed
4 bay leaves
1 teaspoon black pepper
½ teaspoon thyme
Pinch of poultry seasoning
Pinch of ground cloves
Cayenne pepper or hot pepper sauce to taste
Salt to taste
3 ears corn, cut from cob

Cook onions and peppers in oil in heavy skillet until golden. Add squash and continue to cook, stirring, until lightly brown. Add remaining ingredients except corn. Mash the bouillon cubes in the skillet with the back of a wooden spoon. Cook, stirring occasionally, for about 20 minutes. Add corn and cook for 5 minutes longer. Discard bay leaves before serving. Makes 8 or more servings.

Garden Hash

8 strips bacon, diced
1 medium onion, chopped
1 green pepper, seeded and chopped
6 small zucchini, sliced
6 yellow summer squash, sliced
4 medium green tomatoes, coarsely chopped
1 teaspoon sugar
1 teaspoon salt or to taste
¼ teaspoon pepper
1 8-ounce can tomato sauce
1 cup sharp Cheddar cheese, grated

Fry bacon until almost cooked in a large skillet with a cover; drain off all but 2 tablespoons of the drippings. Sauté onion with bacon until golden brown; add green pepper, zucchini, squash, and green tomatoes. Sprinkle with sugar, salt, and pepper; add tomato sauce, and stir lightly. Cover; simmer slowly for 15 minutes. Turn into casserole. Sprinkle with cheese; bake in a 350-degree oven for 25 minutes or until bubbly. Serves 8 to 10.

Squash Casserole

2 pounds yellow summer squash, sliced
1 teaspoon salt
1/8 teaspoon sugar
1 cup water
1/4 cup butter or margarine
1 cup sour cream
1 cup sharp Cheddar cheese, cubed
1/4 teaspoon pepper
1 cup soft bread crumbs, buttered

Add squash, salt, and sugar to water in saucepan; cook for 20 minutes or until tender, then drain in a colander. Return squash to saucepan, add butter, and mash with potato masher. Blend in sour cream, cheese, and pepper. Turn into baking dish; top with crumbs. Bake in a 350-degree oven for 20 minutes or until bubbly and crumbs are browned. Serves 6.

Scalloped Tomatoes

1 1/2 cups stale bread, in coarse pieces
1/4 cup butter, melted
2 cups canned tomatoes
1 teaspoon salt
6 tablespoons brown sugar

Place bread in 9-inch baking dish 2 inches deep; pour butter over bread, and stir to coat pieces. Meanwhile, in saucepan heat tomatoes, salt, and sugar to boiling point; pour over bread. Bake in a 425-degree oven for 25 minutes or until well browned. Serves 6.

Vegetable Casserole

6 small new potatoes, with strip peeled from middle, cooked
6 small carrots, cooked
1 cup green peas, cooked
1 cup cauliflower, cooked
Salt and pepper to taste
1 1/2 cups medium cream sauce
1/4 pound grated American cheese

Place vegetables in casserole; sprinkle with salt and pepper, pour in sauce, and sprinkle with cheese. Heat in a 350-degree oven for 25 minutes or until bubbly. Serves 6.

CHAPTER 8

Salads

The century was heading toward the halfway point
before the tossed green salad became as routine to dining
as knives and forks. Earlier in the century, salad meant
a pineapple slice with mayonnaise and a cherry or a
Waldorf salad. Gradually, congealed salads became
popular. Garden lettuce and dandelion greens were
served in season with sugar-and-vinegar, or hot bacon
dressing. Mayonnaise was made at home. The vast
array of bottled salad dressings now on grocery shelves
arrived largely after World War II.

Superb Green Salad

 2 No. 303 cans French-style green beans
 1 No. 303 can green peas
 ¼ cup stuffed olives, sliced
 1 cup celery, sliced
 1 cup carrots, sliced
 1 cup green onions with some tops, sliced
 1 cup frozen large green lima beans, cooked,
  optional
 ¼ cup salad oil
 ¼ cup vinegar
 ½ teaspoon Worcestershire sauce
 ½ teaspoon paprika
 ⅔ cup powdered sugar or to taste
 1 teaspoon salt

Drain all vegetables and combine. Mix remaining
ingredients and pour over vegetables. Cover and chill
for 4 hours. It will keep for several days. Makes
16 to 18 servings.

Potato Salad

 3 cups potatoes, peeled and cubed
 2 tablespoons oil and vinegar salad dressing
 1 cup celery, diced
 ½ cup sweet pickles, drained and diced
 1 tablespoon onion, minced
 1 teaspoon salt
 ¼ teaspoon pepper
 1 teaspoon turmeric
 ⅛ teaspoon sugar
 ½ to ⅔ cup mayonnaise
 Salad greens

Boil cubed potatoes until just tender; drain.
Pour dressing over hot potatoes; cool, mix in remaining
ingredients except greens. Cover and chill; serve on
greens. Makes 6 servings.

Deluxe Potato Salad

4 cups potatoes, peeled and cubed
3 tablespoons oil and vinegar dressing
3 hard cooked eggs, chopped
2 cups celery, thinly sliced
2 tablespoons green olives, chopped
2 tablespoons pimiento, chopped
¼ cup green pepper, chopped
1 cup green peas, cooked and drained
1½ teaspoons salt or to taste
¼ teaspoon pepper
½ to ⅔ cup mayonnaise
Salad greens

Boil cubed potatoes until just tender; drain. Pour
dressing over potatoes; cool, add remaining
ingredients except greens. Blend thoroughly; pack down
firmly in round bowl, cover and chill for several hours.
Turn out in rounded mound on greens. Serves 8.

Lentil Salad

1 pound lentils, cooked and drained
¾ cup salad oil
¼ cup red wine vinegar
1 clove garlic, minced
¾ cup onion, chopped
Salt to taste
1 teaspoon black pepper, coarsely ground
½ teaspoon Worcestershire sauce
¼ teaspoon hot pepper sauce
4 slices bacon, crisp and crumbled
¼ cup stuffed olives, chopped
Tomatoes, sliced
Onions, sliced

While lentils are still hot, put them into salad bowl and stir in salad oil; cover and cool. Add vinegar, garlic, onion, salt, pepper, Worcestershire, and hot pepper sauce; chill. Before serving, sprinkle with bacon and olives. Place bowl on platter, arrange tomato and onion slices on platter around bowl. Serves 8.

Chicken Salad

2 cups chicken, cooked and cubed
1 cup celery, diced
2 tablespoons stuffed olives, sliced
¼ cup blanched almonds or water chestnuts, sliced
2 hard-cooked eggs
¾ cup mayonnaise
2 tablespoons Durkee's Famous Sauce
Salt and white pepper to taste
Salad greens

Combine chicken, celery, olives, almonds or chestnuts, diced egg whites, and sieved yolks. Add mayonnaise and sauce with salt and pepper to taste. Chill for 2 or more hours to allow flavors to blend. Serve on salad greens. Makes 8 servings.

When the vines were heavy with cucumbers prickly with freshness, we gathered them in the cool of the morning. They were served peeled and sliced with sliced spring onions in vinegar in a bowl.

In the days when veal was cheaper than chicken, cubes of cooked veal were added to chicken salad to stretch the number of servings.

In the root cellar, turnips stored for the winter sometimes sprout white sprouts similar to bean sprouts. The custom in some homes was to gather the precious sprouts to serve as salad.

Farmers' Delight Salad

½ head lettuce
5 green onions with some tops, sliced
10 radishes, sliced
1 medium cucumber, peeled and sliced
1 cup carrots, sliced and cooked
½ cup celery, thinly sliced
1½ cups green peas, cooked or canned
¼ pound bacon
¼ cup bacon drippings
1 tablespoon flour
3 tablespoons vinegar
1½ tablespoons sugar
½ teaspoon dry mustard
½ cup milk
½ cup blue cheese, crumbled
1 small green pepper, cut into rings
2 medium tomatoes, cut into wedges

Break lettuce into bite-size pieces; place in salad bowl with onions, radishes, cucumber, carrots, celery, and peas. Cook bacon until crisp; drain and crumble. Blend flour into hot drippings to make a smooth paste; remove from heat and stir in vinegar, sugar, and mustard. Slowly add milk, stirring until blended; add cheese and crumbled bacon. Pour dressing over vegetables in salad bowl. Garnish with pepper rings and tomato wedges. Makes 4 to 6 servings.

Drunkard's Dream

2 quarts leaf lettuce, shredded
4 radishes
4 green onions, sliced
1 large dill pickle, diced
2 tomatoes, diced
4 slices bacon, fried crisp
1 cup hot red eye gravy (recipe below)

Place lettuce in a large platter or bowl; top with radishes, onions, pickles, tomatoes, and bacon. Just before serving, pour on hot red eye gravy. Makes 6 servings.

Red Eye Gravy

1 cup ham fat, diced
Water
⅛ teaspoon pepper
⅛ teaspoon sugar

In skillet, fry fat slowly until well browned; lift out crisp fat, discard. Pour drippings into measuring cup. Add enough water to drippings to make 1 cup; pour into hot pan, heat. Add pepper and sugar. (If ham is not salty, add salt to salad to taste.)

Spinach Salad

1 pound fresh spinach
½ cup green onions, sliced
¼ cup salad oil
2 tablespoons wine vinegar
1 tablespoon lemon juice
½ teaspoon salt
½ teaspoon sugar
Dash pepper
1 egg, hard-cooked and diced
4 slices bacon, fried crisp

Wash spinach, discarding stems. Pat dry with paper towels, and tear into bowl. Add onions; cover and chill until crisp. Blend oil, vinegar, lemon juice, sugar, salt, and pepper; toss lightly with spinach and onions. Sprinkle with egg and crumbled bacon. Makes 4 to 6 servings.

Fire and Ice Salad

2 large onions, thinly sliced
6 large firm ripe tomatoes, peeled and cut
   into wedges
1 green pepper, cut into slivers
¾ cup cider vinegar
¼ cup water
1½ teaspoons celery seed
1½ teaspoons mustard seed
½ teaspoon salt
2 tablespoons sugar
¼ teaspoon black pepper, coarsely ground

Separate onions into rings and place with tomatoes and green pepper in a shallow dish. Combine remaining ingredients in a saucepan; bring to a boil, stirring to dissolve sugar. Pour hot mixture over cold vegetables. Chill for several hours. Makes 10 to 12 servings.

Vegetable Salad

1 10-ounce package frozen peas, cooked
1½ cups cooked or canned green beans
1 medium cauliflower, cooked tender, broken
   into flowerets
½ cup lima beans, cooked
1 cup carrots, cooked and diced
1 cup celery, minced
1 5-ounce can water chestnuts, drained and sliced
2 green onions, minced
1 2-ounce jar pimientos, drained and diced
½ cup parsley, chopped
1½ cups mayonnaise
2 tablespoons vinegar
1 tablespoon lemon juice
1 teaspoon salt
½ teaspoon pepper
¾ tablespoon curry powder
Salad greens

Combine vegetables. Blend mayonnaise, vinegar, lemon
juice, salt, pepper, and curry powder; toss with
vegetables. Cover; chill for several hours. Serve on salad
greens. Serves 8 to 10.

Congealed Chutney Salad

1 envelope plain gelatin
¼ cup cold water
1¾ cups apple juice
1 6-ounce jar sweet chutney, chopped
Salad greens

Use ¼ cup cold water to soften gelatin. Heat remaining
apple juice to boiling; add to gelatin, stir to dissolve.
Add chutney. Pour into molds; chill until firm. Unmold
on greens. Makes 4 to 5 molds.

Zippy Tomato Aspic

An earlier version made with sieved canned tomatoes
was called tomato jelly.

1¾ cups V-8 juice
1 3-ounce package raspberry-flavored gelatin
2 tablespoons bottled horseradish
¼ teaspoon salt
1 tablespoon lemon juice or vinegar
½ teaspoon celery salt
½ teaspoon Worcestershire sauce
½ cup celery, finely chopped
¼ cup stuffed olives, chopped

Heat V-8 juice to boiling and pour over gelatin.
Stir to dissolve gelatin. Cool to room temperature,
then stir in remaining ingredients. Pour into 6
individual molds and chill until firm. Unmold
on lettuce and serve with mayonnaise. Serves 6.

Orange-Banana Salad

¼ cup orange juice
¼ cup lemon juice
½ cup salad oil
¼ cup sugar
1 teaspoon salt
¼ teaspoon pepper
1 teaspoon paprika
1 teaspoon prepared mustard
½ teaspoon celery seed
1 teaspoon onion, grated
3 oranges, peeled and sliced into cartwheels
2 large bananas, peeled and sliced
Salad greens
⅓ cup pecans or walnuts, chopped
3 tablespoons watercress, chopped

In a bowl, combine orange juice, lemon juice, oil, sugar,
salt, pepper, paprika, mustard, celery seed, and onion;
blend well with egg beater. Pour dressing over orange
slices and bananas; marinate for 30 minutes. Lift
oranges and bananas from dressing; arrange on salad
greens. Sprinkle with nuts and watercress; serve with
remaining dressing. Makes 8 servings.

Citrus Green Salad

1 medium head romaine
1 ripe avocado, peeled and sliced
1 tablespoon lemon juice
2 grapefruit, peeled and sectioned
1 red onion, thinly sliced
Oil and vinegar dressing (recipe below)

Tear greens into bite-size pieces into salad bowl; add avocado sprinkled with lemon juice, grapefruit sections, and onion rings. Toss with dressing. Makes 6 to 8 servings.

Oil and Vinegar Dressing

½ cup salad oil
¼ cup wine vinegar
1 tablespoon lemon juice
2 teaspoons seasoned salt
¼ teaspoon seasoned pepper

Combine all ingredients in jar with top; shake thoroughly.

Pepper Cabbage

4 cups cabbage, shredded
½ green pepper, finely chopped
1 rib celery, finely chopped
¼ cup carrot, grated
1 teaspoon salt
½ cup water
5 tablespoons vinegar

Combine all ingredients. Chill. Serves 6 to 8.

Texas Coleslaw

1½ pound head cabbage
1 medium onion, finely chopped
½ green pepper, finely chopped
¼ cup plus one tablespoon sugar
½ cup salad oil
½ cup vinegar
½ teaspoon dry mustard
1 teaspoon salt
½ teaspoon celery seed

Chop or shred cabbage and place it in a bowl with onion and green pepper. Sprinkle with ¼ cup sugar and toss lightly to blend.

In a saucepan, combine remaining sugar and other ingredients; bring to a boil. Pour, while hot, over the cabbage mixture. Toss to mix. Chill, covered, for at least 4 hours. It will keep for days in the refrigerator. Makes about 2 quarts.

Superb Coleslaw Dressing

    1 cup mayonnaise
    1 small onion, grated
    1½ teaspoons prepared mustard
    1½ tablespoons sugar
    ¾ teaspoon salt
    ½ teaspoon black pepper

Mix all ingredients and use to moisten finely shredded crisp cabbage. Makes about 1 cup.

Mayonnaise

    1 whole egg or 2 egg yolks
    ½ teaspoon dry mustard
    1 teaspoon salt
    2 tablespoons vinegar
    1 cup salad oil

Into the container of the electric blender, put the egg or egg yolks, mustard, salt, vinegar, and ¼ cup salad oil; cover container and flick motor on and off high speed. Remove cover, turn motor on high; immediately add remaining oil in a steady stream. When all the oil is added, turn off motor. Makes 1¼ cups.

Before mayonnaise came in jars, it was made by beating egg and oil with an egg beater in a bowl. The oil was added a drop at a time. Some cooks made mayonnaise by beating the ingredients on a dinner plate with a silver fork. Every time Mama made mayonnaise, children snacked on mayonnaise sandwiches —that is, white bread spread with nothing but mayonnaise.

CHAPTER 9
The Miracle Called Bread

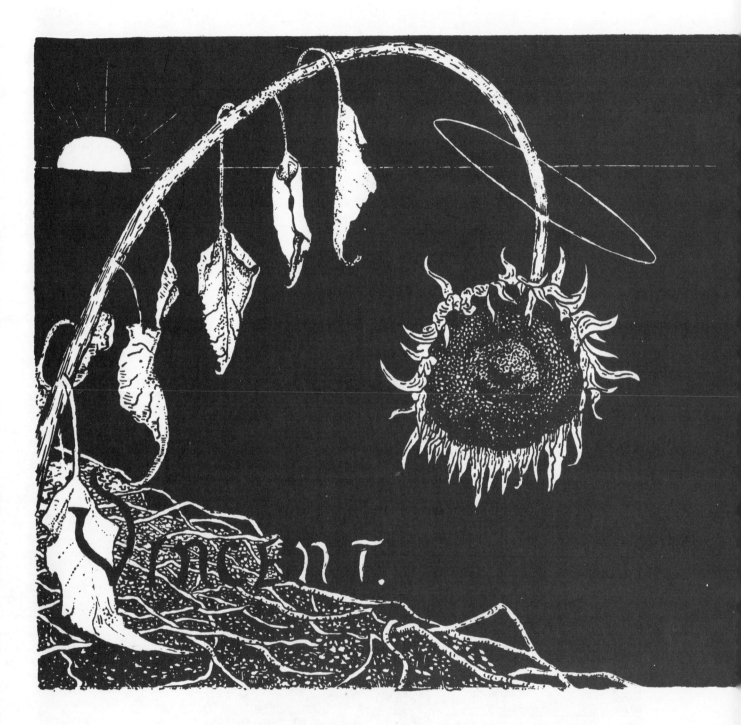

The memory of bread is combined with memories of Rudolph Valentino and Charlie Chaplin in the memoirs of Pola Negri, a well-known movie queen of the twenties. She recalls soups "thick with vegetables and juliennes of meats, and fresh crackling wheat homemade breads to mop up the bottoms of plates."

Kuhn's, a German delicatessen in Chicago, has an assortment of breads to accompany their sausages for a feast which is moveable anywhere. The label on their hearth-baked breads says "Mit der kostlicken kruste." No matter how it translates, it means crumb-licking good.

A bread display was staged in recent years at the Hallmark Gallery on Fifth Avenue. It featured "live" models of the famous breads of the world.

In addition to loaves which are long, round, flat, twisted, and plump, bread comes as rolls, muffins, popovers, Sally Lunn, Boston brown bread, nut bread, sticks, brioches, croissants, and crullers.

Cornmeal appears in bread, hoe cakes, ash cakes, pone, dodgers, biscuits, shortnin' bread (made famous in a song sung by Nelson Eddy in an earlier decade), muffins, hush puppies, spoonbread, and tortillas.

"Ethnic" breads include rings, twists, ovals, rounds, loaves, and horseshoes, giant challah in the shape of a sheaf of wheat, Irish soda bread, Greek bread, Italian bread, Cuban bread, bauernbrot, pumpernickel, Arabic pita, bagels, Hungarian potato bread, Tubo, Swedish limpa, and Danish rugbrød.

This country produces the whitest, lightest, most perfect loaf of bread of any country in the world. To produce this intrinsically American loaf, the beautiful whole grain is stripped of its bran and its germ. It is a monumental achievement, yet had the country not awakened in time to pass enrichment laws ordering that the nutrients removed in milling be put back in chemical form, we would have slowly starved on this white fiasco.

The yeast breads made in the home earlier in the century were good enough to make a meal, as they often did. Yeast works in a way as wondrous as the unfolding of a bud into a flower and yields a scent more enticing than a fragrant rose. Yeast for making bread came from stills and was made from hops, a plant, and potatoes, before the three-cent cake of yeast appeared.

Near the old homeplace there was a federal distillery which operated until prohibition. We bought yeast from the still—it was called still yeast—and when bread made from the yeast was baking, I am sure the aroma reached the next county.

Bakery bread, we called it light bread because it was lighter than homemade bread, was a treat because it was bought at the store. Children treated themselves on a sugar sandwich made on it—that was bread spread with butter and sprinkled heavily with sugar.

Salt-rising bread is made by fermenting potatoes. Sourdough, without which the West might have been lost, can be made from scratch but is most often made with the trusty starter carried in westward-bound wagons and shared by neighbors.

In 1910, 95 per cent of America's bread was baked at home; in 1960, 95 per cent of all bread was baked in bakeries. Now, however, joys and rewards of home-baked bread is part of the renaissance of cooking. Women, and men, are learning that a loaf of yeast bread put into the oven at the moment guests arrive dazzles the appetite more than the aperitif. Home bakers also find that many a frustration can be kneaded into bread.

MARGARET RUDKIN

A typical home baker of a good loaf of bread was Margaret Rudkin, a Connecticut housewife. She baked bread with stone-milled flour and other natural ingredients for the purpose of helping her son, who suffered from allergies. The bread helped her son to such an extent his doctor asked Mrs. Rudkin to bake bread for other patients.

Soon after she started baking in 1937, Mrs. Rudkin's bread became popular with friends and neighbors and led to the start of a substantial mail-order business. A sizeable number of people were willing to pay twenty-five cents a loaf for it, as compared to ten cents for the baker's spongy loaf.

In her home with one helper, Mrs. Rudkin kneaded by hand and baked Pepperidge Farm bread. Rapid growth in sales in a matter of months caused her to move her kitchen to a remodeled garage and from there to abandoned polo stables by February 1940. The line had grown by then to five items and production was in excess of twenty thousand loaves per week. The first modern Pepperidge Bakery opened in Norwalk, Conn., in 1947. Before her death on June 1, 1967, Mrs. Rudkin lived to see a Pepperidge Farm baking empire.

Honey Oat Bread

1 cup water, boiling
1½ cups rolled oats, uncooked
⅓ cup honey
¼ cup margarine, softened
1 tablespoon salt
1 cup sour cream
2 packages dry yeast
½ cup very warm water
2 eggs, beaten
6½ cups flour, sifted, approximate

Pour boiling water over oats; stir in honey, margarine, and salt. Blend in sour cream. Soften yeast in very warm water; add to oats mixture with eggs and 2 cups flour. Stir until smooth; add flour (about 4½ cups) to make a stiff dough (a dough which is no longer sticky). Turn out on lightly floured board; knead until elastic. Cover dough with tea towel or bowl; let rest for 20 minutes. Divide into 2 equal portions; shape each into a loaf. Place each loaf in greased loaf pan; cover pans loosely with plastic wrap. Store in the refrigerator for 2 to 24 hours. When ready to bake; remove from refrigerator. Let stand at room temperature for 10 minutes; bake in a 375-degree oven for 45 minutes or until done. To test for doneness, turn loaf out of pan and tap bottom; if loaf sounds hollow, the bread is done. Turn out on racks to cool.

Just once more I'd like to come home from school and walk into Ma's kitchen when she was ready to take loaves of bread out of the oven. She'd let me break off chunks to eat with butter and jelly.

After grandmother passed away, her big yellow mixing bowl became an heirloom. Those who came after her were content to let the bakery do the baking. A member of the now generation has discovered the joys of breadmaking and the bowl is back in use. I think grandmother would be pleased.

Cheese Bread

1 cup milk, scalded
3 tablespoons sugar
1 tablespoon butter
2 teaspoons salt
1 package dry yeast
2 tablespoons warm water
1 egg, beaten
2 cups sharp Cheddar cheese, grated
4 cups flour, sifted, approximate
1 teaspoon oil

Pour hot milk over sugar, butter, and salt; stir and cool to lukewarm. Dissolve yeast in warm water; allow to stand for 5 minutes, then add with egg to milk mixture, and blend. Add cheese and sufficient flour to make a soft dough. Turn out on lightly floured board; knead. Place in greased bowl; turn to grease dough on all sides. Cover dough; allow to rise in a warm place until double in bulk. Punch down, shape into a loaf, and place in loaf pan. Brush with oil. Cover, and let stand in a warm place until almost double in bulk. Bake in a 350-degree oven for 50 minutes or until done. Makes 1 loaf. Toasted slices served with apple jelly are good reason for making cheese bread.

Sweet Yeast Dough

2 cups milk, scalded
2 packages dry yeast
2 teaspoons salt
½ cup sugar
2 eggs
½ cup plus 2 tablespoons margarine
7 cups flour, approximate

Cool milk to lukewarm; dissolve yeast in ½ cup milk. Let yeast stand for 10 minutes. In bowl, blend salt, sugar, and eggs; add yeast, ½ cup melted margarine, remaining milk, and 7 cups flour or enough to make soft dough. Rub large bowl with 2 tablespoons margarine; turn dough to coat with margarine. Cover with damp towel; place bowl over pan of hot tap water; do not allow bowl to touch water. Let stand in warm place for 2 hours; punch down, and let stand 30 minutes longer. Use for making Swedish tea rings, schnecken or bubble loaf (recipes below). When ready for use, add additional flour; if necessary to prevent dough from being sticky.

Swedish Tea Ring

1 recipe sweet yeast dough
3 tablespoons margarine, melted
1 cup brown sugar, packed
2 teaspoons cinnamon
1 cup raisins
Confectioners' sugar frosting (recipe below)
½ cup pecan halves
½ cup candied cherries, halved

Divide dough into two portions; roll each out on floured board to make 2 9- by 18-inch rectangles. Brush dough with margarine. Spread each rectangle with half of the sugar, cinnamon, and raisins. Roll up the wide side of each like a jelly roll with seams underneath; shape to form rings with seams pressed together. With scissors, cut through rings from edge to center about ¾ inch at 1½ inch intervals. This will allow part of the filling to ooze out during baking. Place on greased baking sheet; let stand for 10 minutes. Bake in a 350-degree oven for 30 minutes or until golden. To prevent hard crust, do not overbake. Immediately spread with frosting and decorate with pecans and cherries placed in frosting. Makes 2 rings.

Confectioners' Sugar Frosting

2 tablespoons water, boiling
1 teaspoon vanilla
1½ cups confectioners' sugar, sifted

Stir hot water and vanilla into sugar; spread on rings. Enough for 2 rings.

Schnecken

½ recipe of sweet yeast dough
¼ cup margarine, melted
½ cup granulated or brown sugar
1 teaspoon cinnamon
½ cup raisins

Roll out dough ¼ inch thick and 15 inches square on lightly floured board. Brush with margarine; sprinkle with sugar, cinnamon, and raisins. Roll up like a jelly roll; cut into 1-inch slices. Place slices in greased 9½- by 13½-inch baking pan. Bake in a 350-degree oven for 30 minutes or until golden brown. Makes 15.

Bubble Loaf

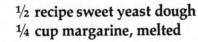

½ recipe sweet yeast dough
¼ cup margarine, melted

Shape dough into 1¼-inch balls; dip each in melted margarine and drop in 8-inch tube pan brushed with margarine. Brush tops with margarine. Let stand for 10 minutes. Bake in a 350-degree oven for 30 minutes or until done. Brush with remaining margarine. Turn out; serve top side up. The loaf bakes with little rounded balls on top, resembling a crown. Use as the centerpiece and invite each person to pull off the tasty baked balls one at a time.

Russian Black Bread

4 cups rye flour
3 cups white flour
1 teaspoon sugar
2 teaspoons salt
2 cups whole bran cereal
2 tablespoons caraway seed, crushed
2 teaspoons instant coffee powder
2 packages dry yeast
2½ cups water
¼ cup vinegar
¼ cup dark molasses
1 ounce unsweetened chocolate
¼ cup margarine
1 teaspoon cornstarch
½ cup cold water

Combine rye and white flours. In a large bowl mix 2⅓ cups flour mixture, sugar, salt, cereal, caraway seed, coffee powder, and undissolved yeast.

Combine water, vinegar, molasses, chocolate, and margarine in saucepan. Heat over low heat until liquids are warm; margarine and chocolate do not need to melt. Gradually add to dry ingredients and beat for 2 minutes. Add enough additional flour mixture to make a soft dough. Turn out on lightly floured board. Cover dough and let rest for 15 minutes; then knead until smooth and elastic. Place dough in greased bowl; turn to grease dough on all sides. Cover and let rise in warm place until double in bulk, about 1 hour.

Turn dough out on lightly floured board, and punch down. Divide in half. Shape each half into a ball about 5 inches in diameter. Place each ball in the center of greased 8-inch-round cake pans. Cover and let rise in a warm place until double in bulk, about 1 hour. Bake in a 350-degree oven for about 45 minutes, or until done.

Meanwhile, combine cornstarch and ½ cup cold water. Cook, stirring, until smooth and thickened. Brush bread hot from the oven with cornstarch mixture. Return bread to oven for 2 to 3 minutes to set glaze. Remove bread from pans and place on wire racks. Makes 2 loaves.

Monkey Bread

A layered yeast bread made of dough rolled out thinly, cut into diamonds, and brushed with melted butter before piling into a tube pan, this is simply a good egg-potato bread with an unusual name. The bread was named by Zasu Pitts, a comedienne, who held her hands as if they were paws, wore little flat hats, and had an "Oh, dear" voice.

> 1 large potato, peeled and diced
> 2 cups water
> 2 packages dry yeast
> ½ cup shortening
> ¼ cup plus 3 tablespoons butter or margarine
> ¾ cup sugar
> 1 teaspoon salt
> 2 eggs, beaten
> 6 cups flour
> ¾ cup lukewarm milk

In saucepan, cook potato in water until soft; drain, and reserve ½ cup liquid. Dissolve yeast in reserved liquid. Mash potato. Cream shortening and ¼ cup butter or margarine with sugar; add salt, potato, eggs, and flour alternately with milk, and yeast mixture. Cover and let rise in a warm place until light. Divide dough in half. Roll out each portion on lightly floured board to ¼-inch thickness. Melt 3 tablespoons butter or margarine; brush on dough. Cut dough into diamond shapes about 2 inches long; place diamonds in layers in a greased tube pan. Fill pan half full; let dough rise until it almost fills the pan. Bake in a 400-degree oven for 30 minutes or until done. If it browns too rapidly, turn heat down to 350 degrees. Makes one large loaf or 2 medium ones.

Challah

4½ to 5½ cups flour
2 tablespoons sugar
1½ teaspoons salt
1 package dry yeast
⅓ cup margarine, softened
1 cup very hot water (120°-130°F.)
4 eggs
1 teaspoon cold water
1 teaspoon poppy seeds

In a large bowl thoroughly mix 1¼ cups flour, sugar, salt, and yeast. Add margarine and hot water. Beat for 2 minutes at medium speed of electric mixer, scraping bowl occasionally. Add 3 eggs, 1 egg white, and ½ cup flour, or enough flour to make a thick batter. Beat at high speed for 2 minutes, scraping bowl occasionally. Stir in enough additional flour to make a soft dough. Turn out onto lightly floured board; knead until smooth and elastic, about 8 to 10 minutes. Place in greased bowl, turning to grease top. Cover; let rise in warm place until double in bulk, about 1 hour. Punch dough down; turn out onto lightly floured board. Divide dough in half. Divide each half into 2 pieces, taking about ⅓ of the dough for one piece and about ⅔ of the dough for the other. Divide larger piece into 3 equal pieces. Roll each of these 3 pieces into a 12-inch rope. Braid the ropes together; pinch ends to seal. Divide smaller piece into 3 equal pieces. Roll each piece into a 10-inch rope. Braid the ropes together; place on top of large braid. Seal braids together at ends. Place on greased baking sheet. Repeat with remaining dough to form second loaf. Beat together remaining egg yolk and 1 teaspoon cold water; brush loaves with egg mixture. Sprinkle with poppy seeds. Let rise, uncovered, in warm place until double in bulk, about 1 hour. Bake in a 400-degree oven for 20 to 25 minutes or until done. Remove from baking sheets and cool on wire racks. Makes 2 loaves.

Featherbeds

The name of the rolls comes from a featherbed, a bed covering made of a quilt cover filled with feathers which makes a plump, lightweight but warm quilt.

 1 medium potato, peeled and diced
 Water
 1 package dry yeast
 ¼ cup warm water
 ⅓ cup sugar
 1 teaspoon salt
 ¼ cup plus 1 tablespoon margarine
 1 egg, beaten
 4 cups flour, approximate

In saucepan, cover potato with water; cook until soft. Drain and reserve ¾ cup liquid. Dissolve yeast in warm water. Pour hot reserved liquid over sugar, salt, and ¼ cup margarine; blend and cool to lukewarm. Mash potato and add with yeast and egg to lukewarm mixture. Blend in 2 cups flour, then another 2 cups flour, or enough to make a dough which is not sticky. Knead on lightly floured board. Place in greased bowl; turn to grease dough on all sides. Cover; let stand in warm place until double in bulk. Punch down; turn out on floured board. Divide in half; shape each half into 12 balls. Place balls in 2 greased 9-inch layer pans. Melt remaining margarine; brush over balls, and let rise until double in bulk. Bake in 375-degree oven for 20 minutes or until lightly browned. Makes 24.

The way ropes of dough are braided to make challah is the same way my older sister braided my pigtails when I was a little girl.

Angel Biscuits

5 cups flour
¼ cup sugar
3 teaspoons baking powder
1 teaspoon baking soda
1 teaspoon salt
1 cup shortening
1 package dry yeast
2 tablespoons warm water
2 cups buttermilk
¼ cup butter or margarine, melted

Sift together flour, sugar, baking powder, baking soda, and salt. Stir in shortening. Meanwhile, dissolve yeast in warm water. Add with buttermilk to flour mixture. Mix well. If necessary, add additional flour to make soft dough. Turn out on lightly floured board. Roll out to ¼-inch thickness. Cut with round biscuit cutter. Brush with melted butter and fold over to make pocketbook rolls. Bake in a 400-degree oven for 15 minutes or until lightly browned. The dough does not have to rise before baking. The dough may be stored in the refrigerator before baking.

Bagels

2 packages dry yeast
¼ cup sugar
2 teaspoons salt
5 to 6 cups flour
1⅓ cups warm water
⅓ cup oil
2 eggs
Boiling water

Stir together yeast, sugar, salt, and 2 cups of the flour. Add warm water and oil to flour mixture and beat until smooth. Blend in eggs, one at a time. Add 1 cup flour and beat for 1 minute. Stir in more flour to make a moderately stiff dough. Turn out onto lightly floured board and knead for 2 minutes. Shape into a ball and place in a lightly greased bowl, turning to grease all sides. Cover and let rise in a warm place for 1½ hours or until double in bulk. Punch down and let rise

again in a warm place until double in bulk, about 45 minutes. Punch down. Turn out onto lightly floured surface and knead until smooth and satiny, about 8 to 10 minutes. Divide dough into 16 equal portions and form each into an 11-inch strip. Shape each into a circle and seal ends securely with water. Place on a lightly floured baking sheet and broil for about 1½ minutes on each side. Then drop into gently boiling water. Simmer for 4 to 5 minutes. Remove from water, and drain. Place on a lightly greased baking sheet. Bake in a 350-degree oven for 45 to 55 minutes or until done.

English Muffins

    1 cup milk
    ¼ cup shortening
    2 teaspoons salt
    1 tablespoon white corn syrup
    1 package dry yeast
    3 cups flour, sifted
    4 tablespoons cornmeal

Scald milk (heat just to the boiling point); combine with shortening, salt, and corn syrup, and cool to lukewarm. Add yeast and flour; blend to form soft dough. Turn dough out on lightly floured board; roll to ¼-inch thickness. Cut with a 3-inch-round cutter or can. Place on baking sheet which has been sprinkled with 2 tablespoons cornmeal; sprinkle remaining cornmeal over the tops. Let rise in a warm place for 1 hour or until double in bulk. Bake on a hot, ungreased griddle about 7 minutes on each side; reduce heat when muffins begin to brown. Makes about 28.

Hamburger Buns

    1 package dry yeast
    ¼ cup very warm water
    ¾ cup milk, lukewarm
    ¼ cup sugar
    1 teaspoon salt
    1 egg
    ¼ cup shortening
    3½ to 4 cups flour, sifted

Dissolve yeast in water; stir in milk, sugar, salt, egg, shortening, and half the flour. Mix until smooth with a spoon; add sufficient remaining flour to make a soft dough which can be handled easily with the hands. Turn out on lightly floured board; knead for about 5 minutes or until smooth and elastic. Place in a greased bowl, turning to grease all sides. Cover and let rise in a warm place for about 1½ hours or until double in bulk. Punch down; let rise again for about 30 minutes or until almost double in bulk. Shape dough into 12 round buns; place on lightly greased baking sheet. Flatten gently; let rise in warm place for 20 to 30 minutes or until double in bulk. Bake in a 400-degree oven for 10 to 12 minutes or until done.
Makes about 12.

Corn Bread

1½ cups cornmeal
1½ cups flour
4 teaspoons baking powder
1 teaspoon salt
3 eggs, separated
1¾ cups milk
6 tablespoons shortening, melted

Sift together cornmeal, flour, baking powder, and salt. Beat egg yolks; blend in milk, shortening, and dry ingredients. Beat egg whites until stiff; fold in. Pour mixture into greased 6- by 9-inch baking pan 2½ inches deep. Bake in a 425-degree oven for 25 minutes or until done.

Deluxe Corn Bread

2 eggs
1 cup sour cream
½ cup salad oil
1 cup canned cream-style corn
1 cup cornmeal
1½ teaspoons salt
3 teaspoons baking powder

Beat eggs. Blend in sour cream, oil, and corn. Combine and blend cornmeal, salt, and baking powder, and add. Blend and pour into a greased 8-inch-square baking pan. Bake in a 375-degree oven for 40 minutes or until done.

Buttermilk Biscuits

2 cups self-rising flour, sifted
1/8 teaspoon baking soda
1/8 teaspoon baking powder
1/3 cup lard or shortening
3/4 cup buttermilk, approximate

To flour, add baking soda and baking powder; cut in lard or shortening until mixture resembles meal. Add milk gradually, blending in to make a soft dough. Turn out on lightly floured board and knead gently—do not knead too much or biscuits will be tough. Pat out dough to 1/2-inch thickness. Cut with floured cutter; place on greased baking sheet. Bake in a 450-degree oven for 10 to 12 minutes or until golden brown. Makes about 12 2 1/2-inch biscuits. (Self-rising flour is a commercial product with 1 1/2 teaspoons baking powder and 1/2 teaspoon salt added to 1 cup flour.)

Cat's Head Biscuits

A logging camp cook developed this recipe to keep from having to pass the biscuit plate so often. The loggers dubbed the biscuits "Cat's Head" because of their size.

4 cups flour
1 teaspoon baking soda
1 teaspoon salt
3 teaspoons baking powder
2 tablespoons lard
1 cup sour buttermilk, approximate

Sift dry ingredients together. Cut in lard. Make a well in the dry ingredients and add enough buttermilk to make a soft dough. Turn out on lightly floured board and knead lightly. Pat out dough and cut with large cutter—a No. 2 tin can will do. Place on a greased baking sheet and bake in a 475-degree oven until golden brown. Makes 16 to 18.

Gingerbread Gems

    1½ cups flour, sifted
    ½ teaspoon salt
    ½ teaspoon baking powder
    ½ teaspoon ground ginger
    1 teaspoon cinnamon
    ¼ teaspoon cloves
    ¼ cup shortening
    ¼ cup sugar
    ½ teaspoon baking soda
    ½ cup molasses
    1 egg
    ½ cup hot water

Sift together flour, salt, baking powder, and spices.
Cream shortening, sugar and baking soda; blend in
molasses and ¼ cup of the flour mixture. Beat in egg
and hot water alternately with remaining flour
mixture. Pour into greased and lightly floured muffin
pans; bake in a 350-degree oven for 15 minutes or
until done. Makes 12 regular-size muffins.

Dumplings

Dumplings deserve a role as important as that of
railroad crossties and spikes in the building of America.
The early settlers followed the practice of their
ancestors from other countries in making dumplings to
stretch the meat, fish, poultry, vegetables, and fruits.
Dumplings are filling and can be made from simple
ingredients, often merely flour and water.

For centuries the Chinese made a translucent dumpling
called *dien hsing,* dough in the shape of a turnover,
filled with meat or other fillings, and steamed or fried.
It is thought that Marco Polo in his travels discovered
dien hsing and carried the idea back to Italy where it
became *ravioli* and *gnocchi.*

The dumplings of this country are generally in three
shapes: balls or dropped dough, strips similar to
noodles, and filled shapes.

Dropped ones include bread dumplings, *butterklosse*
or butter dumplings, matzo balls, *spaetzle* or egg
dumplings, and Russian *vereniki* or pot cheese dumplings. For the liver dumpling, which is German in
origin, ground liver is mixed with egg and bread
crumbs, shaped into balls, and dropped into hot broth
for a hearty main dish.

Philadelphia pepper pot, made of squares of tripe, a cow's stomach with a unique maze-like design, topped with dumplings has been given some credit for helping this country win the Revolutionary War. The Pennsylvania Dutch cook *schnitz-un-gnepp*, smoked ham with dried apples topped with dumplings. In the South, a dish of strips of dough cooked with tender fresh young green peas, seasoned liberally with butter and black pepper, is an old favorite now rarely prepared.

Corn Meal Dumplings

Cornmeal dumplings, also called pot dodgers, are cooked atop stews and green leafy vegetables. To prepare dumplings from corn muffin mix, prepare batter by directions on the box. Drop by the tablespoonful on top of hot stew or green vegetables; cover tightly and steam for 12 minutes.

While gingerbread gems baked, filling the house with a spicy aroma, someone went to the fruit closet for a jar of apple butter made in early autumn in a big pot over an open fire.

Egg Dumplings

In Maine, egg dumplings steamed on top of mature green peas are a favorite.

½ cup water
¼ cup butter
⅛ teaspoon salt
½ cup flour
1 egg plus 1 egg yolk
1 gallon salted water, boiling

In small saucepan, bring to a boil ½ cup water, butter, and salt. With a wooden spoon, stir in flour vigorously until smooth paste forms. Beat in whole egg; when well blended, beat in egg yolk. Using 2 teaspoons form small egg-shaped dumplings. Drop into boiling water and poach for 10 to 12 minutes. Makes about 24.

Chicken and Dumplings

Chicken and dumplings was a routine dish in many homes. There are two different kinds of dumplings served with chicken. One is the dropped dumpling, the other is of the rolled dough variety. The rolled dough cut in strips about an inch wide is dropped into a pot to steam atop stewed chicken. These are called flat dumplings or "slickums."

Toss the subject of chicken and dumplings to any group who lived through the early days of this century and a lively controversy follows. Many mothers served chicken and dumplings but few mothers made dumplings the same way. This is one version:

1 5-pound hen, cut into pieces
4 ribs celery
2 slices onion
2 bay leaves
1½ teaspoons salt
½ teaspoon pepper
7 cups water
2 cups milk
½ cup flour
Dumplings (recipe below)

Place chicken, celery, onion, bay leaves, salt, pepper, and water in large kettle; bring to a boil, simmer covered for 2 hours or until chicken is tender. Add additional water as needed. Lift out chicken; discard celery, onion, and bay leaves. Skim fat from top of broth; reserve.

Into ⅓ cup reserved fat in kettle, blend flour; add 6 cups broth, heat and stir until smooth. Add milk; taste, add more salt and pepper if needed. Add chicken pieces; heat to a simmer. Add dumplings. Cover and steam for 20 minutes.

Dumplings (recipe below)

2 cups flour, sifted
¼ teaspoon celery salt
4 teaspoons baking powder
¼ teaspoon salt
Pinch of sugar
3 tablespoons chicken fat or butter
¾ cup milk

Sift flour with celery salt, baking powder, salt, and sugar. Cut in fat or butter until small even particles are formed. Add milk and blend. Dip a tablespoon first into hot liquid in pot of chicken and then into dumpling batter. Drop the batter by the spoonful on top of the chicken pieces.

For flat dumplings, some cooks used the same kind of pastry used for pies. Others made a dough which was between a pastry and a biscuit dough. Another method was to stir chicken broth into flour with a little salt to make a dough similar to noodle dough.

Dampfnudeln, German steamed dumplings, are raised yeast dumplings. They are served with gravy as an accompaniment to meat or poultry or for dessert with stewed fruit, custard sauce, or jelly.

A sugar dumpling consists of sugar and butter folded or rolled into dough before cooking in sugar syrup or caramel sauce.

Fruit dumplings are made by dropping sweetened batter on top of cooked, sweetened fruits.

Amish cooks make yeast dumplings. These are cooked in a skillet and topped with bread crumbs browned in butter. The dumplings are served with cinnamon sauce.

Cooks with Hungarian backgrounds still make dumplings by enclosing a plum with a cube of sugar nestled in its center in dough. The dumpling is dropped in boiling water to cook. It is served with melted butter or bread crumbs browned in butter, or it is sprinkled with sugar.

The apple dumpling is a culinary wonder. A whole apple, peeled and cored, is filled with cinnamon and sugar and baked or steamed in a coating of tender, flaky pastry. It is served with a cinnamon syrup or cream.

An Old Recipe for Apple Dumpling

"For a boiled apple dumpling, make a 'pretty stiff' paste of 1 quart flour, ¼ pound powdered suet, 1 teaspoon salt and cold water. Roll out one-fourth inch thick. Cut into squares and wrap around a peeled, cored apple.

"Have ready some square cloths, dipped in hot water and floured on the inside. Tie dumpling in cloth with stout string. Boil one hour and serve with plenty of sweet sauce."

My little, round, fat grandmother cut pastry into long strips about an inch wide for dumplings; to carry the strips to the pot, she lined them up over her arm from wrist to elbow, the way a waiter carries a towel. Over the pot, she lifted the strips one by one and dropped them into the hot bubbling stew.

An apple dumpling was a dessert to savor with the eyes before breaking open the tender pastry coating with a spoon. It came to the table in dessert dishes the bottoms of which were filled with syrup spiced with cinnamon.

It was a happy day when green peas grew plump enough on the vines to pick. Shelling the peas, pod by pod, was also a pleasing task with the anticipation of a plate of peas cooked with buttery dumplings.

Strawberry Dumplings

One cook said strawberry dumplings are done "when the lid starts bobbing up and down." She added, but "that isn't a sure sign." The cook cut the pastry circles using a saucer as the pattern.

> ¼ **cup strawberries, capped**
> **2 teaspoons sugar**
> **1 5½-inch round of pastry, the thickness**
>   **used for a pie**
> **Boiling water**
> **Thick cream**

Combine berries and sugar; place on one side of pastry, fold over pastry to cover berries. Pinch edges together to seal or press together with the tines of a fork. Gently drop into 4-inch-deep boiling water in kettle. Cover and cook for about 5 minutes. Lift out with slotted spoon into a cereal bowl. Pour cream over the dumpling. Makes 1 serving.

Sack Dumplings

Make a sack of unbleached domestic (a sturdy cotton fabric). Dip sack in boiling water. Remove and coat inside with flour. Mix 1 quart blackberries, 1 cup flour, ½ teaspoon baking powder, and salt and sugar to taste. Put mixture in sack and tie sack tightly with a string. Drop in boiling water for 1 hour. Serve hot with hard sauce.

Bucket Dumplings

Mix a large tablespoon each of butter and lard. Add 1 pint flour, 2 teaspoons baking powder, 2 beaten eggs, and ⅔ cup milk. Put mixture in lard bucket, smearing it to coat the sides of the bucket. Place 1 quart sweetened blackberries, apples, peaches, or huckleberries in the center. Put lid on bucket. Steam in boiling water for 3 hours. Serve with hard sauce.

211

CHAPTER 10

Before Cakes Came in Boxes

Baseball heroes have their Hall of Fame. The distinguished artifacts of past civilizations are preserved in museums. The magnificent cakes of this country deserve their own Hall of Fame or a spot in a museum. Future generations would be a bit amazed at the replicas of some of the towering glories of the past—the Lady Baltimore, the Lord Baltimore, Atlanta Lane, Japanese fruit, the Brown Front, the Prince Albert, Queen Elizabeth's, the $100 Waldorf Astoria, the Dolly Varden plus the endless chocolate cakes, sponge cakes, gold cakes, white cakes, nut cakes, jam cakes, marble cakes, poundcakes—and just CAKES.

Eighteen different poundcake recipes were included in a cookbook written in 1969 by Mrs. Albert P. Brewer, indicating the popularity of poundcakes. Mrs. Brewer, a home economist, is the wife of the former Governor of Alabama.

Impressive as a museum display of cakes alone might be, the events leading to the moment of eating could not be ignored. These would have to include, for example, a picture of the women of other years sitting in their chairs, big mixing bowls in hand, "working" butter and sugar together by hand until not one grain of sugar was left for the fingers to feel; and other pictures of the baking procedures which followed, always with a bit of mystery. A straw pulled from the broom was used to test the cake for doneness. If the straw, when stuck into the cake, emerged clean, the cake was done, and it was time to turn it out and cover it with frosting. To the kids cake baking meant bowls and spoons to lick. Cakes were left out for everyone to admire before they were cut and devoured. A museum display would be incomplete unless it pictured all the joyous moments of cake baking.

Early in the century, cooks turned out cakes more from knack, word-of-mouth instructions, and watching others bake than from written recipes. Cake recipes often listed ingredients but gave no mixing or baking instructions. This recipe, hand written on a sheet of stationery from Hotel Evans, Winchester, Va., and dated 1900, is an example.

Flour did not come from the grocery store or the general store, it came in 100-pound cloth bags from the roller mill. Papa brought home a sack almost every week and dumped it into the bins of the wooden meal chest which is now an antique.

The quality of eggs which came directly from the nests in the hen house was not predictable as the quality of eggs which come from the supermarket is today. As a precaution against ruining other ingredients with a bad egg, each egg was broken separately into a saucer.

Every weekday after dinner, Mama and us girls would put on clean aprons and sit on the porch and do our embroidery until supper time, but not on Saturday when there were cakes to bake for Sunday.

Pound or Layer Cake

2 lbs. sugar
1½ lbs. butter or butter and cottalene
1 qt. or 20 eggs
1 pt. milk
3½ lbs. flour
½ oz. baking powder
Flavor

Cottalene was a shortening of the period.

This can be used as pound or layer cake. Cost is about
$1.00 or $1.10. Yields nine pounds of cake.

Election Cake

In Hartford, Conn., the custom was to serve election
cakes on election night. One version is made from a
yeast dough rich with butter, eggs, and spices. Studded
with plump raisins and thin slices of citron, the cake
was baked in a tube pan.

This version came from a newspaper clipping yellowed
with age: eighteen pounds of flour, nine pounds of
sugar, nine pounds of butter, ten eggs, three pints of
yeast; four quarts and one pint of milk, two ounces of
nutmeg, two ounces mace, eight glasses of wine, eight
glasses of brandy and nine pounds of raisins. There
were no mixing or cooking directions, or indications of
the amount of cake the ingredients would make. The
following recipe should, however, prove more
functional.

Election Cake

½ cake yeast
½ cup water, lukewarm
1 tablespoon plus ½ cup butter
1 tablespoon plus 1 cup sugar
¾ teaspoon salt
2 cups flour, sifted
2 eggs
1 cup raisins
¼ cup citron, sliced
1 teaspoon lemon rind, grated
1½ teaspoons lemon juice
¾ teaspoon baking soda
½ teaspoon nutmeg
½ cup brandy

Dissolve yeast in water; blend in 1 tablespoon butter, 1 tablespoon sugar, ½ teaspoon salt, and 1¼ cups flour. Cover and let stand overnight. Cream ½ cup butter and 1 cup sugar; add eggs, raisins, citron, lemon rind, and lemon juice. Sift together ¾ cup flour, baking soda, ¼ teaspoon salt, and nutmeg; add to creamed mixture alternately with brandy. Combine yeast mixture and creamed mixture; pour into large greased loaf pan, and let rise in a warm place for about 1 hour. Bake in a 350-degree oven for 1 hour or until done. If desired, frost with confectioners' sugar dissolved in enough warm water to make frosting consistency. Makes 1 loaf.

The Best Poundcake

> ½ pound margarine
> ½ cup shortening
> 3 cups sugar
> 1 teaspoon vanilla extract
> 1 teaspoon lemon extract
> 6 eggs
> 3 cups flour, sifted
> ½ teaspoon baking powder
> ⅛ teaspoon salt
> 1 cup milk

Cream margarine, shortening, and sugar until fluffy. Add extracts and blend well. Add eggs, one at a time, beating well after each is added. Sift together flour, baking powder, and salt. Add alternately with milk to creamed mixture. Pour into large greased and floured tube pan. Bake in a 325-degree oven for 1 hour and 30 minutes, or until cake tests done.

Chocolate Poundcake

> ½ pound butter
> ½ cup shortening
> 3 cups sugar
> 1 teaspoon vanilla
> 5 eggs
> 3 cups flour, sifted
> ¼ teaspoon salt
> ½ teaspoon baking powder
> ½ cup cocoa
> 1¼ cups milk

Cream butter and shortening with sugar; add vanilla and eggs, one at a time, blending well after each is added. Sift together dry ingredients; blend into creamed mixture alternately with milk. Pour batter into a greased and floured tube pan; bake in a 325-degree oven for 1 hour and 25 to 30 minutes or until done.

Before the days of the electric mixer and electric carpet sweeper, women had well-exercised arms from creaming butter and sugar and beating a cake with a wooden spoon. They also beat rugs, hung on the clothesline, by hand with a broom.

Baking a cake in a wood stove with its heat regulated by the kind of wood used and opening and shutting the damper seems like tediousness without equal. The wood stove was a convenience compared to the fireplace where a poundcake in a heavy pan with legs and lid baked in the ashes with hot coals on the lid.

It was like watching a show when our old cook made a cake. First, with a bowl in her lap, she creamed butter and sugar with her fingers until not one grain of sugar was felt. She beat batter with the rhythm of a locomotive. If bits of the baked cake stuck to the pan, she scraped them up and patched the cake back to perfection.

1-2-3-4 Cake

3 cups flour
3 teaspoons baking powder
1 teaspoon salt
1 cup butter
2 cups sugar
1 teaspoon vanilla
4 eggs
1 cup milk

Sift flour once, measure then sift two additional times
with baking powder and salt. Cream butter with sugar
and vanilla; add eggs, one at a time, beating
thoroughly after each is added. Add flour mixture
alternately with milk, beginning and ending with flour.
Pour into 3 greased and floured 8-inch layer pans;
bake in a 375-degree oven for 25 minutes or until cake
tests done. Turn out on racks; cool, frost as desired.

Fresh Coconut Cake

3 layers 1-2-3-4 or hot milk cake
3 tablespoons coconut milk
1½ recipes 7-minute frosting (recipe, page 228)
1 fresh coconut, grated

To obtain coconut milk, poke holes in 3 soft spots in
end of coconut; allow milk to drain out. Dribble 1
tablespoon milk evenly over each warm cake layer.
To prepare coconut, crack into pieces with a hammer.
Place cracked pieces in shallow pan; heat in a
375-degree oven for 10 minutes. Remove shell; peel
off brown portion. Grate meat in electric blender.
Use a portion of grated coconut on frosting between
layers; pat remainder on sides and top of cake.

Snow White Coconut Cake

⅔ cup vegetable shortening
2 cups sugar
3 cups cake flour
½ teaspoon salt
3 teaspoons baking powder
1 cup warm water
1 teaspoon orange extract
8 egg whites
Double recipe boiled white frosting (recipe, page 228)
1 fresh coconut, grated

Sift flour before measuring. Sift three additional times with salt and baking powder. Cream shortening and 1½ cups of the sugar until light and fluffy. Add warm water, ¼ cup at a time. Add extract. Beat egg whites until foamy. Add ½ cup of the sugar gradually and continue beating until stiff. Add flour to creamed mixture alternately with egg whites. Blend until smooth. Pour into 3 greased and floured 10-inch cake pans. Bake in a 350-degree oven for 15 minutes, then increase heat to 375 degrees and bake until done, about 10 to 15 minutes longer. Turn out on racks; cool. Frost with white frosting, sprinkling a small portion of coconut between layers. Pat remainder of coconut on sides and top.

Hot Milk Cake

> 4 large or 5 medium eggs
> 2 cups sugar
> 2 cups flour
> 1 teaspoon baking powder
> ¼ teaspoon salt
> ¼ pound butter
> 1 cup milk

Beat eggs until very fluffy; begin adding sugar, a small amount at a time, and continue to beat until all the sugar is dissolved. Sift together flour, baking powder, and salt; add all at one time to egg mixture and beat only until flour is mixed well. In a saucepan, heat together butter and milk to the point that a finger can be held in the mixture for a second; add at one time to egg mixture and beat only until well mixed. Pour at once into 3 greased (not floured) 9-inch cake pans with a circle of waxed paper in the bottom of each. Bake in a 350-degree oven for 25 minutes or until cake tests done. Turn out on racks and remove waxed paper. For a more moist cake, store layers while still warm with a piece of waxed paper between each in cake box with cover. Makes 3 9-inch layers. Frost as desired.

Seven-Up Cake

The "Uncola" was first introduced as "Bib Label Lithiated Lemon Lime Soda" in October, 1929. This cake made with it has the taste and texture of old-fashioned cakes.

> 1 cup butter
> ½ cup shortening
> 2 cups sugar
> 1 cup eggs, 4 to 5
> 3 cups flour, sifted
> 1 teaspoon vanilla
> 1 teaspoon lemon extract
> 7 ounces Seven-Up

Cream butter, shortening, and sugar together. Add eggs and beat. Add flour alternately with extracts and Seven-Up. Pour into a large greased and floured tube pan. Bake at 325 degrees for 1 hour and 10 minutes or until done.

Rum Cake

2 cups flour, sifted
½ teaspoon salt
½ teaspoon baking powder
1 cup plus 2 tablespoons butter
2⅔ cups sugar
2 tablespoons plus 1 teaspoon rum flavoring
5 eggs, beaten
⅔ cup pecans, finely chopped
1 cup water, boiling

Sift together flour, salt, and baking powder. Cream 1 cup butter, gradually adding 1⅔ cups sugar; continue creaming with the addition of 1 teaspoon rum flavoring until light and fluffy. Add eggs, blend well but do not overbeat. Gently blend in dry ingredients. Meanwhile, line a greased and floured medium-size tube pan with brown paper; coat bottom with 2 tablespoons butter, sprinkle pecans over butter. Spoon batter carefully over pecans. Bake in a 325-degree oven for 1 hour or until done. Meanwhile, make syrup by adding 1 cup sugar to boiling water; boil for 5 minutes. Remove from heat; add 2 tablespoons rum flavoring. When cake is done, remove from oven; immediately pour hot syrup over hot cake. Let stand in pan until cool; when cool, turn out and peel off paper.

Atlanta Lane Cake

1 cup butter or margarine
2 cups sugar
3½ cups cake flour, sifted
2 teaspoons baking powder
½ teaspoon salt
1 cup milk
1 teaspoon vanilla
8 egg whites, stiffly beaten

Cream butter and sugar together until light and fluffy. Sift together dry ingredients and add to creamed mixture alternately with milk and vanilla, beginning and ending with dry ingredients. Fold in egg whites. Pour into 3 8-inch layer cake pans which have been greased and floured and the bottoms lined with greased and floured brown paper. Bake in a 375-degree oven for 25 to 30 minutes or until cake tests done. Turn out on racks to cool. When cool, fill and top with Lane filling (recipe below).

Lane Filling

½ cup buttter or margarine
1 cup sugar
8 egg yolks
1 cup seeded raisins, chopped
1 cup nuts, chopped
2 teaspoons brandy or rum extract

Cream butter and sugar together. Beat egg yolks and add. Cook over hot water, stirring, until thick. Add remaining ingredients. Cool. Spread between layers and on top of cake.

Boiled Raisin Cake

1½ cups seeded raisins
2 cups water
½ cup shortening
¾ cup sugar
1 egg
1½ cups flour, sifted
1 teaspoon baking soda
½ teaspoon ground cloves
½ teaspoon nutmeg
¼ teaspoon allspice
½ teaspoon salt
1 cup pecans, chopped

Simmer raisins in water for 20 minutes; drain, reserving ¾ cup liquid. Cream shortening and sugar; add egg, and blend thoroughly. Sift together flour, baking soda, spices, and salt; add to creamed mixture alternately with cooled, reserved liquid. Stir in raisins and nuts. Pour into 2 greased and floured 9-inch layer pans; bake in a 350-degree oven for 25 minutes or until done. Turn out on racks to cool. Frost with butter frosting (recipe, page 225).

Ambrosia Cake

3 cups flour
2 teaspoons baking soda
1 teaspoon cinnamon
1 teaspoon cloves
½ cup butter
2 cups sugar
3 eggs
1 cup buttermilk
2 tablespoons cocoa
½ cup water, boiling
1 apple, peeled and shredded

Sift together flour, baking soda, cinnamon, and cloves.
Cream together butter and sugar; add eggs, one at a
time, beating well after each is added. Add sifted dry
ingredients alternately with buttermilk and cocoa
dissolved in boiling water. Fold in apple; pour into
3 greased and floured 9-inch layer cake pans. Bake in a
350-degree oven for 25 minutes or until cake tests
done. Turn out on racks to cool; spread filling (recipe
below) between layers and on top.

Ambrosia Filling

Ground meat of 1 fresh coconut
Grated rind and diced pulp of 1 large orange
1 cup raisins, ground
1 cup pecans, chopped
1 cup crushed pineapple, well drained
1 teaspoon vanilla
3 cups sugar
2 cups milk
¼ pound butter or margarine
1/16 teaspoon baking soda
1 teaspoon baking powder

Combine coconut, orange rind and pulp, raisins,
pecans, pineapple, and vanilla; set aside. In top of
double boiler or other deep pan, combine sugar, milk,
butter; stir to dissolve sugar, then cook, without
stirring, to 232 degrees or until a small amount forms
a soft ball in cold water. Remove from heat; add
baking soda and baking powder. Pour immediately into
a large bowl; beat with electric mixer until mixture
begins to thicken, mix in coconut mixture. Spread
between layers and on top.

Classic Spice Cake

In Summit, N.J., Mrs. Helen Bender was famous for thirty years as a music teacher and a cake baker. She baked a great variety of cakes to serve after Sunday afternoon musicales. Spice cake was one of her favorites. This one has old-fashioned taste and texture.

- ½ pound butter
- ½ cup shortening
- 3 cups sugar
- 5 eggs
- 3 cups flour, sifted
- ½ teaspoon mace
- ½ teaspoon allspice
- ¼ teaspoon nutmeg
- ½ teaspoon cloves
- ½ teaspoon salt
- ½ teaspoon baking powder
- 1 cup plus 2 tablespoons milk
- ½ teaspoon vanilla

Cream butter, shortening, and sugar until light and fluffy. Add eggs, one at a time, and continue to cream. Sift together twice the flour, spices, salt, and baking powder. Add to creamed mixture alternately with milk. Add vanilla. Turn into a large greased and floured tube pan. Bake in a 325-degree oven for 1 hour and 15 minutes or until cake tests done.

Applesauce Fruit Cake

- 3 cups flour, sifted
- 1 15-ounce box seedless raisins
- 1 pound candied mixed fruits, diced
- 1 cup candied cherries, halved
- ½ pound pitted dates, diced
- 4 cups pecans, broken
- 2 cups applesauce
- 1 teaspoon baking soda
- 1 cup butter or margarine
- 2 cups sugar
- 3 eggs
- 1 teaspoon nutmeg
- 1 teaspoon cloves
- 1 teaspoon cinnamon
- 1 teaspoon salt

Sift half of the flour over the raisins, mixed fruits, cherries, dates, and pecans. Stir baking soda into applesauce. Cream together butter and sugar; blend in eggs. Sift together remaining flour, spices, and salt; add to creamed mixture. Blend in fruits alternately with applesauce. Pour into greased tube pan lined with greased and floured brown paper. Bake in a 300-degree oven for 3 hours or until done. Cool in pan.

Date Pecan Cake

1 cup flour
1 teaspoon baking powder
⅛ teaspoon salt
1 cup sugar
1 pound dates, diced
1 heaping quart pecan halves
½ pound butter, melted
1 teaspoon vanilla
4 eggs, separated

Sift flour, baking powder, salt, and sugar over dates and pecans; mix in butter and vanilla. Beat egg yolks; add and mix well. Beat egg whites until stiff; fold in gently. Pour into a greased tube pan lined with greased and floured brown paper. Bake at 275 degrees for 1 hour and 15 minutes or until done. Cool in pan.

Carrot Cake

1 cup margarine
2 cups sugar
4 eggs
1½ cups raw carrots, grated
⅔ cup pecans, chopped
2½ cups flour, sifted
4½ teaspoons baking powder
1 teaspoon cinnamon
1 teaspoon mace
½ teaspoon salt
⅓ cup hot water

Cream margarine and sugar until light and fluffy; add eggs, one at a time, beating well after each is added. Stir in carrots and pecans. Sift together flour, baking powder, cinnamon, mace, and salt; add to creamed mixture alternately with hot water. Blend well. Pour into 2 greased and floured 9-inch layer cake pans. Bake in a 375-degree oven for 25 to 30

Often when there was a cake baking in the oven, Mama met us at the kitchen door. She cautioned us to tiptoe lightly through the kitchen in order not to jar the cake and make it fall.

Devil's Food Cake

2½ cups flour, sifted
1½ teaspoons baking soda
¼ teaspoon salt
½ cup cocoa
⅔ cup butter
1¾ cups sugar
1 teaspoon vanilla
3 eggs
½ cup warm water
¾ cup buttermilk

Sift together flour, baking soda, salt, and cocoa. Cream butter, sugar, and vanilla until light and fluffy; add eggs, one at a time, and continue to cream. Add flour mixture alternately with water and buttermilk, beginning and ending with flour. Turn into 3 greased and floured 9-inch layer pans; bake in a 350-degree oven for 25 minutes or until cake tests done. Turn out on racks; cool, frost with seven-minute, fudge, or caramel frosting (recipes at end of chapter).

White Chocolate Cake

¼ pound white chocolate
½ cup water, boiling
1 cup butter or margarine
2 cups sugar
4 eggs, separated
1 teaspoon vanilla
2½ cups cake flour
1 teaspoon baking soda
1 cup buttermilk
1 cup pecans, chopped
1 cup flaked coconut

Melt chocolate in water; blend, set aside to cool. Cream together butter or margarine and sugar; add egg yolks, one at a time, beating well after each is added. Add melted chocolate and vanilla. Sift together flour and baking soda; add to creamed mixture alternately with buttermilk. Fold in stiffly beaten egg whites; gently stir in pecans and coconut. Pour into 3 greased and floured 9-inch layer cake pans; bake in a 350-degree oven for 20 minutes or until cake tests done. Turn out, cool; frost with creamy butter frosting (recipe below).

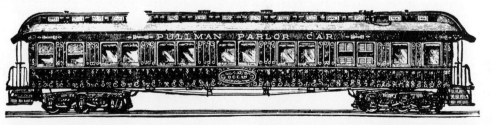

Creamy Butter Frosting

    ¾ cup butter
    1 egg
    6 cups confectioners' sugar, sifted
    2 teaspoons vanilla
    2 to 3 tablespoons cream or evaporated milk

Blend butter and egg thoroughly; continue beating,
adding sugar gradually. Add vanilla and sufficient
cream or milk to make mixture the proper spreading
consistency. Enough for tops and sides of three 9-inch
layers.

Gingerbread

    1 cup shortening or salad oil
    1 cup dark brown sugar, packed
    1 cup dark molasses
    1 tablespoon ground ginger
    1 teaspoon cinnamon
    ½ teaspoon nutmeg
    3½ cups flour
    2 teaspoons baking soda
    ½ teaspoon salt
    1 cup buttermilk

Put shortening or salad oil, sugar, molasses, and spices
in a bowl. Beat well until syrupy. Sift together flour,
baking soda, and salt and add to first mixture
alternately with buttermilk. Put into a greased pan,
8 by 12 inches and 2 inches deep. Bake at 325 degrees
for 40 minutes or until done.

Jelly Roll

1 cup cake flour, sifted
1 teaspoon baking powder
¼ teaspoon salt
3 eggs, separated
1 cup granulated sugar
3 tablespoons hot water
1 teaspoon lemon flavoring
¼ cup confectioners' sugar
1 10-ounce jar red jelly

Sift together flour, baking powder, and salt. Beat egg whites until stiff, gradually beating in ½ cup sugar. To egg yolks, add hot water and flavoring; beat until very light, gradually beating in remaining granulated sugar. Sift dry ingredients over egg yolk mixture; mix gently, then fold in beaten egg whites until blended. Pour into ungreased 9½- by 13-inch baking pan one inch deep. Bake in a 325-degree oven 30 minutes or until cake springs back when touched. Immediately turn out cake on cloth sprinkled with half the confectioners' sugar; spread quickly with jelly and roll up the short side of the cake and jelly. Let stand, seam side down, until cold. Sprinkle with remaining confectioners' sugar. Cut into slices. Makes 8 to 10 slices.

Cheese Cake

The cheese cake served at Lindy's on Broadway on the corner of Fifty-first Street in New York City lingers in the memory of those privileged to enjoy it. Lindy's was filled with patrons when it was open for most of this century. Damon Runyon, the famous newspaperman and writer, sat in a special spot when he was there, and set many of his stories in "Mindy's."

1¼ cups graham cracker crumbs
⅓ cup plus ½ cup butter, melted
1 tablespoon plus 1½ cups sugar
1 pound cottage cheese
1 pound cream cheese
4 eggs, beaten
Juice of ½ lemon
1 teaspoon vanilla
3 tablespoons cornstarch
3 tablespoons flour
2 cups sour cream

For crust, combine crumbs, ⅓ cup butter, and 1 tablespoon sugar; press mixture firmly on the bottom of a 9- or 10-inch spring form pan. For filling, beat cottage cheese until smooth and creamy; add cream cheese, continue beating until smooth. Add remaining ingredients; beat until light and fluffy. Spoon filling over crust; bake in a 325-degree oven for 1 hour and 20 to 25 minutes. Turn off heat; let cake stand in oven for 2 hours. Remove; chill.

Strawberry Shortcake

3 cups flour, sifted
5 teaspoons baking powder
1½ cups sugar
1 teaspoon salt
⅛ teaspoon mace
⅛ teaspoon nutmeg
½ cup shortening
1 egg, beaten
½ cup milk
3 tablespoons butter, melted
2 quarts fresh strawberries
Heavy cream

Sift together flour, baking powder, ½ cup sugar, salt, mace, and nutmeg. With pastry blender or 2 knives, cut shortening into flour mixture. Combine egg with milk; add to flour mixture. Turn out on lightly floured board and knead very lightly to form a ball. Divide ball into 2 parts. Roll out each to form a ¼-inch-thick circle. To make it easy to transfer circles to greased baking sheet, fold each one over into fourths like a handkerchief. Lift to baking sheet and unfold. Brush with melted butter. Bake in a 450-degree oven for 10 to 12 minutes or until lightly browned.

Meanwhile, cap and wash strawberries, reserving large berries for top of cake. Slightly crush remaining berries with potato masher and sweeten with remaining cup of sugar or to taste.

After the drugstore started carrying ice cream, the children took turns going for the ice cream for Sunday dinner. While they were gone, Mama cut the cake to serve with it.

Brush hot baked shortcakes with melted butter. Slide 1 layer onto platter. Top with half the crushed berries. Top with second layer and remaining crushed berries. Garnish with whole strawberries. To serve, cut into wedges. Pour cream over each serving. Makes 12 servings.

Seven-Minute Frosting

2 egg whites
1½ cups sugar
5 tablespoons water
2 teaspoons light corn syrup
1 teaspoon vanilla

In top of double boiler, combine egg whites, sugar, water, and corn syrup; beat until sugar is dissolved. Place over boiling water; cook, beating constantly, until frosting stands in peaks. With electric mixer, it takes 5 to 6 minutes; with egg beater, 7 minutes. Do not overcook. Remove from heat; add vanilla, beat until thick enough to spread. Sufficient for two 9-inch layers.

Boiled White Frosting

1½ cups sugar
2 tablespoons light corn syrup
½ cup water
2 egg whites
1 teaspoon vanilla

In saucepan, combine sugar, syrup, and water; boil until the mixture forms a thread when dripped from a spoon, or to 238 degrees. Meanwhile, beat egg whites until stiff, but not dry. Add hot syrup gradually to egg whites, beating vigorously. Add vanilla; continue to beat until mixture is of proper consistency. Spread on cake. Sufficient for a 2-layer cake.

Caramel Frosting

1 cup buttermilk
2 cups granulated sugar
1 teaspoon baking soda
½ cup butter or margarine
1 teaspoon vanilla
Heavy cream

In a large kettle, combine buttermilk, sugar, baking soda, and butter. Stir mixture over moderate heat until sugar is dissolved. Bring to a boil, cover; lower heat, and boil for 3 minutes. Uncover, insert candy thermometer, and boil to the soft ball stage (238 degrees), stirring. Remove from heat; add vanilla, beat until mixture becomes fudge-like. Beat in heavy cream, a little at a time, until frosting is of spreading consistency. Enough for two 8-inch layers.

Fudge Frosting

4 1-ounce squares unsweetened chocolate
2 cups sugar
1 cup heavy cream
4 tablespoons butter or margarine
1 teaspoon vanilla

In saucepan, combine chocolate, sugar, and cream;
stir over moderate heat until the sugar is dissolved.
Continue cooking slowly, without stirring, to the soft
ball stage (238 degrees). Remove from heat; add butter
and vanilla. Beat until creamy and of spreading
consistency; spread on cake. Sufficient to frost and
fill three 8-inch layers.

Seafoam Frosting

2 egg whites
1½ cups brown sugar, packed
⅓ cup water
Dash of salt
⅛ teaspoon cream of tartar
1 teaspoon vanilla

Combine all ingredients, except vanilla, in top of
double boiler over boiling water; beat with electric
beater until mixture stands in soft peaks, about 7
minutes. Remove from water; add vanilla, continue
beating until slightly cooled. Makes enough for filling
and frosting two 8- or 9-inch layers.

For white frosting our cook beat
egg whites with a wire whisk.
When the hot syrup was ready, she
poured it in a steady stream into
the beaten whites, beating all the
time until the mixture was like a
white cloud.

Mother stacked frosting between
layers of cake as resolutely as a
brick mason spreading mortar.
On Saturday afternoon I would
sneak into the dining room to
look at the cakes on the sideboard.
They looked so high to me as a
little child that I thought I needed
a stepladder to reach the top.

CHAPTER 11

Pies A-Plenty

Our foremothers spent hours rolling pie crusts and crimping the edges with three fingers to make fluted rims. The rolling pin, which Maggie frequently used to threaten her husband Jiggs in the comic strip, has also seen more pie crusts than we should be allowed to think about. With frozen pie shells and pies, however, the rolling pin may well go the way of the whooping crane.

Whatever fruit trees, bushes, vines, and bogs have yielded, cooks have put in a crust or between crusts. Fruit pies come from the oven with a topping of streusel crumbs (a mixture of sugar, flour, and butter), pastry woven into a lattice design, and top crusts.

Crusts with custard and cream fillings, coconut and chess, brown sugar and molasses, jelly and mince have also lined sideboards of many households through the years. Creamy lemon, lime, banana, coconut, and chocolate fillings come beneath billowing meringues. Chiffon pies became popular after automatic refrigerators replaced the icebox.

Potatoes also go into pies. Mashed white potatoes combined with sugar, eggs, and vanilla and dusted with nutmeg make a potato custard pie. A sweet potato custard pie, with more spices, is made the same way.

Pie safes or chests, with doors covered with tin punched with nails to make holes to allow air to circulate, were used in some households. Some tin panels were punched in fancy designs, such as birds in flight. The safe was used to store pies when a number were baked at a time, for instance, on Saturday for the weekend. In the West, the chuck wagon was sometimes called the pie box.

PIE À LA MODE

Apple pie à la Mode originated in Cambridge, N.Y., a small community in the Adirondack foothills. In 1896, a music teacher, Professor Charles Watson Townsend, regularly concluded his dinners at the Hotel Cambridge with apple pie and ice cream. When Mrs. Berry Hall, an employee at the hotel, first saw the creation, she exclaimed, "Pie à la Mode." "A la Mode" was widely used in the 1890s to describe anything extremely fashionable. Later Townsend asked for pie à la Mode at Delmonico's in New York City. They didn't have it, but soon put it on the menu.

Every afternoon after school, in the days before schools had cafeterias, the children headed for the warming closet on top of the wood stove, where there was always some kind of pie.

Pastry

This basic pastry recipe can be used for all the pies that follow, unless otherwise specified.

3 cups flour, sifted
1 teaspoon salt
1 cup lard
1 egg
1 teaspoon vinegar
5 tablespoons ice water

Sift together flour and salt; cut in lard until mixture resembles cornmeal. Beat together egg, vinegar, and water; add to flour mixture. Blend thoroughly. Turn out on wax paper; press into a ball. Roll out thinly on lightly floured board or between two sheets of wax paper. Makes a double-crust 9-inch pie plus a single pie shell.

Apple Pie

1 cup brown sugar, packed
2 tablespoons flour
1/8 teaspoon salt
1 1/2 teaspoons cinnamon
1/4 teaspoon nutmeg
1/4 teaspoon mace
1 tablespoon lemon rind, grated
7 tart apples, peeled and cored
2 tablespoons butter or margarine
1 egg white, slightly beaten
Pastry for double-crust 9-inch pie, unbaked

Combine sugar, flour, salt, spices, and lemon rind; slice apples into mixture, toss to coat. Heap mixture in pastry shell; dot with butter. Top with another layer of pastry, gashed to allow steam to escape; crimp or flute edges to seal. Brush top with egg white. Bake in a 450-degree oven for 10 minutes; lower heat to 350 degrees, and bake for 40 minutes or until done.

French Apple Pie

1/2 cup sugar
1/8 teaspoon salt
2 tablespoons flour
1/2 teaspoon cinnamon
1/8 teaspoon nutmeg
1 teaspoon lemon rind, grated
2 1/2 cups tart apples, sliced
1/2 cup raisins
Juice of 1/2 lemon
1/2 cup confectioners' sugar
2 tablespoons butter
Hot water
Pastry for double-crust 8-inch pie, unbaked

Blend sugar, salt, flour, cinnamon, nutmeg, and lemon rind; sprinkle ⅓ of the mixture in pastry shell. Combine apples and raisins; fill pie. Sprinkle remaining sugar mixture and lemon juice over apples. Cover with another layer of pastry, gashed to allow steam to escape. Bake in a 450-degree oven for 10 minutes; reduce temperature to 350 degrees, and bake 30 minutes longer or until done. Meanwhile, blend confectioners' sugar and butter; add 1 tablespoon hot water or enough to make the mixture of spreading consistency. Spread frosting over top of hot pie.

Apple Pie Without Apples

In the forties a recipe appeared for apple pie without apples. It seems slightly ridiculous, except perhaps for an April Fool. Here is the recipe for the record.

> 2 cups water
> 1¼ cups sugar
> 2 teaspoons cream of tartar
> 18 whole Ritz crackers
> 2 tablespoons butter
> ¼ teaspoon cinnamon
> 1 8-inch pastry shell, unbaked

Bring water, sugar, and cream of tartar to a boil. Drop in crackers; continue to boil for 10 minutes, do not stir. Carefully pour into pastry shell; dot with butter, sprinkle with cinnamon. Bake in 400-degree oven for 20 minutes or until brown.

In the spring every day we looked at the apple tree in the back of the house. Once the pretty little apple blossoms passed the danger of damage by frost, little green apples began to form. As soon as the apples were large enough, we had the first green apple pie of the season.

Peach Crumble Pie

> 6 cups fresh peaches, peeled and sliced
> 1 10-inch pastry shell 2 inches deep, unbaked
> 1½ cups sugar
> 3 tablespoons cornstarch
> ⅛ teaspoon salt
> 1 egg, beaten
> ½ teaspoon almond flavoring
> ½ cup flour
> ¼ cup butter or margarine

Place peaches in pastry shell. Blend 1 cup sugar, cornstarch, and salt; add egg and flavoring and pour over peaches. Combine flour and remaining sugar; cut in butter until fine crumbs are formed. Sprinkle crumb mixture over peaches. Bake in a 375-degree oven for 30 minutes or until golden brown.

Peach Upside Down Pie

1 12-inch square aluminum foil
2 tablespoons butter, soft
⅔ cup toasted almonds or pecan halves
9 tablespoons brown sugar
Pastry for double-crust 9-inch pie, unbaked
5 cups (about 8 medium) fresh peaches,
    peeled and sliced
¾ cup granulated sugar
2 tablespoons quick-cooking tapioca
½ teaspoon nutmeg
¼ teaspoon cinnamon
1 egg white, slightly beaten

Line a 9-inch pie pan with foil; let excess foil overhang edge. Spread butter on bottom of foil; press nuts and 5 tablespoons brown sugar into butter. Fit a layer of pastry over nuts and brown sugar in pie pan. Mix peaches with granulated sugar, 4 tablespoons brown sugar, tapioca, and spices; pour into pastry shell. Cover with another layer of pastry, pricked to allow steam to escape; seal and flute edges. Brush with egg white. Bake in 450-degree oven for 10 minutes; lower heat to 375 degrees, and bake 35 to 40 minutes longer or until done. Turn out upside down.

Deep Dish Peach Pie

1 tablespoon flour
1 cup sugar
8 large peaches, peeled and sliced
½ teaspoon nutmeg
¼ cup butter
Pastry for double-crust pie 9-inch pie
    rolled ⅛-inch thick
Vanilla ice cream or whipped cream

Cut pastry into strips 1-inch wide. In bottom of deep 9-inch-square baking dish, crisscross ⅓ of the pastry strips. Blend flour and 1 tablespoon sugar; sprinkle over strips. Add half the peaches; sprinkle with half of remaining sugar. Dot with half the butter. Crisscross with another third of pastry strips. Add remaining peaches and sugar, sprinkle with nutmeg, dot with remaining butter. Crisscross with remaining pastry strips. Bake in a 450-degree oven for 15 minutes; reduce temperature to 350 degrees, and bake 20 minutes longer. Serve warm with scoops of ice cream or mounds of whipped cream. Makes 8 to 10 servings.

Fresh Strawberry Pie

2 cups flour, sifted
1 cup shortening
1 teaspoon salt
2 tablespoons cold water
1 cup fresh strawberries, crushed
1 cup sugar
1 tablespoon cornstarch
1 quart fresh whole strawberries, washed and
capped
Whipped cream

For pastry, cut shortening into flour and salt. Add cold water to flour mixture, stirring quickly until soft dough is formed. Roll out on lightly floured board to ¼-inch thickness. Fit into 10-inch pie pan. Bake at 425 degrees for 10 minutes or until golden brown. Mix crushed strawberries with sugar and cornstarch. Cook, stirring, until liquid is clear and transparent. Fill pie shell with whole strawberries, points up. Pour hot berry syrup over the berries. Chill. Serve with whipped cream.

Candied Rhubarb Pie

1¾ cups sugar
½ cup plus 3 tablespoons flour
⅜ teaspoon salt
¼ cup butter or margarine
2 tablespoons butter or margarine, melted
1 egg, beaten
4 cups fresh rhubarb, cut in slices about
½-inch thick
1 9-inch pastry shell, unbaked

Blend ½ cup sugar, ½ cup flour, and ⅛ teaspoon salt for the topping. Cut in ¼ cup butter until mixture is like coarse cornmeal. Set aside while making pie. Combine remaining 1¼ cups sugar, 3 tablespoons flour, ¼ teaspoon salt, melted butter, egg, and rhubarb, and turn into pastry shell. Sprinkle with topping. Bake at 425 degrees for about 40 minutes or until filling bubbles up and pastry is brown. If topping and pastry brown too fast, reduce heat to 375 degrees to complete cooking.

Pumpkin Crumble Pie

1½ cups pumpkin, cooked and mashed
    (method below)
¼ cup flour
1 cup granulated sugar
½ teaspoon salt
1 teaspoon cinnamon
½ teaspoon cloves
½ teaspoon nutmeg
2 eggs, beaten
1½ cups milk
6 tablespoons butter
½ teaspoon vanilla
¼ cup brown sugar
½ cup pecans, chopped
1 9-inch pastry shell, baked

In top of double boiler, combine pumpkin, flour,
granulated sugar, salt, spices, eggs, and milk; cook over
boiling water, stirring, until thick. Add 2 tablespoons
butter and vanilla; stir until butter is melted and
blended. Pour mixture into baked pastry shell; top
with mixture of remaining 4 tablespoons butter,
brown sugar, and pecans. Bake in a 350-degree oven
for 10 to 15 minutes or until topping is golden brown.

Baked Pumpkin

For this easy way to cook pumpkin, cut a medium-sized pumpkin into two halves, cutting from stem end down; scoop out seeds and membrane and discard. Place halves, cut sides down, in a shallow baking pan which contains ¼ inch water. Bake in a 300-degree oven for 1 hour or until pumpkin pulp is easily scooped out with a spoon; scoop out pulp and mash.

Pumpkin Pie

3 eggs
3 cups pumpkin, cooked and mashed
1½ cups brown sugar
2 teaspoons cinnamon
1½ teaspoons ginger
¼ teaspoon salt
2 8-inch pastry shells, unbaked

In a large bowl, beat eggs until slightly frothy; add pumpkin, sugar, spices, and salt. Mix thoroughly; pour into pastry shells. Bake in a 350-degree oven for 35 to 40 minutes or until firm.

Raisin or Funeral Pie

An Amish custom was to include raisin pie in a funeral supper, probably because of the somber color of the pie. The pie is not restricted to funeral food. It was a great favorite earlier in the century.

1 cup sugar
3 tablespoons flour
Pinch of salt
1 cup water, boiling
1½ cups seedless raisins
1 tablespoon lemon rind, grated
¼ cup lemon juice
1 tablespoon butter
1 9-inch pastry shell, unbaked

Additional Pastry

Combine sugar, flour, and salt. Add boiling water slowly, stirring constantly. Cook in top of double boiler, stirring over hot water until thick and clear. Add raisins, lemon rind and juice, and butter. Heat, and pour into pastry-lined pan. Cover with strips of pastry to make a lattice crust. Bake at 425 degrees for about 25 minutes or until pastry is browned.

Japanese Fruit Pie

¾ stick margarine, melted
1 cup sugar
⅛ teaspoon salt
2 eggs, beaten
½ cup flaked coconut
½ cup golden raisins
½ cup pecans, broken
1 teaspoon vinegar
1 9-inch pastry shell, unbaked

Blend margarine, sugar, salt, eggs, coconut, raisins, pecans, and vinegar; pour into pastry shell. Bake in a 350-degree oven for 40 minutes or until golden brown and set. Serve warm or cold.

Egg Custard Pie

Baking an egg mixture at a high temperature is contrary to the usual rule of lower temperatures but, for this pie, it works perfectly, producing custard smooth in texture. An added value over the low temperature method is that the top browns beautifully.

2 eggs
¼ cup plus 2 tablespoons sugar
1 teaspoon vanilla
1½ cups milk, scalded
¼ teaspoon nutmeg
1 9-inch pastry shell, unbaked

Beat eggs with egg beater until thoroughly mixed, but not until fluffy. Blend in sugar, vanilla, and hot milk; pour into pastry. Bake on bottom shelf of a 450-degree oven for 20 minutes or until only slightly shaky. Remove from oven. Cool before serving.

Devastating Chocolate Fudge Pie

 ½ cup margarine
 3 1-ounce squares unsweetened chocolate
 4 eggs
 3 tablespoons light corn syrup
 1½ cups granulated sugar
 ¼ teaspoon salt
 1 teaspoon vanilla extract
 1 9-inch pastry shell, unbaked

In top of double boiler over boiling water, heat margarine and chocolate, stirring, until melted and blended; allow to cool slightly. Beat eggs; blend in syrup, sugar, salt, and vanilla. Add chocolate mixture; blend well. Pour mixture into pastry shell. Bake at 400 degrees for 5 minutes, reduce temperature to 350 degrees. Continue baking for 30 minutes or until, when shaken, pie is almost, but not quite, firm.

Lemon Meringue Pie

 1 9-inch pie shell, baked and cooled
 ½ cup cornstarch
 1½ cups plus ⅓ cup water
 1½ cups sugar
 ¼ teaspoon salt
 3 egg yolks
 ½ cup lemon juice
 3 tablespoons margarine
 1 teaspoon lemon rind, grated
 Meringue (recipe below)

Blend cornstarch and ⅓ cup water until smooth. In heavy saucepan or skillet, combine 1½ cups water, sugar, and salt; bring to a boil, stirring to dissolve sugar. Add cornstarch mixture; heat, stirring, until smooth and thick. Beat egg yolks and lemon juice; add to hot mixture. Cook, stirring, for 1 minute. Remove from heat; add margarine and lemon. Stir to blend. Cover with wax paper; let stand until lukewarm. Top with meringue swirled to cover filling completely. Bake in a 325-degree oven for 15 minutes or until lightly browned. Serve meringue pie the day it is baked, preferably within 4 to 5 hours.

Meringue

 5 egg whites
 10 tablespoons sugar
 1 teaspoon lemon rind, grated

Beat egg whites until foamy; add sugar slowly, continuing to beat until stiff. Add lemon rind. Spread on pie.

Apple Kuchen

1 recipe muerbe teig (recipe below)
3 cups tart apples, peeled and thinly sliced
¼ cup sugar
½ teaspoon cinnamon
2 tablespoons butter, melted
1 egg yolk
3 tablespoons cream
Whipped cream or vanilla ice cream

Arrange apple slices in pastry. Combine sugar, cinnamon, and butter; sprinkle over apples. Beat egg yolk and cream; pour over apples. Bake in a 425-degree oven for 20 minutes or until crust is baked and apples are soft. Serve with whipped cream or vanilla ice cream.

Muerbe Teig

½ cup butter
1½ cups flour
1 egg yolk
2 tablespoons water
Grated rind and juice of ½ lemon
2 tablespoons sugar

Cut butter into flour. Beat egg yolk with water; add to flour mixture with lemon rind and juice. Blend. Pat into bottom and up sides of 9-inch pie pan. Fill with apple filling. Bake in a 425-degree oven for 20 minutes or until done.

Shoofly Pie

3/4 cup flour, sifted
1/2 cup light brown sugar, packed
1/8 teaspoon nutmeg
1/8 teaspoon ginger
1/8 teaspoon cloves
1/2 teaspoon cinnamon
1/4 teaspoon salt
2 tablespoons shortening
1 egg yolk, beaten
1/3 cup molasses
1 1/2 teaspoons baking soda
2/3 cup water, boiling
1 8-inch pastry shell, unbaked

Sift together flour, sugar, spices, and salt; cut in shortening until mixture resembles cornmeal. Combine egg yolk, molasses, and baking soda dissolved in boiling water. In pastry shell, place flour mixture and molasses mixture in layers, having flour as base and topping. Bake in a 450-degree oven for 10 minutes; reduce temperature to 350 degrees, and bake 15 minutes longer or until pie is firm.

Brown Sugar Pie

1/2 cup butter
2 cups brown sugar, packed
3 eggs
1 teaspoon vanilla
1 9-inch pastry shell, unbaked

Cream butter and sugar together; add eggs, one at a time, and blend well after each is added; do not beat. Stir in vanilla. Pour into pastry shell. Bake at 450 degrees for 5 minutes; reduce temperature to 325 degrees, and bake 25 minutes longer or until filling is firm.

Chess Tarts

A chess tart is similar to pecan pie, minus the pecans. The name may have originated in Chester, England, or from fillings called "cheese." There is a lemon filling which is called lemon cheese. Another speculation comes from the answer a cook gave when asked what she put in the pie. She replied, "Anything in my chest." (Bins and cabinets used for storing food were once called chests.) Another cook called what she baked "jes' pie."

¼ cup butter
1½ cups brown sugar, packed
1 tablespoon flour
2 eggs, lightly beaten
2 tablespoons water
1 teaspoon vanilla or lemon flavoring
Pastry for double crust pie, unbaked

Cream butter with sugar and flour; blend in eggs, water, and flavoring. Do not beat; a light and fluffy mixture will not produce the desired texture. Pour into 12 to 14 pastry-lined tart pans, filling each ⅔ full. Bake in 375-degree oven for 25 minutes or until filling is firm and pastry is lightly browned.

Coconut Macaroon Pie

2 eggs
1½ cups sugar
½ teaspoon salt
½ cup butter
¼ cup flour
½ cup milk
1 teaspoon vanilla
1½ cups shredded coconut
1 9-inch pastry shell, unbaked

Beat eggs; add sugar gradually, and beat until lemon colored. Add salt, butter, and flour; blend well. Add milk, vanilla, and 1 cup coconut. Pour into pastry shell, and sprinkle with remaining coconut. Bake in a 325-degree oven for 1 hour or until top is browned.

CHAPTER 12
The Cooky Jar

If the cookies in a cooky jar, also called the cooky crock, could talk the way objects talk in animated cartoons they would speak most of the languages of the world. *Pfeffernusse, springerle, lebkuchen, Berliner krantzer, klejner, brune kager, sandkager, kaerlighedskranse, pepparkakor, bizcochos, kourabiedes,* and *Florentines* may sound like words in a world atlas, but they are simply names of cookies. Settlers brought their cooky recipes, cutters, and molds to this country, and their use has continued down through generations who have adapted the old ways to modern equipment and ingredients. A cooky called petticoat tails, for instance, originated in France. When a French princess married an English prince, she took her French chef to England. He made a butter cooky called *petits gateaux tailes*, a favorite of the princess. Spoken in rapid French, the English thought the name was petticoat tails, which is what the cookies are called to this day in England.

Some of the old cooky recipes are as difficult to follow as the names are to pronounce. Directions such as "flavor to taste" and flour to make a "nice" dough are common in the old recipes.

A special cooky, which America took to its heart instantly, is the Toll House cooky developed by Ruth Wakefield at her inn called Toll House in Wakefield, Mass. She started serving her customers a crisp little cooky which contained bits of semi-sweet chocolate chipped from bars. The cookies led to a new product, chocolate morsels or bits.

Sugar Cookies

½ cup shortening
1 cup butter or margarine
2 cups brown sugar, packed
1 cup plus 2 tablespoons granulated sugar
3 eggs
1 teaspoon baking soda
3 tablespoons buttermilk
2 tablespoons vanilla
½ teaspoon salt
1 tablespoon baking powder
6½ cups flour, approximate

Cream shortening, butter or margarine, brown sugar, and 1 cup granulated sugar. Blend in eggs. Dissolve baking soda in buttermilk; add with vanilla to creamed mixture. Sift salt and baking powder with 2 cups flour; add to creamed mixture with sufficient additional flour to make a soft dough. Roll dough at once or chill. Roll out thinly on lightly floured board. Cut with cooky cutters. Sprinkle lightly with sugar. Bake on lightly greased baking sheets in a 325-degree oven for about 5 minutes or just until cookies begin to brown. Makes about 7 dozen.

Tea Cakes

1¼ pounds butter
4½ cups sugar
3 eggs
1 tablespoon water, boiling
8 cups flour
Pinch of salt
½ teaspoon baking powder
1 teaspoon mace

Cream butter and 4 cups sugar together until light and fluffy. Add eggs, one at a time, and continue beating. Add boiling water. Blend in flour, salt, and baking powder. Blend well. Chill dough. Roll out thinly on lightly floured board. Sprinkle tops lightly with mixture of remaining ½ cup sugar and mace. Bake on ungreased baking sheets in a 350-degree oven for 10 minutes or until lightly browned. Run knife under cookies immediately when they come from the oven. Makes about 12 dozen.

Sugar Squares

    1 cup butter or margarine
    1¼ cups sugar
    2 eggs
    2 cups flour, sifted
    ¼ teaspoon baking soda
    ¼ teaspoon salt
    2 tablespoons buttermilk

Cream butter with 1 cup sugar. Add eggs and beat until light and fluffy. Sift together flour, baking soda and salt; blend into creamed mixture with buttermilk. Pour batter one inch deep in a greased 15- by 10-inch baking pan; sprinkle with remaining sugar. Bake in 400-degree oven for 20 minutes or until golden brown. Cool and cut into squares. Makes 24.

Raisin Oatmeal Cookies

    1¾ cups flour, sifted
    1 teaspoon salt
    1 teaspoon baking soda
    1 teaspoon cinnamon
    2 cups rolled oats
    1½ cups seedless raisins
    ½ cup shortening
    1¼ cups sugar
    ½ cup molasses
    2 eggs

Sift together flour, salt, baking soda, and cinnamon. Stir in oats and raisins. Cream together shortening, sugar, molasses, and eggs. Add sifted ingredients and blend. Drop by heaping teaspoonfuls 2 inches apart on lightly oiled cooky sheet. Bake in 375-degree oven for 8 to 10 minutes or until as browned as desired. Makes 5 dozen.

Oatmeal Refrigerator Cookies

1½ cups flour
1 teaspoon salt
1 teaspoon baking soda
½ cup shortening
½ cup butter
1 cup brown sugar
1 cup granulated sugar
2 eggs
1 teaspoon vanilla
3 cups quick-cooking rolled oats

Sift together dry ingredients. Cream together shortening, butter, sugars, and eggs; add vanilla, flour mixture, and oats, and blend. Form into rolls 1½ inches in diameter, and wrap in foil. Chill several hours or overnight. To bake, cut into slices ¼-inch thick; place on ungreased baking sheets. Bake in a 325-degree oven for 10 minutes or until lightly browned.
Makes about 5 dozen.

Gingersnaps

1 cup shortening
1 cup sugar
1 cup molasses
1 teaspoon baking soda
½ cup hot water
1 teaspoon ground ginger
1 teaspoon cinnamon
1 teaspoon ground cloves
5 cups flour, approximate

Cream shortening and sugar; blend in molasses. Dissolve baking soda in hot water; add to creamed mixture. Sift spices with 1 cup flour; add to creamed mixture with sufficient flour to make a stiff dough that will roll easily. Roll out very thin on lightly floured board; cut with cooky cutters. Bake on baking sheets in a 400-degree oven for about 5 minutes. Watch to prevent burning. Makes about 5 dozen.

Gingerbread Men

    4 cups flour, sifted
    1 teaspoon salt
    1 teaspoon baking soda
    2 teaspoons baking powder
    2 teaspoons ginger
    1 teaspoon ground cloves
    1 teaspoon cinnamon
    1 teaspoon nutmeg
    1 cup shortening
    1 cup sugar
    1 cup molasses
    2 egg yolks
    Canned cake frosting

Sift together flour, salt, baking soda, baking powder, and spices. Cream shortening with sugar; blend in molasses and egg yolks. Mix in flour mixture. Cover; chill for several hours or overnight. Roll out small portions at a time to ¼-inch thickness between two sheets of wax paper. Cut with gingerbread man cutter. Place on ungreased baking sheets; bake in a 350-degree oven for 10 to 12 minutes or until done. Remove from oven, and after a minute or two, run a knife under cookies. Cool and decorate with cake frosting. Makes about 16 8-inch cookies.

Joe Froggers

A New England favorite

    7 cups flour, sifted
    1 tablespoon salt
    1 tablespoon ground ginger
    1 teaspoon ground cloves
    1 teaspoon nutmeg
    ½ teaspoon allspice
    ¾ cup water
    ¼ cup rum
    2 teaspoons baking soda
    2 cups dark molasses
    1 cup shortening
    2 cups sugar

Sift flour with salt and spices. Combine water and rum. Add baking soda to molasses. Cream shortening and sugar. Add sifted dry ingredients, water mixture, and molasses mixture, blending well after each addition. Chill dough, preferably overnight. Roll out to ¼-inch thickness on lightly floured board. Cut with 4-inch-round cutter. Place on greased baking sheet. Bake at 375 degrees for 10 to 12 minutes. Let stand on sheet a few minutes before removing to prevent breaking. Store in a covered cooky jar. Makes 24 5-inch cookies.

Soon after cold weather came in late autumn Grandmother had Grandfather help mix up a batch of ginger cooky dough because he had strong hands for the mixing. She kept the dough in a pan on the cold back porch and baked off it until it was gone.

Aunt Tibitha let me help make thimble cookies; she washed her silver thimble and put it on my finger and I'd press it in each cooky ball to make a dent to fill with jelly.

247

Chocolate Refrigerator Cookies

1¼ cups butter
1½ cups confectioners' sugar
1 egg
¼ teaspoon salt
3 cups cake flour, sifted
½ cup cocoa
1½ cups pecans, finely chopped
4 ounces sweet chocolate

Cream butter and sugar; add egg and mix thoroughly. Sift together salt, flour, and cocoa; blend into creamed mixture. Chill dough in refrigerator for about 1 hour. Shape into 2 long, smooth rolls, each 1½ inches in diameter; roll in nuts, pressing nuts into dough. Wrap in foil; chill overnight. Using a thin sharp knife, cut into slices ⅛-inch thick. Bake on ungreased baking sheets in a 400-degree oven for about 10 minutes or until done. Cool. Melt chocolate over hot water; spread chocolate over centers of cookies. Makes about 6 dozen.

Whoopie Pies

A pair of plump chocolate cookies put together with a creamy vanilla filling.

½ cup cocoa
⅓ cup hot water
½ cup margarine or shortening
1½ cups sugar
2 eggs
2¾ cups flour, sifted
1 teaspoon baking powder
½ cup buttermilk
1 teaspoon vanilla

Mix cocoa and hot water to make a smooth paste and set aside to cool. Cream margarine and sugar. Add eggs. Sift dry ingredients together and add to creamed mixture alternately with buttermilk. Add vanilla. Blend in cocoa paste. Drop by tablespoonfuls on greased baking sheet and bake in a 350-degree oven for 12 minutes or until done. Cool and put together in pairs, sandwich fashion, with filling (recipe below).

Filling

½ cup milk
2½ tablespoons flour
½ cup margarine
½ cup granulated sugar
½ teaspoon baking soda
1 teaspoon vanilla
3 heaping tablespoons marshmallow cream
1 cup confectioners' sugar, approximate

Blend milk and flour to make a paste; cook over medium heat, stirring, until smooth and thick. Remove from heat, cool. Add margarine, granulated sugar, soda, vanilla, and marshmallow cream; beat until light and fluffy. Stir in sufficient confectioners' sugar to make stiff enough to spread on cakes.

Chocolate Covered Cookies

1 cup flour, sifted
⅓ cup brown sugar
½ cup butter or margarine
18 maraschino cherries, drained
6 1-ounce squares semisweet chocolate, melted

Mama said store-bought cookies tasted like soap and even after there were several kinds in the store, she kept right on making her own, and said she was building memories for us children.

Combine flour and sugar; cut in butter or margarine until mixture makes coarse crumbs. Press into a greased 8-inch-square baking pan; bake in a 350-degree oven for 20 minutes or until golden brown. Cut while warm into 36 squares; top each with half a cherry, round side up. Spoon melted chocolate over each, allowing it to run off the tip of the spoon over the cherry; cool. Makes 36.

Tuffys

Also spelled toughies, which is suggestive of the somewhat chewy texture.

2 eggs
2 cups brown sugar
1 teaspoon baking soda
2 teaspoons water
1½ teaspoons nutmeg
⅛ teaspoon salt
1½ cups flour, sifted

I was too little to reach the kitchen table so I stood on a box and Grandmother gave me little scraps of cooky dough to roll with my little rolling pin.

Beat eggs until foamy; beat in brown sugar. Dissolve baking soda in water; add to egg-sugar mixture. Sift together nutmeg, salt, and flour; add to egg-sugar mixture. Blend. Drop by the teaspoonful on a greased baking sheet; bake in a 350-degree oven for 8 to 10 minutes or until tan in color. Makes about 50.
The cookies will be slightly cracked and rough on top.

Ambrosia Bars

½ cup butter
1½ cups light brown sugar, packed
1¼ cups flour, sifted
½ teaspoon salt
1 teaspoon vanilla
2 eggs, beaten
1 cup candied pineapple, finely diced
1 3½-ounce can flaked coconut

In a bowl place butter, ½ cup sugar, and 1 cup flour; mix with pastry blender or cut with 2 knives to make fine crumbs. Pat mixture evenly over the bottom of a baking pan 11 x 7 inches; bake in a 375-degree oven for 12 minutes. Combine remaining sugar, ¼ cup flour, salt, vanilla, eggs, pineapple, and coconut; mix well. Remove first portion from oven; gently spoon pineapple mixture over base. Return to oven; bake 20 minutes longer. While warm, cut into bars. Makes about 35.

Nanaimo Bars

1st layer:
½ cup butter
¼ cup sugar
⅓ cup cocoa
1 egg, beaten
1 teaspoon vanilla
2 cups graham cracker crumbs
1 cup coconut, flaked
½ cup nuts, chopped

2nd layer:
¼ cup butter
2 tablespoons instant vanilla pudding mix
3 tablespoons milk
2 cups confectioners' sugar

3rd layer:
3 squares semisweet chocolate
1 tablespoon butter

To make first layer, in a saucepan heat together butter, sugar, and cocoa, stirring until smooth and butter is melted. Add egg and vanilla and remove from heat. Add crumbs, coconut, and nuts, and spread evenly in a buttered 8- or 9-inch-square pan. Place in refrigerator For second layer, cream butter and pudding mix. Add milk and confectioners' sugar. Spread over first layer and chill until firm. For topping, melt together chocolate and butter in a small pan. Spread over second layer. Just before topping is set, cut into one-inch squares. Makes about 64.

Brownies

1 cup flour, sifted
½ teaspoon salt
½ cup butter or margarine
2 1-ounce squares unsweetened chocolate
¾ cup granulated sugar
¾ cup brown sugar, packed
2 eggs
1 teaspoon vanilla
1 cup nuts, chopped

Sift together flour and salt. Over boiling water, melt butter or margarine and chocolate; cool slightly, add sugars, and blend. Add eggs, one at a time, beating well after each is added. Add vanilla and flour; blend until smooth. Fold in nuts; pour into a greased 9-inch-square baking pan. Bake in a 325-degree oven for 30 to 35 minutes or until done; cool slightly, cut into squares. Makes 2½ dozen.

Snow Drop Cookies

Also called meringue surprises.

2 egg whites
¾ cup granulated sugar
1 cup pecans, chopped
1 6-ounce package semisweet chocolate pieces

Beat egg whites until foamy; add sugar gradually and continue beating until stiff. Gently fold in nuts and chocolate pieces; drop by the heaping teaspoonful to make little mounds on a lightly greased baking sheet. Place in a 350-degree oven; turn off heat immediately and leave cookies in the oven for 3 hours or overnight. Makes about 50.

Monkey faces, cookies with raisins for eyes and nose, came out with different, droll expressions and I liked to look at them before eating.

The broom stepped beyond its normal function by providing straws for testing cakes but also by providing a handle over which thin, brittle cookies called broomstick crunch wafers were shaped.

Chess Cookies

½ cup butter
2 cups brown sugar, packed
2 eggs
1½ cups flour, sifted
2 teaspoons baking powder
⅛ teaspoon salt
1 cup nuts, chopped
1 teaspoon vanilla

Melt butter in heavy skillet; add brown sugar, heat over low heat, stirring, until sugar is melted and bubbles. Remove from heat; cool to lukewarm. Blend in eggs, one at a time. Sift together flour, baking powder, and salt; blend into creamed mixture. Add nuts and vanilla. Pour into greased 8-inch-square baking pan; bake in 350-degree oven for 30 to 35 minutes. The cookies puff during baking and sink slightly when cool. Cut into squares. Makes 25 squares.

Kaklingen

A Dutch favorite which is not sweet.

1 pound butter
4 cups flour, sifted
½ cup very cold water
Granulated sugar

Let butter stand at room temperature for about 30 minutes to soften slightly. Cut butter into flour with pastry blender or two knives until mixture forms crumbs about the size of peas. Add water; stir with a fork as in making pastry. Press dough to make a ball; cover and chill overnight. Remove dough; let stand for 15 minutes to soften slightly. With the hands, roll portions of dough into strips the shape of a pencil 6 inches long. Shape to form the figure "8," pressing ends together on the underside. Coat on both sides in granulated sugar in shallow pan. Bake on ungreased baking sheet in a 375-degree oven for 15 minutes or only until brown on bottom side. Makes about 12 dozen.

Hagelslag

1 cup butter
1 cup sugar
1 egg, separated
2 cups flour
¼ teaspoon salt
1½ tablespoons cinnamon
1 tablespoon water
1 cup pecans, chopped

Cream butter and sugar; add egg yolk. Mix well. Sift together flour, salt, and cinnamon; add gradually to creamed mixture. Pat dough evenly into a thin layer in foil-lined 17- by 12-inch shallow baking pan. Blend water with egg white; pour over cooky dough, tilt pan in all directions until dough is well coated—use a pastry brush, if necessary, to spread. Sprinkle with nuts. Bake in 300-degree oven for 30 minutes; turn off heat and leave in oven for 15 minutes. While warm, cut into squares. Makes 70.

Coconut Cookies

1 cup butter or margarine
2 cups brown sugar, packed
2 eggs
3⅔ cups flour, sifted
⅛ teaspoon salt
2 teaspoons baking soda
2 teaspoons cream of tartar
1 teaspoon vanilla
1 3½-ounce can flaked coconut

Cream butter and sugar; add eggs, dry ingredients which have been sifted together, vanilla and coconut. Blend. Drop dough by heaping teaspoonfuls onto greased baking sheets. Bake in a 375-degree oven for 10 to 12 minutes or until lightly browned. Makes about 7 dozen.

At the corner grocery store we bought cookies the shape of rectangles with scalloped edges. A paper sackful cost only a nickel. I liked to dunk the cookies in Postum—children drank Postum the way adults drink coffee.

Before egg beaters were invented, cooky making was a test of muscle and patience. Old recipes say "stir eggs and sugar for one hour."

Brandy Snaps

¾ cup butter
¾ cup sugar
½ cup molasses
2 teaspoons ground ginger
1½ teaspoons brandy
1½ cups flour

In saucepan combine butter, sugar, molasses, and ginger; heat until butter melts, stirring to blend. Remove from heat; gradually stir in brandy and flour. For each snap drop about ½ tablespoon dough onto greased baking sheet, allowing for spreading, since the baked snap measures about 4 inches. Bake in 300-degree oven for 10 minutes; remove from oven and let stand for about 2 minutes. Roll each around the handle of a wooden spoon. Because they become crisp quickly, bake only a few at a time for easier handling. Store in airtight containers. Makes about 4 dozen.

Moravian Love Cakes

It is the custom at the Moravian love feast, which originated in 1727 in Upper Lusatia and brought by immigrants to this country, to serve mugs of coffee and cakes or buns.

¾ cup sugar
¾ cup honey
2 eggs
3½ cups flour, sifted
1 teaspoon baking powder
½ teaspoon cinnamon
¼ teaspoon nutmeg
⅛ teaspoon ground cloves
1 tablespoon lemon rind, grated
1 cup blanched almonds, chopped
¾ cup candied mixed fruit and peels, chopped
1 cup confectioners' sugar
Hot water

Mix sugar, honey, and eggs; add flour, baking powder, and spices which have been sifted together. Stir in lemon rind, almonds, and fruits. Roll out to ¼-inch thickness on floured board. Cut as desired. Place on baking sheets, and bake in a 400-degree oven for about 12 minutes or until golden brown. While warm, brush with confectioners' sugar blended with enough hot water to make glaze. Makes 2 to 4 dozen depending on size.

CHAPTER 13

The Sweet Tooth

The Sweet Tooth

The country store and the city store featured the penny candy counter or jars of candies to attract children with pennies clutched in their little hands. The joy of selecting from gumdrops, chocolate drops, chocolate "babies," candy-coated peanuts called Boston baked beans, nonpareils, strings of taffy and licorice, chewable wax bottles filled with sweet liquids, and jawbreakers was often greater than the joy of eating the candies. As time progressed, the assortment included all-day suckers and the Black Cow, a chocolate sucker.

Candy kitchens which turned out fudge, divinity, and seafoam were common. They continue to this day in a number of cities and are a delight to visit.

Early in the century, candy bars wrapped in paper appeared and found instant popularity at five cents each. The bars were about four times the size of the miniatures designed for present-day Halloween trick-or-treating.

Candy making in the home was a favorite pastime, and a taffy pull was a social event. Kentucky is famous for its cream candy, a pulled sugar candy rich with cream, and similar to pulled mints, considered a necessity for every tea party and wedding reception.

Fudge was popular in the late nineteenth century, and into the twentieth, particularly at women's colleges. Vassar, Wellesley, and Smith colleges had their own recipes. Sometimes the fudge was cooked over the gaslights which hung in rooms from the center of the ceiling and was used as an excuse for late night parties. Later, fudge was prepared in chafing dishes.

Everyone liked striped stick candy flavored with peppermint, wintergreen, and lemon, and even sticks of horehound. Kids stuck a stick of candy into a hole in an orange and sucked. Horehound candy, made from the herb, is soothing to a simple cough or sore throat.

SUGAR PLUMS

Various forms of candy, especially those small in size and oval or round in shape were called sugar plums.

For one version, grind together dried fruits as desired—apricots, apples, peaches, figs, pears, prunes—and fresh or candied lemon rind and walnuts. Moisten with rum and brandy and shape into small balls. Roll in granulated sugar and store in a covered container to ripen.

In another version, a sugar plum is a pitted prune filled with almond paste moistened with sherry and rolled in granulated sugar.

Kids on a trip to the general store usually wrangled a penny's worth of candy. Hard candy, shaped like little fish and tasting of lemon, was a favorite. Adults preferred a stick of horehound.

The candy-store man eked out a living doling out candy, with jelly beans ten for a penny. A kid would demand five whites, three greens, two yellows, and a pink owed from the last purchase.

The Saturday ritual included an afternoon trip to a shop called The Candy Kitchen where we enjoyed the delicious pleasure of spending a portion of our small allowance for a paper sack filled with candy. The ritual ended with the Saturday night bath.

257

The sugar plums children have "visions of" are not the kind with rum, brandy, or sherry. The following version is more suitable for children.

Take small pieces of fondant, flavored and colored to taste; form into olive-shaped balls. Hold one in the palm of the hand, cut it half through and press into it an almond; form the fondant around it, leaving a narrow strip of the nut uncovered. This gives the appearance of a shell cracked open showing the kernel.

Uncooked Fondant

½ cup butter
1 pound confectioners' sugar
4 tablespoons milk, approximate
1 teaspoon vanilla

Cream butter and sugar; add vanilla and sufficient milk to form a consistency that can be shaped with the hands. Tint with food coloring if desired. Shape into small candies. Makes about 1 pound.

Easy Butter Mints

½ cup butter
2 pounds confectioners' sugar
1 envelope unflavored gelatin
¼ cup cold water
16 drops oil of peppermint

Melt butter over hot water to prevent browning; blend in sugar gradually. Dissolve gelatin in water and add with oil of peppermint. Knead until creamy. Tint with food coloring if desired. Roll out and cut with small round cutters. Makes about 2 pounds.

Divinity

3 cups granulated sugar
½ cup light corn syrup
½ cup cold water
Dash of salt
2 egg whites
1 teaspoon vanilla
½ cup pecans, chopped

Place sugar, syrup, water, and salt in pan over low heat; stir until sugar is dissolved. Cook to 232 degrees F. or until small amount dropped in cold water forms a soft ball. Beat egg whites until stiff; continue beating while pouring half the syrup over them slowly.
Cook remaining syrup to 256 degrees F. or until a drop forms a hard ball in cold water; beat egg white mixture slowly while remaining syrup cooks. Add remaining syrup gradually; continue beating until candy is thick enough to drop. Add vanilla and nuts; drop in small mounds on wax paper. Makes about 1 pound.

Seafoam

3 cups light brown sugar, packed
¾ cup water
1 tablespoon light corn syrup
2 egg whites
Pinch of salt
1 teaspoon vanilla
½ cup pecans, chopped, if desired

Combine sugar, water, and syrup—the top of a double boiler makes a good container—and stir over low heat until sugar is dissolved. Continue stirring until syrup boils, then cook without stirring to 256 degrees F. or until a small amount dropped in cold water forms a hard ball. Meanwhile, beat egg whites and salt until stiff but not dry; add hot syrup gradually, continuing to beat until mixture is very stiff. Add vanilla and nuts. Drop in little mounds from a buttered spoon onto wax paper. Makes about 1½ pounds.

Peanut Brittle

½ cup light corn syrup
2 cups granulated sugar
½ cup brown sugar
½ cup water
¼ cup butter
⅛ teaspoon salt
⅛ teaspoon soda
1½ cups peanuts

Combine syrup, sugars, water, and butter in top of double boiler or deep saucepan; cook, stirring occasionally, to 270 degrees F. Continue cooking, stirring more frequently, to 300 degrees F. Remove from heat; stir salt, soda, and peanuts in quickly. Pour onto buttered baking sheet; stretch out thin, and cool. Break into pieces. Makes about 1 pound.

A lady in town made pulled mints for everybody's parties and wedding receptions. She tinted them pastel shades and we served them in little paper bon-bon cups.

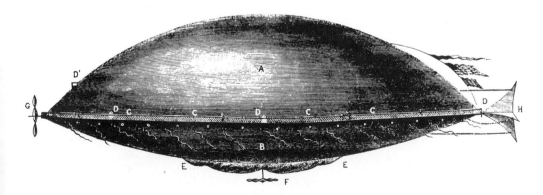

Candied Citrus Peel

3 large grapefruit or 6 large oranges
1 6-ounce package fruit-flavored gelatin
Water
2 cups sugar
1 large stick cinnamon
½ teaspoon whole cloves

Cut grapefruit or oranges in halves. Squeeze juice; strain and use as desired. In saucepan cover grapefruit or orange shells with water; bring to a boil, and boil for 15 minutes. Drain; remove pulp and with bowl of spoon carefully remove moist white membrane. With scissors cut peel into thin strips, about ¼ inch wide. Return peels to saucepan; cover with water and boil again for 15 minutes. Drain. In a heavy skillet, mix gelatin with 2 cups water and 1 cup sugar; add drained peels and spices. Bring to a boil; reduce heat to medium and continue cooking, stirring occasionally, until peels are translucent and syrup is almost all absorbed, about 50 minutes. Remove from heat. Lift peels, a few at a time, with a slotted spoon from skillet and toss in remaining sugar. Arrange pieces in a single layer on trays lined with wax paper; let dry for about 12 hours or overnight. Store in a tightly covered container. Makes about 1 pound.

Clothesline Candy

The name of this sweet comes from the way the candy was cooled in the days before the icebox. It was rolled and wrapped in a cloth soaked in cold water, wrung out, and hung from a clothesline.

3 cups sugar
½ cup light corn syrup
1 cup cream
1 cup nuts, chopped
1 cup dates, chopped
1 teaspoon vanilla extract

Combine sugar, corn syrup, and cream. Stir until sugar is dissolved. Cook to the very firm ball stage (248 degrees F.). Stir in nuts and dates and continue to cook for 3 minutes. Remove from heat, add vanilla extract, and beat until mixture becomes stiff. Form candy into a long roll, wrap in wax paper, and store in refrigerator to chill. Cut into ¼-inch slices. Makes 6 dozen slices.

Stover Fudge

Years ago a surgeon in Bridgeport, Conn., operated on an elderly woman from Springfield, Mass. Upon

recovery the patient shared her special fudge
recipe with the surgeon's wife.

3 eggs
Dash of salt
1 teaspoon vanilla
1 pound confectioners' sugar
1 pound sweet or milk chocolate
2 1-ounce squares unsweetened chocolate
2 tablespoons butter

Beat eggs until thick and foamy. Add salt and vanilla.
Blend in sugar. Meanwhile, in the top of a double
boiler over boiling water, melt chocolates and butter.
Blend chocolate mixture into eggs. Pour into buttered
8-inch-square pan. Chill until firm. Cut into squares.
Makes about 2 pounds.

Horehound Candy

Boil 2 ounces dried horehound in 1½ pints of water
for half an hour; strain. Add 3½ pounds brown sugar
to water. Boil over a hot fire until the mixture is
sufficiently hard. Pour out into flat, well-greased tin
trays and mark into sticks or small squares with a
knife as soon as it is cool enough to retain its shape.
Makes about 3 pounds.

Maple Candy

In New England a popular confection is made by
cooking together 2 cups maple syrup, 1 tablespoon light
corn syrup, and ¾ cup thin cream over low heat to
a temperature of 238 to 240 degrees F. or until a small
amount dropped in cold water forms a soft ball. Cool
to lukewarm, then beat until thickened. If candy refuses
to thicken, add sufficient confectioners' sugar to
produce candy consistency. Add ¾ cup chopped
butternuts and pour into a buttered 8-inch-square pan.
When firm, cut into squares. Makes about ½ pound.

Peach Leather

2½ cups ripe peach pulp, mashed
½ cup sugar plus sugar for sprinkling

Combine pulp and sugar in heavy skillet; cook, stirring,
until thickened. Spread out in a thin layer on oiled
baking sheet; cover with mosquito netting or gauze,
and place in the hot sun to dry for 3 days, bringing it
inside at night. When the leather draws away from the
pan, it is done. Place on board sprinkled with sugar, and
sprinkle sugar over the top. Roll out as thin as a knife
blade, then cut into strips 1½ inches wide. Make small
wafers and roll up; dust again with sugar. Store in
tin box with tight lid.

A sugar tit, made by tying white
sugar tightly in a small square of
clean, white cloth, was used to
pacify a baby. The baby sucked
it the way today's baby sucks a
rubber pacifier.

Mama said that if one grain of
sugar fell from the side of the
pan into the fudge while it
cooked, the fudge would be
grainy. It was my job to wrap a
strip torn from an old sheet
around a fork and after wetting
the strip to wipe the sugar crystals
off the pan so they would not drop
down into the fudge.

CHAPTER 14

Coffee and Other Beverages

Coffee, probably the world's most popular beverage, was discovered in the third century by a goat-herding Coptic monk who noticed his goats were friskier after munching on certain evergreen bushes bearing coffee beans. Modern man and woman turn to coffee for a "friskier" feeling and the coffee-break, or *kaffeeklatsch*, is a way of life in home, office, and factory. A slogan lettered on a handcrafted coffee cup puts it this way: "Good things happen over coffee."

Things have been happening over coffee for centuries. Helen of Troy referred to it as a "magic draught." In the sixteenth century women drank it to ease labor pains, and the seventeenth-century Englishman, Sir Thomas Herbert, credited coffee with "dispelling melancholy, drying tears, allaying anger, and producing cheerfulness." The philosopher, Montesquieu, said that coffee "sometimes enables very stupid people to do clever things."

Coffee came to the home earlier in this century as coffee beans, sometimes green and requiring roasting. The coffee grinder was a standard piece of kitchen equipment. Now specialty coffee shops offer burlap bags of various kinds of coffee beans for customers who select a special blend and the coffee grinder seems to be regaining its popularity.

Boiled Coffee

To 1 cup medium-ground coffee add 1 tablespoon egg white, slightly beaten. Mix with ½ cup cold water. Pour into an enamel coffee pot, add 6 cups boiling water, stop up spout with soft paper, and boil for 3 minutes. Pour out 1 cup to clear spout, return that to pot, add ½ cup cold water, and set over slow fire for 10 minutes. Serve in warm cups with hot cream. Makes 7 cups.

Another way to prepare boiled coffee is to put a heaping tablespoon of ground coffee for each cup of cold water in an enamel pot. Bring to a boil slowly. Let boil gently for 5 minutes. Remove from heat. Add ½ cup cold water and let stand a minute to allow grounds to settle.

Irish Coffee

Irish coffee was introduced to this country in 1953 at the Buena Vista Bar, built in San Francisco in 1901, and became instantly popular.

> **1½ ounces Irish whiskey**
> **1 teaspoon sugar**
> **Hot coffee**
> **2 tablespoons whipped cream, sweetened**

Put whiskey in coffee cup; add sugar, stir to dissolve. Add hot coffee to almost the top of the cup. Spoon whipped cream over the top. Makes 1 serving.

COFFEE IN NEW ORLEANS

No place in New Orleans is so closely associated with coffee as the Morning Call, an unpretentious stand opened in the French Market in 1870. The coffee is enriched with chicory and served with boiled milk, never cream.

COFFEE WITH SCHLAGOBERS

It was customary in Vienna, Austria, to drink coffee with *schlagobers* (whipped cream) and background music by Strauss. Edward Danziger a Viennese candy-shop proprietor who fled Nazi persecution and escaped to America, opened a small coffee shop in Chapel Hill, home of the University of North Carolina. Here he served Viennese coffee, tall glasses of hot coffee topped by cold whipped cream. Danziger's is still in Chapel Hill, but the coffee is no longer served.

Viennese Coffee

> **8 ounces hot coffee**
> **2 tablespoons whipped cream, sweetened**

Pour coffee into tall, thick, flared glass—to prevent breakage, pour over an iced teaspoon in the glass. Top with whipped cream. Serve at once. Makes 1 serving.

The wonderful fragrance of coffee hangs over Magazine Street in New Orleans, where coffee is roasted and blended by importers. It sets the nostrils to quivering.

On the farm the one thing we had to buy was coffee. Grandma always bought it green and roasted it to her own liking and sense of smell.

President Theodore Roosevelt, after a visit to Hermitage, the home of Andrew Jackson, returned to nearby Nashville where he dined at Maxwell House, a center of social and diplomatic life in the South for fifty-five years. The president was so delighted with the coffee which ended his meal, he is said to have exclaimed over his empty cup, "That was good to the last drop!"

Coffee Punch Royale

    1 cup sugar
    3 quarts hot coffee
    Bourbon
    2 quarts vanilla or coffee ice cream

Add sugar to coffee; stir to dissolve. Chill. Pour mixture into punch bowl. Add 1 to 3 cups bourbon depending on the amount of spiking desired. Beat in 1 quart ice cream. Spoon remaining ice cream on top. Makes 44 half-cup servings.

Coffee Grog

    1 tablespoon butter or margarine
    ⅓ cup brown sugar, packed
    ⅛ teaspoon each: cinnamon, nutmeg,
        allspice, and cloves
    4½ cups hot coffee
    1 tablespoon rum extract
    ¾ cup light cream
    6 twists lemon peel
    6 twists orange peel

Blend butter, sugar, and spices; add hot coffee, stir until sugar is dissolved. Add extract and cream; pour into 6 mugs with a twist of lemon and orange peel in each. Serves 6.

PERFECT COFFEE ACCOMPANIMENTS
Sour Cream Coffee Cake

    1 cup butter or margarine
    2 cups sugar
    ½ teaspoon vanilla
    2 eggs
    2 cups flour
    1 teaspoon baking powder
    ¼ teaspoon salt
    1 teaspoon cinnamon
    1 cup pecans, chopped
    ½ cup golden raisins
    1 cup thick sour cream
    Cinnamon sugar

Cream together butter and sugar until light and fluffy. Add vanilla and eggs, one at a time, creaming well after each egg is added. Sift together flour, baking powder, salt, and cinnamon. Add nuts and raisins, mixing until well coated. Add dry ingredients to creamed mixture alternately with sour cream. Blend well—the batter should look like whipped cream tinged with honey. Turn into greased and floured bundt pan. Sprinkle with cinnamon sugar. (It fits a bundt pan, the one shaped like half a pumpkin with ridges, which measures 10 inches across top.) Bake in a 350-degree oven for 60 minutes or until cake tests done. Leave in pan for at least 1 hour before turning out. Turn out and sprinkle with more cinnamon sugar.

Peach Kuchen

2 cups flour, sifted
¼ teaspoon baking powder
½ teaspoon salt
1 cup sugar
½ cup butter or margarine
12 fresh peach halves, peeled
¼ teaspoon nutmeg
¼ teaspoon cardamom
2 egg yolks
1 cup heavy or sour cream

Sift together flour, baking powder, salt, and 2 tablespoons sugar; cut in butter or margarine until mixture resembles coarse cornmeal. Spread and pat in an even layer over the bottom and up a portion of the sides of an 8-inch-square pan. Arrange peaches, cut side up, on pastry; sprinkle peaches with mixture of remaining sugar, nutmeg, and cardamom. Bake in a 400-degree oven for 15 minutes; mix egg yolks and cream, pour over peaches. Bake 30 minutes longer. Makes 9 servings.

ICED TEA

Iced tea was discovered by accident by an English tea merchant at the International Exposition in St. Louis in 1904. Richard Blechynden was trying to interest visitors in his hot tea on a hot, sweltering day in July. No one was interested, so finally he put ice in the tea urn. The drink was an instant success.

The English smile at iced tea, which they find strange. They say, "First you make hot tea, then you put ice in it to make it cold, sugar to make it sweet, lemon to make it sour, say 'here's to you,' and drink it yourself."

For supper on the days when Mama had the woman's club or the ladies' aid society meeting at our house, we had what was left of the fancy sandwiches served with a tureen of chicken or corn chowder and a rich, gooey dessert she made for the ladies.

A vital part of the tea service was the silver container for sugar cubes and a little pair of silver tongs for lifting the cubes into cups of tea. A hostess asked each guest how many lumps of sugar. Another use for lump sugar was a pocketful to treat the horses.

Russian Tea

1 cup sugar
4 cups water
1 3-inch-stick cinnamon
1 teaspoon whole cloves
3 tablespoons dry tea
1 cup orange juice
1 12-ounce can pineapple juice
½ teaspoon orange rind, grated
½ teaspoon lemon rind, grated

In saucepan, combine sugar, water, cinnamon, and cloves; bring to a boil and simmer for 10 minutes. Add tea; remove from heat and let stand, covered, for 5 minutes. Strain; add remaining ingredients. Heat but do not boil. Serve hot. Makes about 8 cups.

Lemonade

6 lemons
1½ cups sugar
2½ quarts water
Ice cubes

Roll lemons with the hands, breaking cells to release juice. Slice one lemon thinly; with a wooden handle pound ½ cup sugar into the sliced lemon. Slice remaining lemons thinly onto first lemon; add remaining sugar. Let stand for 30 minutes; add water and stir. Add ice cubes. Makes 3 quarts.

Canteen Iced Tea

During World War II, volunteers operated canteens where soldiers went for recreation and refreshments. In this recipe sugar rationed during the war was stretched with saccharin.

½ cup loose tea
8 sprigs fresh mint, if available
6 to 8 quarts water
8 whole-grain saccharin tablets
1 cup lemon juice
2 cups sugar

Steep tea and mint in 2 quarts boiling water for 5 minutes. Meanwhile, dissolve saccharin in 4 quarts cold water; add lemon juice and sugar, and stir until sugar is dissolved. Strain tea into saccharin mixture. Makes 6 to 8 quarts.

Mint Tea

4 sprigs fresh mint
8 to 12 whole cloves
3 quarts water
1 ounce loose tea
Juice of 8 lemons
Juice of 6 oranges
1 46-ounce can pineapple juice
2 cups sugar or to taste

Add mint and cloves to water; bring to a boil, and simmer for 10 minutes. Remove from heat. Add tea; cover and allow to steep for 10 minutes. Strain and while still hot, add fruit juices and sugar, stirring to dissolve sugar. Chill and serve over ice. Makes about 6 quarts.

Blackberry Acid

A beverage from before the days of bottled soft drinks.

5 ounces tartaric acid
12 pounds blackberries
1 gallon water
Sugar

Sprinkle tartaric acid over berries. Add water. Let stand for 48 hours, then strain without mashing berries. To each pint juice, add 1 pound sugar. Stir well and then bottle. Makes 8 quarts.

Strawberry Acid

A delightful summer beverage.
Dissolve 4 ounces citric acid in ½ gallon water, and pour it over 2 gallons ripe crushed strawberries. Let stand for 24 hours, and then strain. To each pint juice, add 1 pound sugar. Boil well for 5 minutes, then let stand for 3 days before bottling. When ready to serve, add 2 tablespoonfuls to a glass of ice water. Makes 4 quarts.

THE SALOON

In the early part of the 20th century Americans drank in quantity. An English visitor commenting on American drinking habits said that "gin sling, brandy smash, whiskey skin, streak of lightning, cocktail, and rum-salad" were consumed morning, noon, and night by persons who of a similar class in England would no more think of going into a gin shop than robbing a bank.

The saloon, so familiar a part of western movies and westerns on television, was a symbol of evil incarnate.

Women in and out of the Women's Christian Temperance Union (WCTU) crusaded against drink. The best-known crusader was Carrie Nation (1846-1911) who was most active in the 1890s. With a few hymn-singing women, or alone, she would march into a saloon, sing, pray, hurl vituperations at all "rummies" present, and smash fixtures and the stock with hatchets. She called her rampages the "hatchetation of joints." One must remember there were no television sets in saloons, which means saloon patrons were no doubt highly entertained by the hatchet woman.

PRAIRIE OYSTER

Since the egg tends to soothe by counteracting the action of alcohol on the body, this is a favorite remedy for the morning after.

Break an egg into a wine glass, taking care not to break the yolk. Pour ½ teaspoon or more of vinegar gently down the inside of the glass. Sprinkle with salt and pepper. Drink so the egg is swallowed first and then the vinegar.

Later versions add Worcestershire sauce, catsup, and hot pepper sauce.

PROHIBITION

The boozeless regime began at midnight January 10, 1920, and ended in December, 1933. The era brought into being a new kind of criminal, the bootlegger. Among the most famous was Al Capone, whose annual estimated earnings were $60 million.

The illegal saloon, the speakeasy, flourished and lawbreakers guzzled bathtub gin and home brew, whiskey distilled at home. There was discreet drinking from teacups during Prohibition, even in public places.

A book, **Prohibition Punches,** published in 1930 offered nonalcoholic suggestions. The introduction to breakfast punches presented this thought, "The day should always be begun with a vision of green hills and newblown roses, to fill the thoughts with freshness and whisk away the cobwebs—like the clean sweep of a broom." Before the dinner hour "when purple shades have fallen and the afterglow lingers touching the world with unreality, one's cocktail should reflect the purple blood of grapes, the lush richness of the raspberry, the amber of apple or ginger juice."

Locust Beer

Gather the long black pods of locust and cut away the hard part. Break the remaining portion into pieces and place in layers with a few crushed ripe persimmons or dried apples in a stone crock or wooden keg. Cover with hot water and place a weight on top. Let stand in a warm place for several days. It does not ferment. Drink soon, as it does not keep well. A layer of straw placed in the bottom of the keg acts as a filter if the beer is to be drawn out through the bottom.

A bowl of punch for the men was often provided at musicales. Men who did not care for the music found it more palatable after slipping by to the punch bowl filled with offerings like this one.

Wabash Punch

   3 gallons water
   1½ pounds dry tea
   1 gallon whiskey
   1 quart rum
   1 quart jug curacao
   1 gallon sweet Catawba wine
   1 quart lemon juice
   2 pounds sugar
   6 bottles champagne

Make tea by soaking dry tea in cold water overnight. Combine with remaining ingredients; stir to dissolve sugar. Serve over ice. Makes about 7¼ quarts.

During Prohibition somebody could always get a little corn likker, moonshine, white lightnin', or rot gut.

Corn likker is traditionally bottled in Mason jars called fruit jars whether filled with likker or kraut. Men often took a swig right from the jar which supposedly left a slight imprint on the nose, a basis of the expression, "I grew up with a ring around my nose."

269

Lalla Rookh Punch

1 cup sugar
5 eggs, separated
¾ cup brandy
¼ cup rum
1 quart heavy cream, whipped
½ teaspoon grated nutmeg

Combine sugar with egg yolks in a saucepan. Cook
gently, stirring constantly, until slightly thick. Remove
from fire and allow to cool. Add brandy and rum.
Fold in whipped cream and stiffly beaten egg whites.
Blend in nutmeg. Put into a mold, pack in ice and salt,
and freeze. Makes 8 to 12 portions.

Mineral Water

Apollinaris or other mineral water was served after
the meal and it was "welcomed," partly because water
was less pure than it is today and partly because
mineral waters were regarded as medicinal. Grocers
stocked them because they "drew a good class of
trade." Apollinaris water came from the Apollinaris
Spring in Prussia.

Mineral springs in the United States included
Bear-Lithia Springs, Va.; Blue Lick Springs, Ky.;
Bokert Springs, Mo.; Buffalo Springs, Va.;
Londonderry Lithia Springs, N.H.; Manitou Springs,
Colo., Richfield Springs, N.Y.; Sharon Springs, N.Y.;
White Sulphur Springs, W. Va.; and Yellow Sulphur
Springs, Va.

Springs attracted many visitors, some stayed for
months at a time, others went to collect demijohns of
the water to bring home. A demijohn is a very large-
bodied bottle with a small neck, often protected by a
wickerwork covering. Some hold as much as five
gallons.

CHAPTER 15

The More We Get Together

OUTINGS IN THE TOURING CAR

"The way to see the world is not by following the beaten tracks of the Baedecker guide books but by the honk honk and smooth running mechanism of an up-to-date automobile." That was the decision in 1909 of Mrs. Harriet White Fisher of Trenton, N.J. She set out in July of that year with three companions, "piloting" her own touring car on a trip around the world which took one year. Also in the party were Honk, a bulldog, and Billiken, an ape. Mrs. Fisher, the widow of U.S. Naval Captain Clark Fisher, was the owner and operator of a successful anvil factory in Trenton. After her world tour, she became the wife of Silvano Albert Andrew, an officer in the Argentine Navy.

Others toured in the touring car but over less ambitious courses. The following list of emergency supplies was recommended to motorists in the days before the service station.

> 2 2-gallon canvas water bags
> 4 pounds hardtack
> 4 ½-pound cans meat or fish
> 2 pounds sweet chocolate
> 2 cans fruit

OUTING SUPPLIES

The grocer of the first decade was advised to stock up on outing supplies. Appropriate articles were crackers and sweet biscuits, cheese, butter of the very best quality in screw-top glass jars, pickles, olives, candy, salmon, sardines, tongue, deviled meats, pilot bread for chowder or coffee. (Pilot bread or ship biscuit is another name for hardtack, large hard biscuits of plain dough, kiln-dried.)

Also recommended were collapsible camping kits including cups, chafing dishes, and a stove, "the whole fitting closely together and capable of being packed in a big boiling pot or fitted into a box that may be slung over the shoulder."

Cars back in 1904 weren't the durable machines they are today. You were lucky if you took a 10-mile trip without breaking down.

For a Sunday afternoon outing in the touring car, Ma packed a large basket of food, even a home-stuffed sausage, and put it on the rear seat beside me.

PICNICS

From the shores of Maine to the beaches of the lake in Salt Lake City, and from down into mysteries of the Grand Canyon to the Big Sur on the edge of the Pacific, Americans carry picnics year after year. The book *Menus For Every Occasion* (1927) called the disease "picnicitis." It stated: "At least once every year entire families get an attack of picnicitis. And when the disease makes its attack the automobile dealers, the street-car companies, the boat corporations, the owners of camps, the manufacturers of canned goods, the bakers of crackers, etc. play the role of doctor by making the patient or patients comfortable while the malady runs its true course."

In the days before paper plates, picnic hampers came fitted with white enamel plates, cups and saucers, bone handled knives and forks, together with glass and metal containers for foods. Such hampers, made of wicker, belong to the era of the touring car.

Picnic Favorites

Deviled Eggs

6 hard-cooked eggs
1 tablespoon lemon juice or vinegar
¼ cup butter, melted
¼ teaspoon salt
⅛ teaspoon pepper
½ teaspoon celery salt
½ teaspoon dry mustard
1 teaspoon onion, grated

Cut eggs in half lengthwise; scoop out yolks, mash thoroughly with a fork. To mashed yolks, add seasonings. Pack into shells. Makes 12 halves.

Roast Beef Buns

2 tablespoons mayonnaise
2 tablespoons bottled horseradish
2 tablespoons prepared mustard
Thinly sliced roast beef, medium rare
12 small rolls

Blend mayonnaise, horseradish, and mustard; spread on rolls. Fill rolls with several layers of roast beef. Makes 12 buns.

Pimiento Cheese

½ pound Cheddar cheese, cubed
1 2-ounce jar pimientos, undrained
⅛ teaspoon salt
1 teaspoon lemon juice or vinegar
½ cup mayonnaise

Grind together cheese and pimiento or blend in electric blender; blend in remaining ingredients. Makes about 1½ cups or enough for 5 to 6 sandwiches.

Stack Pie

Stack pies belong to the days of basket dinners prepared for outings. A basket had to feed family and friends, so there was room only for the base of one pie in the basket. Pies were therefore stacked on top of each other. The stack pie recipe below is for chess pie.

Pastry for 4 or 5 9-inch pie pans
10 egg yolks
3 cups sugar
1½ cups butter, melted
1 cup cream

Line 4 or 5 pie pans with pastry. Make the one that will be used on the bottom of the basket the usual depth of a pie; make the others less deep. Beat egg yolks until light and lemon colored. Cream in sugar, beating again until light. Add butter and cream. Pour 1 cup of mixture into each unbaked pie shell, adding a little more to the bottom pie. Bake in a 350-degree oven until fillings are firm. Allow pies to cool in their pans. Run a spatula around the crusts, slide the pies out, and frost with caramel frosting (recipe below). Stack the pies on top of one another.

Caramel Frosting

Cook together 2 cups brown sugar and 1 cup cream until the mixture reaches the soft ball stage (when a small amount dropped in cold water forms a soft ball). Beat until creamy. If the frosting gets too hard, beat in more cream.

Everytime I pack a picnic with paper plates, I think of Mama's fitted wicker picnic basket filled with white enamel plates and cups, glass boxes, and salt and peppers, and her round white linen napkins with scalloped edges.

Best Yet Cupcakes

4 squares unsweetened chocolate
1 cup margarine
¼ teaspoon butter flavoring
1½ cups pecans, chopped
1¾ cups sugar
1 cup flour
4 eggs
1 teaspoon vanilla

In saucepan, melt chocolate and margarine over medium heat; add butter flavoring and pecans. Stir to coat pecans; remove from heat and blend in sugar, flour, eggs, and vanilla. Pour into 18 baking cups set in muffin pans. Bake in a 350-degree oven for 25 minutes or until done. Frost. Makes 18.

Frosting for Cupcakes

4 squares unsweetened chocolate
1 cup margarine
1 egg
1 teaspoon vanilla
1 pound confectioners' sugar

In saucepan, melt chocolate and margarine; remove from heat, and add remaining ingredients. Beat until thick enough to spread.

SUGARING OFF

In Vermont, the land of the sugar maple, the custom is to have a sugaring off "in the sugar bush" when the sap flows. It is a social occasion where the hot syrup is poured on snow to make cold, shiny brittle that is half-warm, half-cold, a waxy mixture called leather aprons, frogs, and sheepskins.

To counteract the sweetness of "sugar snow" the menu includes sour cucumber pickles, hard-cooked eggs, doughnuts, coffee, and hot soda biscuits for dunking into hot syrup and cheese.

SUGAR ON SNOW

Boil maple syrup in a large cooking pan to 230 degrees, watching carefully to prevent boiling over or scorching. Pour syrup slowly, a little at a time, over snow packed firmly in metal pie plates. Eat it at once with a fork before it loses its waxy texture. A gallon of syrup and a bushel of snow will take care of 30 appetites.

Fruit Plate with Maple Syrup

  1 fresh pineapple, peeled and cored
  6 fresh purple plums, halved and seeded
  1 grapefruit, peeled and sectioned
  2 oranges, peeled and sectioned
  2 large red apples, unpeeled
  2 fresh pears, unpeeled
  2 bananas, peeled and sliced diagonally
  Lemon Juice
  1 cup grapes, seedless or halved and seeded
  2 cups maple syrup
  ½ teaspoonful cardamom
  ¼ cup rum

On six plates, arrange pineapple cut into fingers, plums, grapefruit and orange sections, apples and pears cut into wedges, and banana slices; sprinkle apples, pears, and bananas with lemon juice. Add grapes. Heat together syrup, cardamom, and rum; spoon hot over cold fruits. Serves 6.

SNOW CARNIVALS

In winter the ice carnival with ice skating contests, bobsledding, tobogganing and winter hikes was a feature of those areas with cold climates. A picture from early in the century shows a "Merry crew spilled from a toboggan rushing at railroad speed." In the same period, at a carnival at Saranac Lake, N.Y., an ice palace of the dimension of the palace in Disneyland was built of blocks of ice and illuminated "in a blaze of glory" at night.

WIENER ROASTS

Roasting wieners over an open fire has been largely replaced by the charcoal grill, except for camping groups.
For a "wienee" roast, there is the fun of searching for sticks and sharpening the end to spear the wiener which will become slightly charred.

Mustard for Hot Dogs

  2 1⅛-ounce boxes dry mustard
  1 cup granulated sugar
  1 cup cider vinegar
  2 eggs

In top of double boiler, blend mustard and sugar; stir in vinegar. Let stand, covered, overnight. Place over boiling water, and cook for 10 minutes. Beat in eggs, one at a time. Blend thoroughly; remove from heat. Cool. Makes about 1 cup.

The maple sugar maker gave his constant attention to the golden liquid seething in the kettle. He tested it constantly, plucking threads of it from his stirring stick, and trailing them around in cups of cold water. If the threads were waxy to the touch, the sugar was not yet ripe; but as soon as one broke crisply between his fingers, that was the moment to take the kettle off the fire.

OYSTER ROASTS

Roasting oysters requires a special roasting pit about a foot deep for holding a bed of glowing coals. Over the pit, about six inches above the ground, should be a sheet of metal like metal roofing.

Wash the mud off the oysters and allow one bushel for 15 guests. Dump oysters on metal sheet that is almost red hot. When hot, the oyster shells open. Shovel onto a table with a hole in the center for the shells. Provide melted butter and seafood cocktail sauce for dunking. Cotton work gloves for the hands are a good idea as the oysters are hot.

Another delightful way to eat oysters is at the stand-up raw bars in New Orleans. Eat as many as desired and pay by the number of empty shells. There are similar outdoor bars on Long Island and other coastal areas.

OYSTER PARLORS

In Cincinnati, and no doubt in other cities, oyster parlors were popular meeting places and no dinner was considered proper if oysters were not included on the menu. An "oyster express" of fast wagons carried the bivalves packed in water-soaked straw from Baltimore to Pittsburgh where they were loaded on boats to travel the remainder of the way down the Ohio River.

Clambakes

The clambake is the Northeast's most glamorous seaside rite—comparable to a beef barbecue in Texas, a fish fry in the South, a salmon barbecue in the Pacific Northwest, and a luau in Hawaii. It is a political and fraternal occasion.

Sipping clam broth whets the appetite as luscious pink lobsters, bundles of pale green corn, clams, sweet potatoes, and onions mingle with seaweed steam in a pit under a sheet of canvas held down by rocks. The bakemaster presides over the bake. When the bake is "undone," the gorging begins. The feast is finished off with watermelon.

When New Englanders went west to settle the country, they kept up the social custom of clambakes hundreds of miles from the ocean, and without a hint of a clam on the menu. Clambakes in the Midwest featured giant stacks of fried chicken, "roasting ears" of corn, sometimes called "rosen" ears, baked with mealy white potatoes in the ashes.

FISH FRIES

Wherever fresh fish is abundant, especially in the South, the custom is to have a fish fry. Fish is fried in big iron skillets over fires and served with fried corn bread or hush puppies and cole slaw.

CHICKEN STEWS

Chicken stews are held in churches and schools but the most distinctive are those staged at tobacco barns.

In the days before oil burners, the big green leaves of tobacco strung on thin poles were cured to golden brown by heat from fires stoked by wood. This meant someone had to stay on duty 24 hours a day for days. To relieve the monotony of the fire watcher, a chicken stew was staged, and a few still are, at the tobacco barn. Chicken is stewed in a big iron wash pot and seasoned with butter, salt, and pepper and to some extent with the rich aroma of the wood burning under the pot. The stew is thickened with flour and served in soup bowls with crackers. Corn from a nearby field is roasted in the ashes of the tobacco barn fire. Accompaniments are endless homemade pickles, pies, and cakes.

Chicken Stew

The old tobacco barn version adapted to the modern kitchen.

    1 3-pound broiler-fryer
    Water
    1½ teaspoons salt
    ½ teaspoon pepper
    3 cups milk
    ¼ cup butter, softened
    ¼ cup flour
    Crackers

Place whole chicken with water to cover in a pot; add salt and pepper, and bring to a boil. Simmer for 1 hour or until it is easy to remove meat from bones. Lift chicken out of broth; allow to cool enough to handle, and pull meat from bones. Shred meat; discard skin and bones. Meanwhile, allow broth to boil to reduce volume by ⅓; add chicken and milk. Blend butter and flour; add a small amount of hot liquid, then combine both mixtures. Heat, stirring, until smooth and thickened—do not allow to boil. Serve with crackers to crumble into stew. Makes 6 servings.

HUSKING BEES

In autumn when the harvest was in, the fields on farms where corn was the leading product were covered with the corn stalks tied into clusters. The corn from the stalks required husking before being taken to market. As was the custom in combining work with fun, husking bees were staged to get the corn shucked.

A girl who happened upon a red ear of corn in her shucking thereby earned the right to demand a kiss from the young man of her choice. Songs, dancing, and refreshments followed the husking.

QUILTING BEES

Homemade patchwork quilts not only provided warmth, but also an opportunity for social get-togethers before the commercially made blanket was widely used. A quilt consists of pieces of fabric—cotton, silk, or wool—cut into patterns and sewn together, often by hand, to make a design. Some designs include intricate embroidery like featherstitching. Usually, only one side of the quilt, the top side, is pieced. The bottom side is made of a single fabric.

Top and bottom are put together with a layer of cotton between them for warmth. All three layers are then stretched on a frame and tacked together. A number of ladies gather for this job at a quilting bee. Often they bring along a pot luck, or covered dish lunch.

FIDDLERS' CONVENTIONS

In the days when no sound of music was brought into the home by radio or television, there were always those in a community who had a fiddle and were able to get sounds from it by sawing with a bow. Fiddlers gathered for fiddlers' conventions. Some groups performed from chairs placed in a flatbed wagon which served as a stage. Guests shared picnic baskets and fellowship flowed to the sounds. A fiddlers' convention might well be called the rock festival of its day.

BARN RAISINGS AND WHEAT THRESHINGS

When labor was dependent more on pairs of hands than on machines, neighbors "pitched in" to help each other with chores such as putting up a new barn or threshing wheat. Frontier families were largely self-contained units. Visiting was rare, but when there was a need for all to get together, the word got around and whole families piled into wagons with an abundance of food for a barn raising or a wheat threshing, which were social occasions and hard work.

For one barn raising, a group of women in the Pennsylvania Dutch country brought a hundred lemon pies, twenty cakes, two hundred light rolls, endless loaves of crusty bread, forty fried chickens, five roast geese, several gallons of applesauce, and jars of the seven sweets and seven sours.

BOX LUNCHES AND SUPPERS

The shoe box, often covered with wallpaper or drawings, has been the container for many meals away from home. Lunch packed in a shoe box is a Kentucky Derby tradition. Those who attended the Chautauqua sometimes took supper in a shoe box. A box supper party is an old money-making and beau-getting scheme staged by church, school, or social groups. Girls packed supper for two in one box which was auctioned off to the highest bidder. The man who bought the box was entitled to share it with the girl who packed it.

COUNTY FAIR

Part of the celebration of the harvest is the county and state fair, where farmers enter produce, poultry, and livestock in competition. Ladies take jars of jams, jellies, preserves, and fruits to vie for blue ribbons. They also take an array of cakes to make the eyes bulge and to titillate the taste buds. Those who do not enter the competition come to look at the perfection of the winning items.

The midway, covered with sawdust, offers sideshows, freaks, barkers, bingo games, egg-throwing contests, shooting galleries, rides, hot dogs, cotton candy, and apples-on-a-stick. A fair often includes harness and other horse racing, vaudeville-type performances at the grandstand, and fireworks.

Best-of-the-Show Cake

4 cups minus 2 tablespoons cake flour, sifted
2 teaspoons baking powder
¾ teaspoon salt
1 cup plus 1 tablespoon cocoa
1¼ cups butter
3 cups sugar
2 teaspoons vanilla
5 eggs, separated
1 teaspoon baking soda
1½ cups buttermilk

Sift together flour, baking powder, salt, and cocoa.
Cream butter; add sugar gradually and continue to
cream until light and fluffy, add vanilla and beaten egg
yolks. Stir baking soda into buttermilk and add to
creamed mixture alternately with dry ingredients,
beginning and ending with dry ingredients. Beat egg
whites until stiff and fold in gently. Pour into 4 greased
and floured 9-inch layer pans. Bake in a 350-degree
oven for 30 to 35 minutes or until cake tests done.
Turn out on racks; cool and frost with fudge frosting
(recipe below.)

Fudge Frosting

3 cups sugar
3 tablespoons light corn syrup
Dash of salt
1 cup milk
4 squares unsweetened chocolate
⅓ cup butter
1 teaspoon vanilla

Place sugar, corn syrup, salt, milk, and chocolate in a
large saucepan; cook and stir over medium heat until
sugar dissolves, then cook stirring occasionally until a
small amount when dropped into cold water forms a
very soft ball or to 232 to 234F. Remove from heat; add
butter and vanilla. Cool to lukewarm or 110F. Beat until
frosting is creamy and just begins to hold its shape;
spread quickly on cake, if too thick, add sour cream.

Candied Apples on a Stick

2 cups sugar
½ cup light corn syrup
¾ cup water
Red food coloring
8 to 12 apples
8 to 12 wooden sticks

In saucepan, combine sugar, syrup, and water; cook, stirring, until sugar is dissolved. Continue cooking, without stirring, to 300 degrees on the candy thermometer or until the syrup is brittle when tested in cold water. Remove syrup from heat; place pan in another pan of hot water. Add red food coloring to make desired shade. Insert sticks into apples; hold each apple by stick, and coat well with hot syrup. Place apples on wax paper to cool.

CIRCUS UNDER THE BIG TENT

Today the circus comes to town quietly and performs indoors. It offers excitement but nothing compared to the days of the three-ring circus which performed under the big top. When the circus arrived, somehow the whole town sensed it. There was a preview parade to stimulate interest and people gathered to watch the hoisting of the tent.

THE HORSEY SET

Those who follow the horses and those who chase foxes are a special breed dedicated to the good life with good food in Lucullan abundance. The country's best known horse race is the Kentucky Derby. Irvin Cobb (1876–1944), a humorist and writer, wrote about the Derby. This reprint hangs in the Kentucky Derby Museum: "It is not horses alone that are running at Churchill Downs on that spring day every year. Tradition, by-gone romance, dimmed echoing poetry, the ghosts of ancient glories and ancient ideals and ancient heroes, they're all there speeding down the homestretch and past the grandstand and on into the sunset's gilded afterglow of vanished yesterdays. In my end of the State we worship a fast horse, else we wouldn't be true Kentuckians. But with us the outstanding sports are still what they have always been—voting the Democratic ticket and running for office."

Cobb described the track as "a bracelet of molten gold encircling a greensward that's like a patch of emerald velvet—all the pretty girls in the state turning the grandstand into a brocaded terrace of beauty and color such as the hanging gardens of Babylon never equalled."

His description concludes: "Until you go to Kentucky and with your own eyes behold the Derby you ain't never been nowheres and you ain't never seen nothin!"

For the Kentucky Derby and the Maryland Hunt, a lavish breakfast is served in mid or late morning and the table is replenished until early afternoon.

Kentucky Derby Day Breakfast
Mint Juleps or Whiskey Sours
Canapés of Caviar
Anchovy Paste, and Chutney
Chicken Croquettes with Mushroom Sauce
or
Country Fried Chicken
Shoestring Potatoes
Ham Biscuits
Tomato Aspic
Assorted Relishes
Fresh Strawberry Ice Cream in
Individual Meringue Shells
Coffee

Another menu includes:
Tomato Juice Cocktail
Hot Brown Sandwich
Bibb Lettuce with
Maple Syrup Salad Dressing
Fresh Asparagus
Transparent Pie
Iced Tea   Coffee

Hot Brown Sandwich

This famous sandwich is an open-face sandwich of toast topped with sliced white meat of chicken, a rich cream sauce, crisp bacon slices, and garnished with a mushroom cap.

For the white meat of chicken, cook one or more hens in enough water to cover with a few peppercorns, salt, and a bay leaf. When cool, cut breast into thin slices. Use the dark meat for another purpose.

For each sandwich, cut crusts from 2 slices of toast. Place 1 slice of toast in a shallow baking dish. Cover with sliced chicken. Top with liberal portion of sauce. Heat in hot oven or under broiler until bubbly. Top with crisp bacon and garnish with mushroom cap. Cut second slice of toast in half and place on sides of plate.

The sauce for the sandwich is a combination of the following two sauces.

Bechamel Sauce

$\frac{1}{3}$ cup butter or margarine
$\frac{1}{2}$ medium-size onion, minced
$\frac{1}{3}$ cup flour
3 cups milk
1 teaspoon salt
Dash of cayenne
A few sprigs of parsley
Dash of nutmeg

Melt butter in saucepan. Add onion and cook until golden brown. Blend in flour. Add milk and seasonings and cook, stirring, until thickened. Strain.

Mornay Sauce

2 cups Bechamel Sauce
2 egg yolks
$\frac{1}{2}$ cup grated Parmesan cheese
1 tablespoon butter or margarine
Whipped cream

Combine Bechamel and egg yolks in top of double boiler. Cook, stirring, over boiling water until thickened. Add cheese and butter and blend. For each $\frac{1}{2}$ cup sauce, fold in 1 tablespoon whipped cream.

Maryland Hunt Breakfast

Bourbon and Branch Water
Scrambled Eggs in Cream
Country Sausage with Fried Apple Rings
Creamed Sweetbreads and Oysters
Capitolade of Chicken
(Chicken Hash)
Kidney Stew
Bacon and Fried Tomato Slices
Waffles
Hominy Pudding
Broiled Salt Roe Herring
Baked Country Ham
Spoon Bread   Beaten Biscuits
Buttermilk Biscuits   Jellies
Apple Butter   Honey   Damson Plum Preserves

Country Sausage with Fried Apple Rings

Shape bulk sausage into patties and fry in a skillet until done. Drain off excess sausage drippings and slice cored, unpeeled apples into the drippings. To keep the apples intact in rings, fry only one layer at a time. Sprinkle with brown sugar and cook, turning carefully, until done.

Bacon and Fried Tomato Slices

For bacon and fried tomato slices, both firm red and green tomato slices are used. Coat the slices in flour or cornmeal seasoned with salt and pepper. Brown quickly on one side in hot bacon drippings in a skillet. Turn and brown on the other side. Serve plain or with cream gravy.

Chicken or Turkey Hash

3 tablespoons butter
1 tablespoon flour
½ cup milk
1 egg yolk
⅓ pound pork sausage meat
½ cup onions, chopped
2 cups cooked chicken or turkey, chopped
2 tablespoons parsley, minced
½ cup soft white bread crumbs
½ teaspoon lemon rind, grated
Salt and pepper to taste

Make a cream sauce of 1 tablespoon butter, flour, and milk over low heat. Add a small amount of the sauce to the egg yolk and then blend in remainder of sauce. Set sauce aside.

In a skillet, cook sausage meat, stirring until browned. Remove meat from pan and cook onions in sausage drippings until golden. Thoroughly drain sausage meat and onions, and discard drippings. Combine sausage, onions, chicken, parsley, bread crumbs, and lemon rind with salt and pepper to taste. Add sauce.

Turn into a skillet which contains remaining 2 tablespoons butter. Cook a few minutes longer. Makes 4 to 6 servings. Superb with spoon bread.

Steeplechase Pickled Shrimp

As served from a tailgate at a steeplechase.

2 pounds shrimp, cleaned and cooked
¼ cup catsup
½ cup cider vinegar
2 teaspoons sugar
2 teaspoons salt
½ teaspoon dry mustard
2 tablespoons Worcestershire sauce
½ cup salad oil
5 to 6 drops hot pepper sauce
1 bay leaf
1 large white onion, thinly sliced

Blend catsup and vinegar; add remaining ingredients, except shrimp. Pour mixture over shrimp; cover, chill for 24 hours before serving. Makes 6 to 8 servings.

Club Meetings

Earlier in the century almost every community had a woman's club, a group formed to work on projects to improve the community and at the same time provide social occasions. The meeting of a woman's club, a church or fraternal auxiliary, and ladies aid society was concluded with refreshments. Hostesses brought out their best china for what they called "refreshment plates." A typical plate included fancy sandwiches, a salad and/or dessert, small cakes, and salted nuts. After the coming of the automatic refrigerator with its ice trays, many refreshment plates featured frozen fruit salad.

Frozen Fruit Salad

> 1½ cups mayonnaise
> 12 ounces cream cheese, softened
> 2 teaspoons lemon rind, grated
> ¼ cup confectioners' sugar
> 1 17-ounce can fruit cocktail, well drained
> 1 large banana, diced
> 2 cups fresh blueberries
> 2 cups heavy cream, whipped
> Lettuce

Blend mayonnaise and cream cheese; add lemon rind, sugar, fruit cocktail, banana, and blueberries. Fold in whipped cream; pour into trays and freeze. Cut into squares; serve on lettuce. Makes 8 servings.

Florida Orange Swirls

3 egg whites
¼ teaspoon cream of tartar
⅛ teaspoon salt
¾ cup sugar
Orange filling (recipe below)

Beat egg whites until foamy; add cream of tartar and salt; beat until stiff, but not dry. Gradually add sugar, beating until very stiff. Cover baking sheet with heavy brown paper or aluminum foil. With spoon or pastry bag, pile meringue into 6 rounds each about 3 inches in diameter on baking sheet. Make a 2-inch depression in the center of each. Bake in a 275-degree oven for 1 hour. Cool. Fill with orange filling. Garnish with orange sections. Makes six servings.

Orange Filling

3 egg yolks
2 tablespoons sugar
⅛ teaspoon salt
6 tablespoons frozen orange juice concentrate,
    thawed and undiluted
1½ teaspoons orange rind, grated
1 cup heavy cream, whipped
18 orange sections, sweetened

Beat egg yolks in top of double boiler; add sugar, salt, and orange concentrate. Cook over boiling water, stirring constantly, until thickened. Remove from heat; add orange rind and chill. Fold in whipped cream. Spoon into shells.

Before radio and television, groups gathered in homes for an afternoon or evening of singing or listening to musical selections performed on the piano, and possibly other instruments, and soloists. Refreshments were served.

A leaflet called "The Hostess," published in 1905 by the Randolph Confection Co. of Saint Louis, Mo., suggested managing a musicale as follows:

"For a Christmas musicale arrange your rooms as richly as possible. Borrow rugs, screens, palms, pillows, and tables from rooms which will not be used, and convert your whole drawing-room floor into cozy nooks, with tête-à-tête corners. Holly and mistletoe may be used for the principal decorations, but sweet-smelling flowers should abound. Red and white roses, or red and white carnations, would carry out the color scheme admirably.

"In the different rooms have various small tables; upon one of them place a Russian samovar for tea, sliced lemon, fancy cakes, and crystalized fruits; in another room have a coffee urn, wafers, dainty sandwiches, and salted nuts; in another room could be placed a punch bowl with Christmas punch, sweet cakes, and marguerites; and still another table could be used for an English tea service, English fruit cake, and various delicious cakes typical of that country. Or one could have a table with hot chocolate, fancy cake, and coffee frappé.

"Each table should be decorated with flowers and with red-shaded candles. The hostess should ask four or five of her friends to serve at these tables and tell them what her color scheme is to be, so their gowns will correspond."

THE SOCIAL TEA

The afternoon tea was a pleasant way to entertain brides, newcomers, and friends. For the occasion, the best of everything was brought out—the best lace or cutwork linen tablecloth, the best Madeira or linen tea napkins, the best china, and a shining tea and coffee service.

Asking someone "to pour" was considered bestowing an honor on that person. The beverages served often included both tea and coffee from the dining room table and punch from the punch bowl in another room.

The menu included fancy sandwiches, ribbon sandwiches, checkerboards, rolled sandwiches, calla lily sandwiches, tiny tarts, the household's best cookies and fancy cakes.

Guests came dressed in their finest silk, crepe de chine, gorgette, voille, and foulard with hats and gloves, white kid if possible.

Iced Crackers or Marguerites

A tea table favorite.

> **3 egg whites**
> **1 pound powdered sugar**
> **1 pound English walnuts, in the shell**
> **1 pound pecans, in the shell**
> **Salted crackers**

Beat egg whites until stiff. Blend in sugar. Shell nuts and add finely chopped or ground nut meats. Pile on salted crackers and place in a moderate oven to brown lightly.

Pumpkin Tea Bread

1½ cups sugar
1½ cups flour, sifted
¼ teaspoon baking powder
1 teaspoon baking soda
¾ teaspoon salt
2 eggs, beaten
1 teaspoon cinnamon
1 teaspoon nutmeg
1 teaspoon ground cloves
½ cup salad oil
½ cup water
1 cup pumpkin, canned or cooked
½ cup pecans, chopped

Combine all ingredients in mixing bowl; stir to blend. Batter does not have to be completely smooth. Pour into greased and floured 9- by 5-inch loaf pan. Bake in a 350-degree oven for 1 hour and 15 minutes or until loaf tests done. Makes 1 loaf.

Tea Rolls

2 packages dry yeast
½ cup water, lukewarm
¼ cup sugar
½ cup milk, scalded
1 teaspoon salt
½ cup plus 2 tablespoons butter, melted
3 eggs, beaten
4½ cups flour, sifted, approximate

Stir yeast into water; let stand for a few minutes, then add sugar. Pour hot milk over salt and ½ cup butter; let stand until lukewarm, add yeast, eggs, and flour to make a soft dough. Turn out on floured board; knead lightly. Place in bowl, cover; let rise in a warm place until double in bulk; punch down. Roll out dough on floured board to ¼-inch thickness; cut with 2-inch-round cutter. Fold each piece in half with top slightly overlapping bottom. Place on baking sheet, and brush with remaining melted butter; let rise in warm place until almost double in bulk. Bake in a 425-degree oven for 15 minutes or until done. Makes about 4 dozen.

Rosettes and Timbales

Timbale irons come in various molds or shapes.

A rosette is a crisp timbale made by dipping an iron into batter and then frying the batter-covered iron in hot deep fat. Rosettes dusted with powdered sugar were popular with tea.

1½ cups flour, sifted
¼ teaspoon salt
2 teaspoons sugar
2 eggs
1 cup milk
Deep fat for frying

Sift together flour, salt, and sugar. Beat eggs and milk; add to flour mixture, and beat with egg beater. Heat deep fat to 365 degrees or until it browns a 1-inch cube of bread in 1 minute. Dip mold into hot fat; allow to heat for 30 seconds. Drain; dip into batter allowing batter to come to the top of the mold but not over the top. Place in hot fat to cook until browned; lift out, use fork to pry timbale from mold. Makes about 12. Dust with powdered sugar or use as base for creamed peas, chicken, or mushrooms.

Summer Tea Dance Menu

Assorted Canapés
White Grape Juice
Chicken and Asparagus Tips in Patty Cases
Finger Sandwiches
Watermelon Pickles
Cucumber Aspic in Lettuce Cups
Poundcake
Glazed Pecans
Hot Coffee   Iced Tea

Christmas Tea Dance Menu
Tomato Bisque Served in Cups
Chicken Salad
Ham Biscuits
Pistachio Ice Cream and Raspberry Ice
Coconut Balls
Fruit Cake
Hot Coffee   Russian Tea
Candied Peels   Spiced Nuts
Cluster Raisins

THE FIVE O'CLOCK TEA

The Century Cook Book (1904) has a chapter of
instructions to a hostess on the proper way to serve the
five o'clock tea. These are some of those instructions:

"The tea must be properly prepared. Tea tied in a swiss
muslin bag or a silver tea ball is used and the tea pot
often nestles in its own cozy. After the proper
preparation of the tea which includes scalding out the
pot before making tea, the attractiveness of the table
and the delicacy of the china are the next things to be
desired. Tea does not taste as well taken from a coarse,
large or heavy cup. The cups may all differ from one
another, but each one should be small and thin. The
cloth may be as elaborate as one wishes, but it must
above all be spotless, unwrinkled and dainty.

"A dry biscuit or a thin piece of bread and butter is
usually offered with the tea. Fresh unsalted butter is
preferable, but any of the fine butters may be used.
Three kinds of bread may be used—white, graham,
and Boston brown bread, and all may be served on the
same plate. In some homes, the bread and butter tastes
of roses, violets, clover or nasturtiums. The flavor is
obtained by shutting the fresh butter in a tight jar with
the blossoms for several hours. The flavored butter is
spread in the ordinary way on the bread, which has
been treated also to a bath of flowers."

CHOCOLATIERE

Mrs. Rorer's Everyday Menu Book of 1905 described
the popular chocolatiere as follows: "A chocolatiere is
usually given in the afternoon, although it may be
given in the evening. Chocolate is served in every
conceivable form. All the invitations are on chocolate-
colored cards. The decorations are brown; in the
autumn shades of leaves are especially appropriate.
The young ladies receiving are dressed in chocolate-
colored costumes; plain full skirts, white aprons and
little Dutch caps."

Chocolate Cake Squares

2 cups flour
2 cups sugar
½ teaspoon salt
½ cup margarine
½ cup salad oil
1 cup water
6 tablespoons cocoa
1 teaspoon baking soda
½ cup buttermilk
2 eggs
1 teaspoon vanilla

Sift together flour, sugar, and salt. In a saucepan, combine margarine, salad oil, water, and cocoa, and bring to a boil; pour over flour mixture. Stir baking soda into buttermilk; add to flour mixture. Stir to blend. Beat in eggs and vanilla. Pour into greased and floured 18- by 12-inch baking pan 1 inch deep; bake in 350-degree oven for 20 minutes. Meanwhile, make frosting (recipe below).

Frosting

½ cup margarine
6 tablespoons evaporated milk
2 tablespoons cocoa
1 pound confectioners' sugar
1 teaspoon vanilla

In saucepan, melt margarine; remove from heat, and blend in remaining ingredients. Spread over hot cake. When cool, cut into squares. Makes about 40 squares.

BEFORE CHARCOAL

Before the advent of the charcoal grill, it was customary to barbecue over a fire of wood in a pit. For one steer it took a pit similar to a grave and somewhat larger.
Pits were packed in various ways. One started with a layer of oak and hickory wood which burned for six hours. Fine stone was placed on top the hot coals and the meat, wrapped in paper and burlap, was placed on the stone. Covered with tin and dirt, it was cooked for 12 hours.

Barbecue in Texas and the Midwest means beef, in the Southeast it means pork. Whichever it is, a politician had better like barbecue if he wants to get elected, as it is the favorite food for rallies.

Pork is barbecued over wood coals in a shallow trench. The meat is placed on a rack and brushed with a sauce as it cooks "as tendah as a mother's love."

A "no-tomato" sauce is preferred for pork. This one is also good on chicken.

Barbecue Sauce

> ½ pound butter or margarine
> Juice of 2 lemons
> 1 cup vinegar
> 3 tablespoons salt
> 1 teaspoon black pepper

Combine all ingredients. Enough for 5 broilers.

THEN CAME CHARCOAL

After World War II, beef became plentiful and was steadily improved in quality to the point that a good steak was available in every supermarket. Backyard chefs, encouraged by their women, started building charcoal fires and smoke signals of "Come and Get It" went up all over America.

Alphabetical Index

Index by Category